Contents

Contents

Production management

Financial and accountancy management

Macroeconomic and other environmental factors

Contents

Marketing management

Introduction

Very few men are wise by their own counsel or learned by their own teaching. For he that was taught by himself had a fool for his master.

Ben Johnson

The value of a Guide such as this is that it distils many of the key areas of the subject, and the more frequently asked questions with corresponding answers, into an easily digestible and fairly succinct form. It is a reference facility based on the core material of A-level business studies, on several of the modules, and on many aspects of the GNVQ courses. It can act as an *aide-mémoire* both for those studying the foundations of the subject and for those working on the more difficult assignments, as well as providing a catalyst for further research and reading. Its aim, of course, is to help to boost the final grades.

The essays and calculations in this Guide give explanations of many of the key topics and subject areas. The book will therefore be helpful for revision, particularly when a specific subject area in the syllabus has been completed. The essays illustrate many of the more relevant and important points to bring out, and identify the places where students may begin to go wrong in their answers, not least by omitting relevant evaluation, mature judgement and deeper under-standing. The essays in this book will, in addition:

- analyse questions in order to identify the examiner's requirements;
- suggest how students can optimise the marks awarded;
- exemplify the skill development from lower-order skills to the higher levels;
- comment on the additional factors that might need to be considered;
- alert students to common pitfalls;
- refer to similarly worded questions in order to develop a more flexible approach to answering the questions.

They are certainly *not* intended to be 'model' answers, for, it could be argued, there is no such thing as a model answer, especially in social sciences such as business and management studies. Indeed, most of the questions selected would each require several full-scale chapters if they were to be answered completely. There are, however, key points in all subjects that need to be brought out, expanded and developed. It will be useful to remember the mnemonic DEEE: define, explain, expand, exemplify.

The essays, as a collection of relevant topics, aim to add depth and to improve understanding as well as to bolster and improve the basic knowledge. They will help the student to encapsu-late, within the answer, the main factors and interrelated connections that need to be explained, expanded and exemplified if the highest grades are to be achieved.

It is not enough to have a good mind; the main thing is to use it well.　　　**Descartes**

The Language of Business Studies

Business studies uses the vocabulary of the many subjects of which it consists: finance, marketing, operational research, industrial psychology, production management, statistics, human resource management, economics and so on. Students should not be put off by some of the terminology found in business and management textbooks or articles. It often conveys a very precise meaning and is, therefore, to be welcomed. Don't be reluctant to use it. Practise using it. It will show to others, and especially to examiners, that you know what you are talking about — but only, of course, if you use the terminology (and the various techniques and theories) in the right context.

However, some of the jargon to be found in some publications or overheard in the board room, in schools and in universities is remarkably unintelligible even to the most intelligent and articulate of people. So, as Oliver Holmes advises, 'a word is not a crystal, transparent and unchanged; it is the skin of living thought and may vary greatly in colour and content according to the circumstances and time in which it is used'. Get into the habit of choosing and checking your words very carefully; buy, and then use *frequently*, an ordinary dictionary and a business studies dictionary. The more accurately you can express yourself, the more credible your material will be.

How to Study

No revision aid can be a substitute, of course, for either greater explanation by your teacher or purposeful reading of appropriate and comprehensive textbooks. But never 'read' a textbook on its own, except when you are browsing through it. When you are working through it, following its contents very carefully, have by you a scrapbook and lots of sharpened pencils; make frequent notes — headings, balloons, spider diagrams — and begin to link the various themes as you read them and attempt to understand them. Tease out the themes, wrestle with the concepts — and make notes of the ones you don't understand so that you can ask your teacher later.

Frequent and short sessions of study are much more effective than infrequent, long ones. You might also consider that we learn and remember:

- 10% of what we read;
- 20% of what we hear;
- 50% of what we see and hear;
- 80% of what we say;
- 90% of what we say and do simultaneously.

So simply reading the material is not enough. We have to work actively at it. Use the method or technique that suits you best. As an example, it might be useful to dictate your own notes into a small battery-operated tape-recorder, or even take it into the classroom to record your teachers (with their permission).

All business studies A- and AS-levels now have a common 'core' of material; thereafter, the examinations, the forms of assessment and the subject content may vary. Nonetheless, there is great similarity in the subject areas covered. In business studies all A and AS courses are required to encourage students to:

- develop a critical understanding of organisations, the markets they serve, and the process of adding value. It should involve consideration of the internal workings and management of organisations and, in particular, the process of decision making in a dynamic external environment.
- be aware that business behaviour can be studied from the perspectives of a range of stakeholders, including customer, manager, creditor, owner/shareholder and employee — and that business studies draws on a variety of disciplines. Students should understand that these

perspectives and disciplines are interrelated (SCAA, 126744 — *Subject Cores For Business Studies*, 21 January 1997).

When You Start the Syllabus

Whichever board's examinations you are taking, and whatever the form of that assessment or examination — whether mainly at the end of two years or at the end of each module, and whether in coursework, assignments or projects, or a combination of these — try to get into the habit of being methodical in your studies from the very beginning:

- Use and develop your own subject vocabulary book.
- Start writing 'crib' cards from day one.
- Write up your notes periodically and frequently.
- File and organise your work in an orderly manner.
- Start revising as soon as you start your course!

As the course progresses, your notes will expand voluminously; your teachers will give you handouts, you will collect tables and photocopied material and you will have lots of homework! File it all sensibly. Colour code it, perhaps by using coloured page tabs, coloured dots, stars or different-coloured folders — any method you choose, as long as you know where to find your material and topics.

At the beginning of the course, your teachers may well have given you the examination board's syllabus (you *must* use this as the course progresses; tick off the topics as you cover them) and a scheme of work showing what you will be covering each term. The syllabus content will gradually unfold, but at times it may seem a little overwhelming. There seems to be so much to understand, and that is the key word — 'understand' — for as your understanding increases, so too will your confidence. Don't, however, be disheartened if it all seems too much. It will all begin to fit into place in due course.

Business studies is not a single subject. It is a multidisciplinary, integrated subject and that is what makes the area such an exciting field of study, for there is something in it for everyone. Some prefer the human resources part of the syllabus, others enjoy the marketing aspects, and yet others prefer the more numerate requirements associated with operational research, accounting or statistics. If you are taking a modular form of examination, you will be able to choose some of the areas that you think you will prefer.

The newcomer to the subject requires a reasonably comprehensive source to which to turn. There are many excellent textbooks on the market, mostly written by teachers who know how to get the best out of their students. More often than not, however, one's own notes are the most important source of information, for they will expand and develop and evolve, complete with your own peculiarities and hieroglyphics, as your teachers present the subject and as you undertake various assignments. Keeping one's own notes and writings in good order therefore makes sound sense.

The Syllabus and Business Decision Making

Many factors influence business decision making. The external and internal forces that determine a firm's *modus operandi* — the way the firm works — are infinite. The dynamic environment in which firms exist and co-exist, interact and operate, is like a kaleidoscope of colour — forever changing, moving and coalescing, and often with unpredictable results. The world in which we live is far from predictable. This unpredictability increases uncertainty, and where uncertainty increases, so too does risk. Simplistically, there is an inverse relationship between certainty and risk.

Any business studies course, at whatever level, seeks to understand businesses and the environment in which they operate, in order to minimise that risk. Most business studies courses have, as their central theme, the concept of decision making and how decisions can be optimised.

It could be argued that a manager's fundamental task is to minimise risk while attempting to optimise returns. This is achieved through planning, co-ordinating, monitoring and controlling. To minimise risk, therefore, we must make outcomes more predictable. To do so requires an arsenal of information and an armoury of experience, but such experience must be built upon a sound foundation of relevant knowledge and understanding, such as is presented in any business or management course. Nonetheless, the enormous advances in management techniques and the complexity of computer simulations and mathematical modelling have not eliminated intuitive judgements: the areas complement each other.

Revision and Examination Requirements

In examinations the foolish ask questions that the wise cannot answer.   **Oscar Wilde**

One goes to university to read for a degree — 'Henry Allen, Edinburgh, reading Modern History with Management Studies'. But the reading starts now; must start now! However, it is not enough to read: one must also revise — frequently. Increasing your knowledge and especially your understanding consists of:

- *reading* the material from your course and any related material, articles, comments — in textbooks, papers, journals, newspapers. Make notes of what you read and file them for future use and revision.
- *reflecting* on what you have read. Does it make sense? Do you agree with it? Does it add to your understanding? So what?
- *reciting* it back to yourself. Intone it into a tape recorder. Summarise the material. See if you can reproduce it in your own style — in your own way.
- *reviewing* your notes, your assignments, your homework. What did you get right? More important still, perhaps, what did you get wrong, and why?

There are several, very good reasons why you should revise frequently:

- Writing and producing revision notes requires you to select relevant material and to add additional notes and ideas that may have come up since you first made the original notes.
- It gives you a chance to organise and pull together all your material and your time and, indeed, your revision schedule.
- It requires that you focus and concentrate as you revise.
- It helps you to see the connections between topic areas and to integrate the material.
- It disciplines you into thinking about the material and grappling with the more difficult concepts.
- It helps to identify weaker areas of which you might be unsure, and which you can then check subsequently with your teachers.
- It improves your confidence.
- The results and benefits of the revision process are cumulative.

Long before the final examination or, indeed, your school or college examinations, as often as possible and besides any work that your teachers may give you, practise your answers — preferably under a self-imposed time constraint. Work through previous examination papers and be ruthless with yourself! Don't kid yourself that you know it when you come to check your answer with the textbook, or that you will know it by the time the examination arrives. If you don't know it now, or can't understand it now, be honest with yourself and seek help and clarification — now. Note and revise again the areas you forgot or got wrong, and rewrite your answer. Fill in the gaps in both your knowledge and understanding. Concentrate your attention on one thing at a time. That way you will not only get through more work, but you will do it more thoroughly.

As you progress up the academic ladder of examinations, you will find that there's an increasing emphasis on the need to demonstrate what teachers and examiners call 'higher-level skills'.

You will have to demonstrate, first, a basic working knowledge and understanding of the language of the subject and the many concepts introduced during the syllabus. You must also demonstrate your ability to recall the facts and concepts. It does not take a great deal of intelligence to recall rote-learned facts and figures, but you must be able to do it, even if it means learning the material 'parrot fashion'. However, it is not *enough* to learn them in this manner; you must be able to analyse, interpret, apply and evaluate this multitude of facts, knowledge and theories.

To get the highest grades, you have to demonstrate:

- *knowledge*. You know the facts. You can identify, list, name, outline and state.
- *understanding*. You can explain, extend, generalise, exemplify, infer, summarise and estimate.
- *application*. Now you can demonstrate, relate, use, compare and prepare.
- *analysis*. You are able to select, discriminate, illustrate, separate and distinguish.
- *synthesis*. At this stage you can classify, compile, design, modify, reorganise, formulate, reconstruct and substitute.
- *evaluation and judgement*. Now you are reaching the highest level of the higher-order skills. You can appraise, compare, contrast, interpret, explain and expand.

Coursework and Project Requirements

You must be able to find, collect and discriminate between raw data, convert this data into information and put that information into some kind of order for subsequent numerical and pictorial presentation. An analysis and interpretation of that information will then be required. Interpretation is a higher-order skill because it requires evaluation and judgement. It answers the vital question: 'So what?' I have analysed the information. What does it all mean? What are the consequences? What are the implications? *So what?*

The Schools Curriculum and Assessment Authority (SCAA) states that coursework 'is carried out by candidates during their course of study, is normally assessed by the centre and moderated by the awarding body, and contributes to the final grade awarded. Coursework is appropriate for the assessment of certain skills that cannot be fully assessed under controlled examination conditions.'

In most subjects coursework is limited to 25% of the total marks for the AS-level and 20% of the total marks for the A-level. In undertaking your coursework you will need to turn to many sources of reference and conduct a great deal of research. Read what one author says about the subject and then find out what another author has said, and then another — and yet another. One lead leads to another lead! It's a little like detective work. This approach is mainly eclectic, i.e. you are gathering the ideas and findings of a number of people to *synthesise* your own thoughts, opinions and conclusions. Above all, you must address the problem that has been set. Your project or coursework must answer the question posed in the first place.

However, you must not simply regurgitate what others have said or what you have read about that subject area. You must select and evaluate such information. In doing so, you will show that you are also capable of making additional judgements and, further, that you can assemble the arguments in favour of those judgements. In effect, you must produce the evidence for what you are claiming to prove. Don't forget to include your bibliography, references and sources of information.

You may even have to suggest a solution, after considering the evidence you have collected and the analysis you have undertaken. Your information and analyses must, therefore, be comprehensive, thorough and relevant. A well-known maxim in information technology is 'garbage in, garbage out' (GIGO); such a maxim applies just as well to course and project work.

But it can be very bewildering. One writer will present a *thesis* — an original thought about something. Another writer will present the *antithesis* — the opposite. You will have to take many of these opposing ideas — theses and antitheses — and then synthesise your own interpretation and explanation of that phenomenon. In doing so, you must carefully balance the arguments, especially if you are going to come to a conclusion or recommendation at the end of your work. You must be able to show an understanding of the suitability of various analytical techniques in an attempt to solve particular problems. It is important that you are also able to recognise the limitations of such techniques.

In business and management studies you must demonstrate the integrative nature of the different subjects you will study. For example, what might appear to be a sound financial or operational research solution might not be appropriate because, say, of the personnel implications and the industrial relations difficulties that could arise.

Coursework, assignments and projects provide an opportunity to assess your abilities under conditions where time and a good memory are not key imperatives. Projects are extended pieces of work that are more difficult to evaluate than the usual and more familiar examination answers, but it is important that you do well in them because they may contribute 20% or 25% of the total marks available.

Here are some areas and requirements for which the marks will be awarded:

- The skill with which the 'problem' or investigation has been put into context, defined and considered.
- The skill and relevance with which the objectives have been set and met.
- The data and information gathered, their relevance and your methods of collection.
- The theoretical base of the work, your attempts to compare and contrast, and your recognition of the limitations of the methods and techniques that you use.
- The depth and breadth of the analysis undertaken and the appropriateness of your analysis.
- Your interpretation of the results of the analyses.
- The conclusions that must arise from your interpretations and your analyses. You may be expected to propose solutions or make recommendations.
- The effectiveness of your communication and, in particular, the layout of your assignment, the illustrations, explanations and labelling, the bibliography and sources, as well as spelling, punctuation and syntax.

Care with Language

In business and management, there is rarely one definitive, absolute solution; rarely is anything certain. Business, in theory and practice, is an area of compromise. So in your writing you can rarely be categorical (unless, of course, you are answering a numerical question). The answer may be exact, but your conclusions, based on that answer and other factors, may not be so definite. So it is probably best to avoid words and phrases such as 'obviously', or 'the firm will go bust/lose out', or 'the firm will make/lose money'. Only the Royal Mint (legally) makes money! And it's not true to say that 'in a recession all firms will make a loss'. Some firms may do very well in a recession, such as the liquidators! So rephrase your answer: 'In a recession some/many firms may/are likely to make a loss.' Leave yourself some latitude.

You must, of course, be able to communicate in an accurate and effective manner. Among many other things, the examination board imperative requires reasonably neat and reasonably legible scripts, with good punctuation and spelling. Draw *big* diagrams, if appropriate, and tabulate, tabulate, tabulate whenever possible. Make it easier for the examiners to mark your scripts! Unless absolutely necessary, throw away your colouring pencils. In the examination you have not got time for very detailed or pretty diagrams or models, and, in any case, this is not an examination in design and technology or art.

Examination Technique

Although most candidates are usually well prepared for the event, and despite the mountains of advice and help that all will have received from teachers and tutors, a few candidates will ignore or forget some of that excellent advice and make fundamental mistakes — not so much, perhaps, in their answers (although that might also happen!) as in examination technique. A careful and methodical approach to the examination can make quite a significant difference to the final marks.

Buy yourself a highlighter pen! Use it frequently in the examination room to highlight the key words — the command words — in the question paper or case study. What exactly does the examiner wish me to do? Identify and highlight just that.

In the examination room:

(1) Allocate your time and stick to that allocation
Note the number of marks awarded for each question and for each subsection of the question, and allocate your time accordingly. Do not spend 20 minutes trying to get just 2 marks — which require no more than a couple of sentences — and leave yourself with only a further 20 minutes in which to get the other 23 marks! Suppose you have to answer four questions, you allocate 40 minutes to each question and there are 25 marks for each question. The bulk of your marks will probably come in the first few minutes that you spend on the answer, e.g.

- the first 15 minutes — say, 9 marks;
- the second 15 minutes — say, 7 marks;
- the final 10 minutes — say, 3 marks.

That's 19 marks so far: you're heading for a grade B — good.

You can see, however, that it becomes disproportionately harder to get more marks as you use up the time because you are having to draw on those higher-level skills. Nonetheless, you still think you might be able to squeeze another mark or two out of your answer. If you were now to overrun the time that you have allocated, say by a further 10 minutes, you might, indeed, get another one or two marks, but you could have started on your next question, spent that 10 minutes on it, and obtained 7 or 8 marks instead. So, resist the temptation to hang on to a question. *Discipline yourself in the exam room!*

When the invigilator gives permission to start:

(2) Read the instructions (rubric) with great care
Note how many questions you must answer and note any special instructions.

(3) Scan the entire question paper quickly
Then read it again, but carefully this time, and start planning and thinking about which questions you are likely to answer. Eliminate the impossibles! Put a question mark by those that appear ambiguous or possible. Tick the *definites* and prioritise them. Providing you number your answers correspondingly, you can tackle the questions in any order you choose. Many find it helpful and confidence building to choose the least difficult question and answer it first.

(4) Check and highlight the key words in the question using your highlighter pen
For example, consider the question 'What are the major obstacles to corporate planning and how can they be overcome? Compare and contrast the various approaches to company planning.' Here the key words are 'obstacles', 'planning' and 'overcome', and the command words 'compare and contrast'. So that is exactly what you must do — compare *and* contrast — and consider the advantages and disadvantages.

(5) Note any limitations in the question
For example, 'Discuss the advantages of decentralisation...' (not the disadvantages).

(6) Note the operational verb (the command word) and do precisely as the examiner asks
You may be asked to compare, contrast, discuss, explain, evaluate, define, interpret, justify, outline, review, summarise, etc. In the question 'Discuss and evaluate the weaknesses of the classical approach to management', you are required to present the arguments *for* and *against* some point of view, to consider the merits of the arguments and to come to some judgement — some opinion. To answer the question 'Evaluate the use of operational research techniques to a practising manager', present the strengths and the weaknesses of these techniques. In other words, do as you are asked. Do not summarise if you are asked to discuss. Do not evaluate if you are asked to define.

(7) Plan, plan, plan your answer
Jot down absolutely anything that comes to mind and which might be even faintly relevant to the question. As you think of one thing, that will lead you on to another area — a sort of word association. Some of the ideas and data that you think of may prove to be of little use; they may prove to be irrelevant to this particular question. Never mind. Write them down for now. You can always discard them later. Marshal your words and ideas into some kind of rational sequence.

Now follow your plan; lead the examiner sequentially through your answer to a conclusion (usually). Be relevant and avoid padding and waffle! Examiners will spot it instantly. They will not penalise you for it — they are not allowed to — but you will be penalising yourself by using up valuable time. So answer the question that the examiners *have* set; not the one you think they *should have* set! Make sure, before you start answering, that you understand the question.

Double-check it. Use diagrams or models if they help your explanation, but do not waste time on elaborate and detailed construction.

(8) Data-response questions and case studies

In data-response questions and case studies, study the data — the charts, diagrams, graphs and tables — very carefully.

Note trends in the data, identify major disparities and differences, highlight the areas and statements that you think are likely to be important. Refer to the data, to prove your point, when constructing your answer.

(9) Read through your answer

Amend the answer where necessary and leave some space at the end for afterthoughts and relevant points or observations that may come to mind. Underline where necessary, particularly in numerical answers, to help the examiners identify the key stages and the development of your answer. Do remember that, in a numerical answer or a data-response question particularly, even if you get the final calculation wrong, you can and will score marks for each correct stage that you have gone through and demonstrated correctly. It is important, therefore, that the examiners can understand each stage and can see how you have developed your calculation if they are to award you progressively more and more marks.

(10) If your timing goes wrong

If you begin to run out of time, consider using short notes and bullet points. An answer in this form will certainly earn some marks. If necessary, use short, punchy paragraphs. But, whatever you do, do not panic.

(11) Case studies

Case studies are searching and comprehensive. They test not only knowledge of business and management principles, but also the ability to relate those principles to the data and comments presented. Read the case study several times; read it quickly at first and then go through it more slowly, highlighting key words and phrases. Identify the problems from the data supplied. Get the feel of the case study. Make sure that you use the information given in the case study itself to support your answers. Try not to express your answers in vague terms; relate them to the case study in question. It is perfectly acceptable, indeed desirable, to use relevant theory, but if one question is about, say, low morale in the factory, do not write several pages about Herzberg. Do not simply copy into your own answer large tranches of material from the case study; refer to it, perhaps quote from it, but do not simply copy it. Neither do you need to copy or repeat in your answer the question that has been set. Read the material very carefully (use your highlighter pen!), for there are invariably clues within the text. The case study material is designed to help you answer the questions set, and little, if any, of it is redundant.

(12) Finally, constructing your response

An essay tends to follow a traditional structure. It is built on paragraphs, each dealing with one or two connected themes and linking sequentially with the next paragraph. There should always be a general introduction to the essay and there should always be a conclusion that originates from the evidence presented. Essays give candidates an opportunity to develop a theme in great detail, to bring in the interconnections, to show the implications and to discuss the philosophy behind the topic area. They reveal evidence of deeper reading, further study, and analytical and judgemental skills.

Except in the case study paper, the questions set in business studies exams rarely consist of a single question with a single theme. They are often broken down into subquestions, some of which have numerical requirements, but others of which are more descriptive — almost mini-essays. The full question may involve several topic areas. This is deliberate, of course, for one particular question may test more than one skill and, indeed, give you several opportunities to demonstrate your skills, knowledge and understanding. But such a question will not allow you to roam with quite the same liberty that a full essay question might. For example, the first part of the question may be mainly numerical and require you to solve a network analysis or decision tree analysis problem. The subsections may then, however, ask questions about the limitations of such techniques, or about distribution channels, location factors, employees and change, market research, cash flow, economic considerations and so on. You still need to know and understand the issue in depth, but you have to get to the key points and consequences more quickly.

The most common cause of failure in examinations is not lack of knowledge, but an inability to pick out the points asked for. So, ask yourself whether you have answered — really answered — the question set. If you have spare time at the end of the examination, you can return to the question and your answer. But do remember also that the marks available and shown on the question paper are usually proportional to the amount of time you should spend on that question or subquestion.

There tends to be less emphasis by most examination boards, nowadays, on the importance of extended essay writing, and more emphasis on 'business reports'. However, that does not diminish the requirements to be able to draft and craft an argument with the consummate skill of an artist — a writer. Indeed, part of the assessment itself requires that candidates should be able to select when to write in a concise report format and when to use extended prose.

Writing anything is a highly individual exercise; it is very personal. To some, writing an essay or report seems to come easily — the words just flow. Yet others seem to have to spend ages deliberating, perhaps on a single paragraph that refuses to convey what the author has in mind. But the plain fact is that, if you know and understand the subject, the words will certainly come more easily. There are basic rules of writing, of course, and for those who are not geniuses — for geniuses rarely stick to the rules — these rules can be easily learned and applied. Indeed, you will have spent most of your school life learning those rules. One must practise and then practise — and then practise again — just like learning to play the cello or to play football or snooker.

The most valuable sources of support, however, are your teachers who have groomed you for the past two years or so. When in any doubt, ask their advice. Use their knowledge and experience to your own ends. They will appreciate that. And if it all gets too much, just remember that Confucius probably had the right idea:

In all things, success depends on previous preparation and without such preparation there is sure to be failure.

Wise words, indeed! Good luck.

General Management

Question 1

With an example, show what you understand by the term 'added value'. What are the implications of this idea for the nation's economic growth? Suggest how this concept is of importance to the business community.

Tackling the question

This kind of question gives the candidate several opportunities to display not only basic business knowledge, but also a deeper understanding of how the business community and business activity fit into the overall national, macroeconomic scene. However, there is so much potential scope that it would be very easy to drift off into all sorts of areas which, while very interesting, are not directly relevant to the question posed. The main thrust of your answer should be to show how added value and wealth creation are at the root of all economic activity, and how they are optimised by combining resources in the right way. You should also show how the equitable distribution of the added value can be related to productivity bargaining at both local and national levels. Productivity is the central theme that dominates most management and political discussions. Crudely, it's about getting more and more from less and less. Control is central to the management process and it is based largely on planning, measuring the outcomes of that planning and then taking corrective action when outcomes do not match expectations. The added value calculation is a precise and open way of measuring both national and corporate performance. In a sense, added value or adding value is what business and management studies are all about. It is a core theme.

Answer

Guidance notes

A method of calculating the actual value of the output of a company and being able to compare the value of that output with other companies is a basic economic requirement. It is also an extremely useful concept in measuring the achievements and productivity within a company. The added value concept has become more widely used in recent years and, indeed, has spread to the service industries as well, including the public sector, such as in the measurement of educational and health achievements. Although the concept is simple, however, there is no agreed or precise definition of the term. The Institute of Chartered Accountants defines it as 'the wealth the reporting entity has been able to create by its own and its employees'

Think about this for a moment. In a sense, it's the very reason why businesses — any business — exist. If a business does not or cannot add value, why is it in existence? Far better to end it and use the resources more productively elsewhere.

A useful mnemonic, and one which will help to discipline your answer, is DEEE — define, explain, expand, exemplify. You do get marks for giving examples that help to illustrate whatever point you're making.

And here's a simple example. It shows the examiner that you can use the concept and that you can put it into context. If you do give a numerical example, there's no point in making it too complicated or too long, but do keep it neat and tidy so that the examiner can follow it easily.

I've resisted the temptation to give examples of stock valuation techniques, although I might have been tempted to mention the basic methods, such as LIFO and FIFO. But would they add to the answer? I think not.

efforts'. Generally, it is accepted that added value is the difference between the value of the goods produced (or services rendered) and the costs of the materials and other services that have to be purchased — such as professional advice, marketing, power and telephone costs and depreciation.

It is important to note that the costs in calculating the added value do not include direct labour or fixed cost items such as leasing charges, interest charges, rents and the business rate. These particular costs are deducted from the calculated added value to show the net profit before tax and dividends, as in the following example:

Sales revenue	£250,000
less	
Raw materials and component parts	£80,000
Marketing, advertising, legal fees, etc.	£55,000
Depreciation	£10,000
Added value	£105,000
less	
Labour charges	£45,000
Fixed costs	£22,000
Net profit before tax and dividends	£38,000

The ratio of labour cost:added value = $45,000/105,000 \times (100) = 43\%$

In assessing the cost of the component parts and raw materials, it will be apparent that companies may value stock in different ways, but, providing the method of valuation is consistent, the relative figure can be obtained to give the annual added value, which is a useful indicator of the firm's output and particularly its productivity. Effectively, added value measures the additional value given to the basic raw materials through the combination of fixed assets, personnel skills and management competence.

The value of anything is related to three factors:

- scarcity (supply and availability);
- transferability (can it be transferred from seller to buyer?);
- utility (the usefulness that the potential purchasers believe they will get from that product).

The actual price that customers are willing to pay for the product, therefore, is simply a quantified reflection of that value.

It is the amount of money they are prepared to part with to satisfy some anticipated utility. However, this price — any price — must be seen in relation to the changes in the elasticities of demand caused by the price itself, by incomes, and by promotional expenditure on that product. The higher the price that the customer is willing to pay for the product, the greater the added value that can be realised and the greater the wealth that the company is able to create. The relationship between customer satisfaction and the creation of added value is so important that the most successful companies are market oriented and customer centred. There can be no added value at all unless a customer buys the product. The significance of this is that any change in perceived utility will affect the perceived value, and any change in perceived value will be reflected ultimately in the price that a customer is willing to pay.

Businesses, and especially the marketing departments of the business, can markedly influence the actual and potential consumers' perceptions of the 'usefulness' of a product, not least through the management of the marketing mix elements. The usefulness of the added value concept is especially significant when analysing intra-firm performance by departments, divisions or even individual operatives, and inter-firm comparisons over a period of time, which leads to trend analysis. Frequent assessment and comparison of the added value achieved gives a greater degree of management control and an opportunity for remedial action to take place.

In a stable economy there is a fairly constant relationship between labour costs and added value. It is the shop-floor employees who primarily create the added value. As an incentive, it would seem sensible, therefore, that the employees should receive a proportion of the additional value achieved through their increases in productivity. An increase in productivity is, in effect, to get more from the same resources, or the same amount from fewer resources, so reducing the average unit cost. The added value concept therefore gives a greater opportunity to introduce rational and transparent productivity payment schemes.

For example, if 10 people, each earning £200 per week, produce a total of 2,000 units per week, the labour cost per unit is £1.

If two people now leave and the remaining eight are still able to produce 2,000 units per week, the labour cost per unit

Value must always be related to the price a product will fetch, but you shouldn't mention price without mentioning elasticity in the same breath. Similarly, consumers' interpretation of value is related to their perceptions of satisfaction that they will get by buying and owning that product or service. Do remember, however, that you're answering a business studies question and not an economics one. So be careful of using too much economic theory unless, of course, the question specifically asks for it — and this question doesn't.

We must assume, of course, that the reader knows what is meant by 'trend analysis'; in any case, resist the temptation to explain it, for that isn't what the question's about. However, don't hesitate to introduce key concepts and relevant and specialist terminology if it adds knowledge, understanding or judgement to your answer. You've only one chance to show the examiner what a clever person you are. So, if in doubt, put it in — but watch your timing.

Productivity increases and productivity measurement are the important features and we don't want to detract from them. In a sense, productivity is exactly what this essay's all about. The whole objective of 'productivity' is to reduce the average unit cost. If that can be reduced, then the added value can be increased, assuming the price remains the same. But then, that depends on other factors — not least, elasticity, competition, the marketing mix, market segments, and so on.

There are, or could be, other recipients of an increase in productivity — not least the owners of the company, who want some reward for risking their financial investment.

falls to £0.80. While there has been no increase in production, there has been an increase in productivity (i.e. the same volume of output from fewer resources). The price of the product could now be reduced to stimulate sales, or the company and the employees could share, on a fair basis after negotiation between management and unions or employees' representatives, the £400 reduction in labour costs. Furthermore, an intent to share additional added value may help to overcome resistance to change, reduce the potential for industrial conflict (given that over 50% of industrial conflicts have to do with payment), and increase shareholders' confidence through additional dividends.

And here we can turn from the firm to the country as a whole, and the idea of how the whole country can increase its wealth and the value of its GDP.

It is precisely this concept of adding value and increasing productivity that is at the root of both corporate and national wealth creation. The wealth of the nation, measured by the gross domestic product (GDP), is the monetary value of all the goods and services a country produces. Economic growth, which is invariably one of the government's key economic objectives, is the percentage increase in total output of the economy at constant prices. Such increases mean that real incomes have improved. It is only by creating wealth, and distributing that wealth equitably, that a country can improve the standard of living of all its inhabitants, improve employment opportunities, and meet the aspirations of the community in terms of improved social infrastructure, better health care and education facilities, and a reduction in poverty through the redistribution of wealth.

The essay now begins to go deeper; it begins to show judgement and evaluation. The higher marks are awarded for this kind of 'so what?' analysis. The top-grade candidates ask the questions 'What if...?' and 'So what...?' They begin to show intellectual curiosity, which leads them on to deeper things.

We live in an interdependent society and many talk of 'the global village'. Industry and commerce need the infrastructure and the social and protective services provided by central and local governments. Governments and society need the added value created by the business sector. Every activity of a firm must somehow add value if the company is to optimise its final profits and increase its wealth creation. This concept, however, may require a company to undertake value analysis and value engineering. In other words, can the actual cost of the product be reduced without compromising the functions of that product?

This is an interesting concept and a useful one with which to conclude the essay. Again, it shows a wider appreciation of

However, adding value should not stop with the product. An increasingly successful company will itself increase in value, and therefore corporate value creation should be the primary, preferably quantified, objective of all senior managers. Such value-creating behaviour should be encouraged throughout any commercial organisation.

what businesses are all about — the *raison d'être* of most businesses.

Related questions

1   What is the difference between an increase in productivity and an increase in production? Consider how productivity might be achieved within a commercial organisation, and suggest how the benefits of such productivity might be distributed.

2   It is sometimes alleged that the UK is falling behind its international competitors. What measures do governments tend to use to gauge such comparisons? Suggest what the limitations of such measurements might be.

3   Explain the difference, if any, between value engineering or value analysis and added value. Consider how a deliberate policy of changing from labour intensity to capital intensity may improve productivity within both a firm and a country.

4   Why is such emphasis placed on increasing productivity and what are the possible implications for the employees?

Question 2

Consider how a company may be brought into existence and define the purpose of the Articles and Memorandum of Association. Explain the advantages of limited liability. Differentiate between bankruptcy and liquidation, and suggest what some of the causes might be.

Tackling the question

The first two parts of this question are fairly straightforward. Clearly, this basic knowledge must be a core area in any business studies syllabus. Questions about forming a company might also offer an opportunity to talk about raising funds, the differences between a private limited company and a public limited company, the stock market requirements, and even share prices and why they rise and fall. On a similar note, it might be useful to mention units of business ownership, business expansion and business confidence. The latter part of the question is, however, a little more subtle. It is looking for a deeper understanding of insolvency and gives an opportunity to explore bankruptcy and liquidation in some depth, and with them, the importance of liquidity and working capital. It would be legitimate to consider how working capital might be controlled through solvency or liquidity ratios and how such capital rises and falls with the volume of sales.

Answer

There are two main ways by which a company may be brought into existence:

- by statute, i.e. by a special Act of Parliament (e.g. an Enabling Act to 'privatise' state-owned corporations);
- by registering under the Companies Act of 1985.

Unless you're doing a 'business law' module you won't need to know in great depth the many Acts of Parliament that affect businesses. But it's useful to know and appreciate the existence and background of some of the key ones.

In the last 20 years or so a number of companies have been created through an Enabling Act of Parliament to transfer public utilities (such as British Gas and the water boards) and state-owned corporations (such as British Telecom and British Airways) to the private sector. The majority of companies, however, come into existence by completing the formalities required when registering under the Companies Acts of 1985 and 1989, and the Business Names Act of 1985.

This method does not create a company, but it lays down a process by which companies may become incorporated, i.e. the business now becomes a corporation (*corpus:* body). The business is born and becomes a single legal entity. The company has rights and duties in the eyes of the law. However, this new company has been made by the law and can only be 'unmade' — or die — through the processes of law. A company's directors, shareholders and employees may all die, but the company will not be 'dead' until the law says it is, for a company is a legal 'person' separate from those who own it or started it. Just like a human being, a company must have a name and, as a separate legal entity, can sue and be sued.

The actual process is much more complicated than this, of course, but you don't need to get into the 'nitty gritty'; you're certainly not doing an A-level or GNVQ in Company Law and, in any case, the question doesn't seek an explanation of the process of 'liquidation'.

A company is brought into existence through the process of registration with the Registrar of Companies in Cardiff. Certain key documents must be filed with the Registrar. Furthermore, a company cannot make contracts until it has been incorporated. All companies must have a written constitution, which must include the Memorandum of Association and the Articles of Association.

The Memorandum of Association states the purposes for which the company exists, and must show:

- the company's name, which must also appear on all business letters, trade catalogues, etc.;
- the registered office — to be shown on all company literature;
- the company's objects — the scope and nature of the business envisaged (the objects of the company must be legal);
- the liability of the members — all contracts should be signed 'for and on behalf of' the limited company;
- the authorised share capital.

These are the two most important documents and, even if you can't remember precisely what they contain, you should certainly know of their existence, why they exist and what their purposes are. One has to do with the actual purpose of the business and the other has to do with the regulation of that business: how it's to be governed.

The Articles of Association are concerned with the regulation of the company's internal affairs. They will show:

- the share capital — how much is authorised, issued, paid up and reserved (NB 'Reserve capital' is quite different from 'capital reserves'. Reserve capital is the amount remaining unpaid on the issued share capital, which can be called up if the company goes into liquidation. Capital reserve constitutes the money that is realised on sale of 'capital', i.e. assets, such as land or buildings);
- provision for the transfer of shares;
- provision for the meetings of its members;
- the arrangements for the appointment and removal of directors;

The 'separate legal entity' concept is the key point. There may be 10,000 shareholders, the owners of the company, but the law can't put them all in the dock if the company is sued. So, in a sense, the company becomes a person. That process, however, doesn't disbar the directors of a company or the trustees of a charity from certain legal obligations that fall on them as individuals. Incidentally, do remember that companies are liquidated, not 'liquidised': that's what happens to food for babies!

At this point we can begin to consider why companies should become limited when they are 'incorporated' — from the Latin *corpus*, meaning a body or substance: literally, to make a 'body' — and then go on to explain what 'limited' means.

This is a very important point that is sometimes overlooked. Even if the owners, the shareholders, have limited liability, the company doesn't. It must still pay all its dues and debts, and if that means breaking up the company and selling off bits of it — its fixed and/or current assets — at net realisable value, then so be it. But it's usually a last resort, used when everything else has failed.

Even the media talk about companies becoming 'bankrupt'. It's not true: it can't happen, and it's a careless use of the term. People, not limited or unlimited companies, are made or declared bankrupt by a court of law. It's a personal state of affairs — like measles or mumps!

In each of these I give the reason why bankruptcy or liquidation

- the powers of the directors;
- provision for dividends and reserves.

Provided all the documents are in order, and the business name chosen is still available and has not been used by another company, the Registrar will issue the Certificate of Incorporation. The company is effectively born. From now on the company — as a public or private limited company — must file annual returns and accounts with the Registrar and, on payment of a small fee, any member of the public can obtain a photocopy of the accounts of any private or public company.

Companies may be registered with limited or unlimited liability. In the latter form of company, the shareholders will be liable for all the company's debts if it goes into liquidation. There are very few unlimited companies, although there are a few advantages for such an organisation. For example, an unlimited company does not have to file its accounts with the Registrar of Companies and so can keep its activities secret. The company itself, however — the legal entity — is always fully liable and has unlimited liability. In practice, this means that sufficient of the fixed and current assets, such as buildings, vehicles, machinery and unsold stock, must be sold — liquidated, turned into cash — to pay off the company's debts.

The debts must be paid off in a strict order laid down by the law. If a company does not have enough assets to pay off its debts, it will be dissolved by voluntary or involuntary liquidation. However, while a company goes into liquidation, a person, such as a sole trader, is declared bankrupt. They are both insolvent, but there are two forms of insolvency: legal insolvency occurs when a company (or person) is unable to obtain sufficient cash to pay its debts; technical insolvency occurs when the company is unable to pay its debts at a particular time. In legal terms, no company can be made bankrupt. Bankruptcy is a personal state of affairs. The bankruptcy procedure is set out in the Insolvency Act of 1986. People who are unable to pay their debts may apply to a court for a bankruptcy order; alternatively, the person's creditors may apply to the court.

The main causes of bankruptcy or liquidation include:

- losses through debts that are irrecoverable. The balances of debtors (people or companies who owe the company) become higher and higher, and effective credit control becomes difficult to implement. Giving excessive discounts to attract customers and 'penetrate' the market may make the problem worse.

- too much reliance on trade credit, coupled with insufficient working capital. Firms can actually overtrade. They are so busy completing their orders, buying raw materials and paying wages and other costs that they cannot get the revenue collected fast enough. Inevitably, the firm resorts to overdrafts and loans and goes deeper into debt. Overtrading is a common cause of insolvency. The company expands too fast before sales have translated into hard cash. For example, a sales campaign might generate a higher level of sales, for which supplies have to be purchased. The inward cash flow is inadequate to service the outward cash flow requirements. In effect, the management ignores profit in search of turnover, and ignores cash in search of profit. Simply to expand trade on the same terms will require proportionally more working capital; increased sales will lead to an increased number of debtors and increased stockholding costs in the form of raw materials and component parts.
- defective accounting and costing systems, and inadequate information systems;
- insufficient fixed and working capital to maintain the business and to match competitors' technological advances;
- mismanagement, including carelessness, poor supervision, recklessness, fraud and extravagant living.

occurs, followed by a short explanation and the consequences. In business report writing, the use of bullet points and explanatory paragraphs is perfectly acceptable. You should avoid long, descriptive prose. In any case, in the exam you haven't got time to write a novel.

Although there is an enormous amount of regulation of companies, whether public or private, there are clearly major advantages associated with the act of incorporation — limited liability, separate legal entity, transferability of shares, tax advantages — such that many sole traders and partnerships may ultimately become incorporated.

The need to conclude the answer becomes apparent, so start to conclude.

Related questions

1 Compare and contrast the legal structure and objectives of joint stock companies and public corporations. Would it make economic sense to renationalise some of the privatised utilities?

2 Consider the various legal forms of business ownership, and suggest how and why sole owners of a business may decide to become private limited companies.

3   Explain the process of seeking a stock market flotation, and discuss the advantages of becoming a public limited company rather than a private limited company.

4   What is the purpose of the Alternative Investment Market? Of what use is this market to the small business, and how does the owner of such a firm gain access?

Question 3

Show how the various approaches to management have evolved and consider what effect, if any, such approaches may have had on management styles today.

Tackling the question

This could give rise to a very comprehensive and over-long answer if we're not careful, so we shall have to be quite selective. There are, after all, many 'approaches to management'. I've chosen to answer this question using a chronological approach to the development and evolution of management thinking. This is a rational, and probably the easiest, way of doing it. What is required is a broad knowledge of the various conventional models of management, and of how one idea led to another as more and more research was undertaken, and as the study of 'management' became more respectable. It is an opportunity to compare and discuss the key merits and inadequacies of the various approaches. It is important to remember, however, that we have the benefit of hindsight! At the time, many of these management approaches were quite revolutionary. Many, if not all, have stood the test of time in one form or another. Mention should also be made of areas where the various approaches generally overlap, such as the concern for improved productivity.

Answer

Guidance notes

The development of modern management thinking is viewed generally as dating from the end of the nineteenth century, with the emergence of large-scale industrial organisations and the management problems that developed.

The early classical writers placed emphasis on structure and on a set of rules of management as a direct means of improving productivity. They were concerned to develop rules that would render management less susceptible to the personal ambitions of the employees. They tended to base their theories on the assumption of the rational behaviour of employees, who would wish to maximise their wages. This approach is associated with the work of people such as Taylor and Fayol.

A major contributor to this approach was F.W. Taylor, said to be the 'Father of Scientific Management'. He considered that all

It's perfectly acceptable to weave your answers to the parts of a question throughout the answer, rather than addressing each individual part in a separate and distinct block. But you have to ensure, of course, that you have actually answered each part of the question.

Identify the key features of the approach, and then give examples of those who became renowned in that specific field — some of the approaches are better known by their author or originator than by their management title. 'Taylorism', for example, is a synonym for 'scientific management' but there were many contributors to this approach other than Taylor himself. And then discuss the pros and cons of that particular approach.

Taylorism became a standard approach for many companies, particularly and understandably in the USA, but it spread across the industrial world almost like a religion — and with it came many disciples, each of whom made some small but often very significant contribution. Therefore, we have to be selective, otherwise we could end up writing an essay only about scientific management, or one of the other major approaches.

work processes could be analysed into separate tasks and that, by the application of scientific methods, it would be possible to find the 'one best way' to perform each task. In effect, all uncertainty would be removed from the task. Each job would be broken down into its component parts; each part would be timed and analysed; and then these parts would be rearranged to produce the most efficient method of working. Taylor believed in the rational, economic motivation of man — the workers would be motivated to work harder because they would obtain higher wages by working in the most efficient way. Both the company and the individual employees, therefore, would benefit financially.

Taylor was concerned with finding methods for the more efficient control of work and he set out a number of principles as a guide to managers. An array of scientific management techniques has been left to today's management. They form the basis of many productivity deals and they are characteristic of many assembly-line companies. These practices include work study, organisation and methods for improving office systems, payment by results, piece rate systems, job evaluation and the foundations of ergonomics — fitting people to machines.

Other classical writers were more concerned with improving the organisation's structure as a means of increasing efficiency. Among the most publicised is the work of Fayol. He advocated 14 basic principles of management. However, the idea of sets of principles to direct managerial action has been subject to much criticism because, it is argued, individual initiative and flexibility are reduced.

The weakness of the classical approach, and its attempts to prescribe exact ways of doing things, is that it leads to an unresponsive organisation, rather than a flexible, proactive one. Managers tend to 'go by the book' instead of using their experiences and initiative. In addition, individual employees are not encouraged to think and be innovative. In many ways, it is argued, such workers are no more than extensions to a machine: they supply the muscle power only. The most significant charge against such systems is that, in the attempt to minimise risk and increase control, the workplace is 'de-humanised'. Workers become alienated from the product. They cannot identify with the end-product.

During the 1920s more attention began to be paid to the sociology of the workplace and to the behaviour of employees, particularly within groups. In the USA a significant turning point in the development of human relations studies came when Elton Mayo and his team undertook research at the famous Hawthorne plant of the Western Electric Co., Chicago (1924–32).

The original investigation was concerned with the effects of the intensity of lighting on the workers' productivity. The results of these tests were inconclusive, for productivity increased even when the working conditions were made worse. This prompted a series of additional experiments. The conclusion, after many years of research, was that the increased interest that the researchers had shown had led to a phenomenon that became known as 'the Hawthorne effect'. In addition, the research revealed the enormous influence that the informal groups — with their establishment of group norms and their measures to achieve group conformity — could have on the formal, organisational objectives. The Hawthorne experiments thus generated new ideas concerning work groups and leadership, and placed particular emphasis on the importance of personnel management — or human resource management, as it is called today.

This approach emphasises the importance of the informal organisation that will always be present within any formal organisation. The human relations writers argued that people go to work to satisfy a complexity of needs and not simply for wages. They emphasised the importance of the social, or affiliation, needs of individuals and the importance of the group in influencing individual behaviour at work. The Hawthorne experiments, while not without their critics, have been described as one of the most important of all social science investigations. Critics of the approach, however, have termed it 'cow sociology' — keep the workers happy and they will give more 'milk'.

In the systems approach, attention is focused on the total work organisation and on the subsystems that collectively make up the whole system. The sociotechnical systems approach continues to view the organisation as a whole, but goes further in that it studies the organisation in terms of the interaction between the technical and the social or human variables within the system. Changes in any one part of the system, technical or social, will have an impact on other parts of the system.

The sociotechnical system — any system, in fact — is concerned with the transformation or conversion process itself, i.e. turning raw materials into finished goods. It is also concerned with the distinction between the needs and demands of the human part of the organisation and the needs of the technical requirements. The balance between these two elements must be correct. The concept of sociotechnical systems arose from the work of Trist and Bamforth in the postwar coal-mining industry in Durham.

Here I'm emphasising the key points of this approach and the philosophy behind it, but this is an enormous topic, so we shall have to watch how much we write and how deep into the subject we go. The key point is: how and why did this approach differ so much from the scientific management ideas?

The systems approach brings us well up to date. There have been and are (and will be) many more approaches and variations on a theme, but they have not caught the imagination as much as those earlier approaches. In fact, we can ruminate on how and why a new idea becomes a management fad, and when it becomes a respectable doctrine embedded in the evolution of management history.

Here is a definition of a system. Examine it. It's in three distinct parts. Understand each one.

Viewing the organisation as a system recognises that a change in any subsystem may modify behaviour in other subsystems and, ultimately, the whole system — the firm itself — given that the system is a set of interdependent parts, all of which have needs and will exhibit behavioural patterns if these needs remain unfulfilled.

These writers were mainly concerned about the employee in his or her work environment, and part of the environment must be the management style that operates in the place. In a sense, they were alerting management to how it might better meet the needs and aspirations of employees. In a nutshell, they were suggesting how managers could be better managers. Almost every textbook on management will mention one or more of these people.

Under the heading of human relations studies can loosely be identified the work of those writers in the 1940s to 1960s who adopted a more sociopsychological orientation and showed particular concern for the personal adjustment of the individual within the work organisation, and the effects of group relations and leadership styles. This group of writers, which includes Maslow, McGregor, Likert, Herzberg and Argyris, is often, and much more correctly, categorised under the separate heading of 'neo-human relations'. Much of this work has emphasised the need for any task to possess some intrinsic motivational factor, the need for an individual's positive image to be reinforced, and the importance of participation and consultation in the decision-making process. Empowering the workforce to take decisions has introduced a much greater degree of industrial democracy.

The various approaches to management represent a progression of ideas, each building on from others and adding to them. The different approaches are not in competition with each other and no one approach should be viewed as if it were the only approach, replacing or superseding earlier contributions. Each approach has its advantages and disadvantages.

The need for management, whatever its style or approach, will remain for purposes of planning, control, co-ordination and direction. The development of autonomous work groups has not eliminated a hierarchical structure, although there is a considerable trend and emphasis towards flatter and less hierarchical structures. The debate about management style still hinges not on whether the function of management is necessary, but on how it is to be fulfilled.

Related questions

1   Compare and contrast the various approaches to management, identifying the advantages and limitations of such approaches.

2   'The main approach to the management of assembly-line factories has changed little since the days of F.W. Taylor. Nothing else will work as well.' How far do you think this is true? What alternatives are there?

3 'There is probably no one best way of designing organisations.' Discuss this statement, demonstrating how the contingency theories of Lawrence and Lorsch may support this argument.

4 What were the major conclusions of Burns and Stalker, and what implications do they have for commercial organisations?

Question 4

Discuss, with examples, the importance of corporate planning and the establishment of corporate objectives. What factors are likely to influence the firm's objectives and how might a company identify its strategic direction?

Tackling the question

This question is looking for a bird's-eye view of the company, without focusing too much on individual departments. Imagine yourself as one of the board of directors, asking questions such as 'What business are we in?' and 'Where are we going, and how do we intend to get there?' Any question about corporate planning will certainly refer to objectives and strategy, and strategy is a result of a response to the environment. Some gurus talk of 'mission statements', but it must be accepted that someone in the business, such as the managing director, needs some kind of 'vision'. So the question is a philosophical one rather than an examination of specific management techniques or theories — although there is some of that in it too. The planning process needs to be examined together with the variables and constituents within that planning process.

Answer

Few, if any, companies do not engage in corporate planning of some sort, however casual. Corporate planning is a systematic and disciplined study, designed to identify the objectives of the firm, identify appropriate targets, identify relevant constraints and devise practical plans of action.

Although this point is probably very obvious, it's still worth saying — and letting the examiner know that you know it. In the exam, don't take anything for granted.

Every firm is unique in some way, and so too is every market. Although there are common areas between companies, they produce a multitude of different products and they have many different customers with diverse requirements. What might be considered sound planning for one company, therefore, may be quite inappropriate for another firm, with a different philosophy and approach, serving another market. Nonetheless, basic ground rules of corporate planning have been established.

There are fundamental reasons why corporate planning should occur in any organisation, irrespective of its size, culture or operations, including:

- to ensure survival;
- to maximise or, more realistically, to optimise profits;
- to discharge the firm's social and other responsibilities;
- to motivate its executives and management and to inspire confidence in its workforce;
- to grow;
- to compete;
- to control, monitor and adjust its operations.

However, like most business practices and philosophies, planning has both its advantages and disadvantages.

The advantages can be summarised as:

- better and more effective delegation of action;
- improved bases for control;
- possible economies of scale through streamlining and the avoidance of duplication of action;
- minimising of mistakes;
- more purposeful action.

The disadvantages or 'costs' include:

- the expense involved in both setting up and running such a system;
- the time factor involved, particularly for middle and senior management;
- the inflexibility of a draft plan once it has been agreed;
- uncertainty of forecasts — there is, inevitably, an element of risk.

Do remember that for every advantage in business studies or social sciences someone will think of a disadvantage: the pros and the cons. You should state those as well. It shows you're trying to present a balanced picture.

Planning is, perhaps, the most basic of all managerial functions, since it involves selection from many alternative courses of action for the enterprise as a whole and for each department within that enterprise. It has been said that the purpose of every plan and all derivative plans is to facilitate the accomplishment of enterprise objectives. Plans alone cannot make an enterprise successful; action is required. Without plans, however, action becomes merely random and incoherent activity. Clearly, the firm must define its strategic objective, preferably in quantifiable terms for the achievement or progress to be accurately measured. Therefore the strategic and, indeed, the tactical objectives must be cast in terms of:

- purpose — why are we doing it?
- timing — when are we going to do it?
- resources — what are we going to use to do it with?

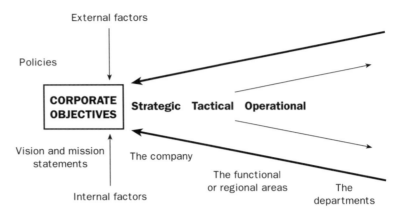

Figure 1 The hierarchy of goals

Many people have a stake in every company, not just the owners or managers. Of course, some have a very big stake, not least in money terms, and others will have a much smaller stake — such as the local community — but they do all have a stake or interest. It usually doesn't do anyone any good if a company goes out of business.

It is necessary, of course, to put a plan into action and it is important to consider what constraints and limitations are likely to affect the achievement of the objectives. In this latter regard, many agencies share some interest in the firm.

Externally, the following stakeholders may influence a firm's objectives: shareholders, employees, customers, the community, management, the government and competitors' actions. Internal departmental claims will include production, personnel, finance, research and development, marketing and the trade unions. All of these stakeholders have an interest in the overall objectives of the company, but their personal or departmental goals may be considered by them to be more important.

If a specific department is considered — say, the production department of an engineering company — its tactical and ideal-istic goals might be: to achieve long production runs, to set production at or above a certain level, to achieve low produc-tion costs, to establish easy production scheduling and to maintain a stable number of employees and expertise. However, the customer will be more concerned about: the quality of the product, the quantity and availability of the product, lead times and delivery dates, price and value for money, after-sales service, warranties and guarantees. The aims of the various stakeholders may, therefore, be incompatible. The differences will have to be reconciled.

Corporate planning and the setting of goals cannot sensibly be undertaken without adequate and relevant information. Unfortunately, information may be deficient in two ways. First, all decisions are taken about the future; therefore there is doubt and uncertainty. Second, the firm may be incapable of collecting the information it requires, or of making use of it even if it does get the information.

There are other factors and variables involved. Information is expensive to collect and yet the planners — whoever they are — need the information at the right time and in the right place if the information is to be really meaningful. They must evaluate the information and analyse it before they can identify and produce alternative courses of action. When the plans are finalised it is necessary to determine that such plans are implemented effectively and correctly. There needs, therefore, to be an element of control. Planning and control are the Siamese twins of management: the firm separates them at its peril. Yet the more control is imposed, the less delegation there can be. The more one increases, the more the other decreases. There is an inverse relationship between the two.

Throughout business studies you will find that this is a key point. If a company — or a person — is to optimise its decision making, it can't do so unless it has an adequate supply of data, which is then turned into information. Hence the importance of research of any kind.

The broad strategic objective of a light engineering company, for example, might be to concentrate upon the major product line and become worldwide, leading distributors in that field. First, however, the subgoals must be identified and achieved as steps along the way. An engineering company's subgoals might consist of:

- acquiring manufacturing facilities in, say, the EU and Japan;
- disposing of a secondary product not closely related to the main line;
- re-engineering some products to permit local production of bulky parts;
- strengthening the marketing effort and sales force in, say, Latin America, Australia and the USA;
- raising long-term finance by equity rather than loans.

Having presented a bird's-eye view of the whole company, we can start to think about how just one department might carefully plan and put its own tactical goals in focus, and what it needs to do to start the ball rolling.

These subgoals will in many cases be quantifiable, and can be more easily measured and controlled. Vague aspirations will be much more difficult to control and to realise.

In other words, realistic short-term targets can be established as steps towards the more ideal long-run, strategic objectives. It is important to distinguish between hopes and expectations, and between ambitions and realistic targets.

Corporate planning must be comprehensive and formal because it must embrace all aspects of the company and not just a chosen few departments or divisions. It must also be formal because growth and survival require scripted, detailed

The time dimension is important, of course. It makes sense to set the objectives in quantified terms, but by when does the firm expect to achieve all the subgoals? Everyone in the company needs some kind of time scale, and if they are not going to meet that deadline then someone will have to rethink.

plans and not just entrepreneurial flair. Corporate planning is an attempt to navigate the course of the company and to formulate its future strategy. It achieves this by producing short-term and long-term objectives. Sometimes, however, the objectives are not fully thought through, often expressed as aspirational levels, and often stated in non-operational (i.e. woolly and abstract) terms.

But objectives, once formulated, do tend to be stable — not least because there is often insufficient time for all the members of the planning committee to alter those objectives.

Related questions

1   How can a company ensure that it is continuing to pursue its objectives and follow its chosen strategies?

2   How far should the needs of individual managers and the organisation be taken into account when designing a new management information system?

3   How far do you think that relevant and adequate information is essential in order to optimise decision making?

4   Discuss how past performance might be able to improve tomorrow's results. What implications does the history of results have for strategic planning and corporate objectives?

Question 5

Consider the factors that might be considered by the management of a company which is attempting to determine in which part of the country it should relocate.

Tackling the question

The question is asking for more than a straightforward list of factors that need to be considered. What about the underlying costs — the obvious costs and the not-so-obvious costs? And what of the employees? How are they going to react? Are any likely to be made redundant? How would a move affect the local communities and the employees' families? That might be another cost. Morale may be affected, and the unions are not going to be happy about workers losing their jobs. It is important to stress why companies set up initially and, perhaps even more importantly, why they decide to relocate somewhere else.

Answer

In most cases the decision to move is forced by current lack of space associated with increasing turnover, inadequate production facilities and stockholding requirements. The reasons for relocation are many. It may make sense for a company to move closer to better road and/or rail links, or to an international airport to improve supply. The lease on an existing building may be about to expire, or the company may wish to present a different or improved company image. The company may wish to rationalise the organisation, to create a better working environment and to reduce its rental costs. Around 65% of relocating companies give business expansion as the reason for moving. Inner-city costs and congestion follow close behind.

Companies that simply do not have the time or inclination to handle the relocation decision themselves can save themselves a great deal of money and effort by using an agency to advise them. In the United States 70% of all company moves are handled by relocation agencies.

An appraisal of alternative location possibilities may involve the firm in considerable expenditure — a cost that has to be set

Guidance notes

The obvious location factors are the kind of items you might have learned in GCSE Geography — nearness to markets, resources, transport; but you will have to go deeper than that. In any question you need to be thinking of the magic word — 'implications'!

Incidentally, don't confuse 'locational factors' with statistical 'measures of location', such as the mean, median and mode, or else you'll really be off on the wrong track.

These specific location factors are fairly obvious, but you still need to know them. Don't forget to include the pros and cons of each location and site. Every location has some disadvantage. Tell the examiner what it is.

against the likely gains from getting a better location. There is also another cost: namely, that of the time taken up in the decision-making process and in the preparations for production at the new location. In effect, there may be a time lag in manufacturing, which can be very expensive in terms of lost sales. This being so, a factory that is available for production today may be chosen in preference to one that will eventually be a better prospect, but which cannot yet begin production.

A city location offers advantages in that it is an existing natural centre for road, rail or water transport. Facilities will have been devised and refined for the receipt of raw materials and the dispatch of processed goods to the customer. There is likely to be a flow of abundant and continuous labour, and networks of municipal or other public services, such as electricity supply, police and fire brigades, are available. There is also some gain in having available the professional services of the city in such matters as financing, the purchase of raw materials and the handling of export documentation. An additional advantage for the firm with limited resources of its own is that maintenance services, supplies of bought-in parts and subcontractors are likely to be readily available. On the other hand, the price of land in a city location is certain to be high and it may be difficult to secure a site suitable for the type of buildings needed. City-centre business rates may be prohibitive. Competition for skilled labour may cause wages to be higher than an alternative location. The conduct of the business could be subject to stringent planning regulations.

A suburban site, however, may hold out the inducement of less expensive land and buildings. The industrial estates that are now a distinctive feature of expanding towns offer special sites to manufacturing firms in search of a location. Premises on such an estate may be available, either for sale or tenancy, while the company that owns the estate may also lend on a mortgage to further the construction of a plant. Known as trading or factory estates, these areas are planned to accommodate a variety of industries rather than one specific area of production.

In a move to a rural area, assuming planning permission can be obtained, it may be possible to acquire land cheaply with the prospect of developing a purpose-built plant, with further space to expand. The burden of the business rates may be less heavy than in congested conurbations. Rural sites can meet the requirements of large independent establishments in a number of ways and it may be socially desirable for some plants, e.g. oil refineries and nuclear power stations, to be isolated from high-population areas. However, obtaining and retaining an adequate supply of trained labour may present difficulties.

Many firms have to compete internationally if they are to survive, and they rely heavily on the export markets. For a British firm, a production or assembly plant on the mainland of Europe may prove to be the most profitable and convenient proposition. On the other hand, there has been a significant influx of both Japanese and American companies into the UK during the past two decades, so that such companies might have a foot in the European door. Where a complex network of factories exists, however, the search for lower costs and competitive price advantages may lead to rationalisation of manufacturing and distribution facilities on the mainland of Europe.

> I think this is a very useful point to bring out. How many candidates will think of a location overseas? Yet it's a perfectly valid answer, especially when we talk of 'the global village', a single currency, the EU and harmonisation. What's so special about setting up in the UK? Why not eastern France?

Ultimately, it is the examination of costs that is the most relevant factor. Other things being equal, a firm will set up its establishment in an area where wage costs are comparatively low, and in a development area. A company already in production must weigh up the possibilities of transferring all or part of its operations. However, if most or all the existing employees are to be transferred, then extensive consultation with them must take place. Presentations should be made to groups of staff, detailing the features of the new area and the availability of schools, hospitals and housing. Indeed, some companies hire or set up specialist services — such as house buying and selling — specifically for their employees. The company may offer some form of compensation — financial or otherwise — to transferring employees. In addition, it may need to call for voluntary redundancies or consider severance pay to those employees who will be leaving the company.

> Unless there really are exceptional circumstances — such as highly specialised labour that simply isn't available anywhere else — cost has to be the main factor, but I would add 'potential' to that. OK; it's expensive now, but look at the benefits we're going to get in five or ten years' time — we're into corporate strategy now.

Comprehensive capital investment appraisal is needed to determine whether it will ultimately be commercially viable to relocate an enterprise. In those areas where the government particularly seeks to encourage further industrial expansion, additional investment grants may be available.

The costs, availability and transportation of raw material also need to be considered. Where perishability or other types of deterioration are a feature of material, it might seriously restrict the potential area of operation open to a producer. An example of this would be market gardening of fresh vegetables, where not only must the soil be suitable, but the accessibility of markets must be such that the crop will arrive in first-class condition. Often, a cost of greater significance than the purchase of raw material itself is that of specialist transportation, such as refrigerated vehicles. The effects on overheads of setting up on a new site include service costs and administrative and communication costs. The cost of transporting the finished product, delivery services, the need to replace damaged consignments and delays in replenishment must all entail a further reduction in the net return.

Government measures tend to change quite frequently, and it's sometimes difficult to keep up with them. A visit to your local 'Business Link' office might be useful if you're in any doubt — particularly if the syllabus requires coursework or projects.

Various forms of government intervention greatly influence the siting of a new plant. Government policies tend to have three main objectives. First, they are designed to counteract an excessive concentration of people in particular towns and cities. Second, the government is trying to develop areas currently dominated by declining industries. The final aim is to develop regions depressed because of their dependence on low-income, extractive industries, such as agriculture, forestry and fishing. The government's policies consist of a variety of financial inducements designed to encourage firms to move to the assisted areas, together with a form of deterrent to expansion elsewhere. Government grants may be available to help firms meet the cost of training labour in development and special development areas.

Planning and implementing a company relocation consists of a series of overlapping steps; it is not one single step. It will require considerable location analysis, site selection and relocation planning.

Related questions

1 What factors do you think should be taken into account when deciding how far a company should be decentralised? Explain the likely effects on managerial autonomy.

2 The eventual outcome of a SWOT analysis should be a strategic plan. Explain how such analysis may be useful in corporate relocation.

3 What are the major steps in corporate decision making? Explain the key considerations at each stage and the importance of collecting appropriate data. How do data differ from information?

4 What measures does the government currently employ to persuade companies — both national and overseas — to invest in areas of high unemployment in the UK?

Question 6

Discuss the role and importance of small businesses and comment on the problems that they tend to encounter.

Tackling the question

This is a favourite question in one form or another. The majority of businesses are small businesses by anyone's definition. It would be useful to give some indication of the growth and the demise of such businesses and to consider why many small businesses do not survive. The assistance offered by local councils and central government does tend to change or vary depending partly on political whim but, more especially, on the availability of support finance. There are main themes — with, perhaps, local variations on those themes — but the economic climate must be a major one. For example, the central government has recently introduced financial support for rural shops — such as village post offices — by not charging them as much for their business rates, but most of the funding comes from the local taxpayers.

Answer

Guidance notes

Recent figures have shown that on average 1,400 new businesses are registering for VAT each month — the highest figure ever recorded. Over 96% of all businesses in the UK employ fewer than 200 people. These companies provide 20% of all business turnover and 35% of all private-sector jobs. Although a particular strength of the smaller firm lies in its ability to satisfy the requirements of a local market, a significant feature today is the increasing international dimension to small business development and its management. In considering size and what constitutes a 'small' firm, the Bolton Committee of 1971 set a variety of cut-off levels of employment or turnover (e.g. 200 employees in manufacturing; annual turnover of £50,000–£185,000 in retailing; 25 employees in construction). According to the criteria used, some 46% of small firms were in retailing, and 43% of all small firms' output was in manufacturing.

Small firms provide many benefits to the community and possess several advantages. They are a stimulus to increased competition: the more independent firms there are in a

Here are the advantages of the small firm, but you must go on to explain why they are advantages, what benefits the community gets, and how they benefit the nation as a whole.

particular industry, the greater the competition and the lower the price will be. Small firms have a better record of industrial relations, with fewer industrial conflicts, partly because there are more opportunities for the staff to become personally involved in the success of the firm. Managers or owners are able to exercise much greater control over the operation of the company and to take a greater interest in their employees. They often succeed because the entrepreneur-owner has great motivation and commitment, which may be difficult to foster in a larger organisation. Small firms are often a source of technological innovation: a study in the USA showed that small firms come up with 4 times as many innovations per research and development dollar spent as medium firms, and 24 times as many as big firms. Small firms tend to be labour intensive, rather than capital intensive, and tend to create jobs. Another study in the USA revealed that, between 1969 and 1976, 88% of new jobs were provided by small businesses.

Research shows that small firms can achieve great success in 'niche', unexplored markets and make substantial profits, at least until the big firms decide to enter the same market. In addition, small firms can often get a product to the market place faster than the larger businesses. As small firms are less hampered by bureaucratic structures, decision making can be much quicker and more flexible. In consequence, they may be able to adapt more quickly than larger companies. In addition, of course, small firms frequently provide the 'personal touch' that may be characteristically absent in larger organisations.

And similarly with the disadvantages or, at least, the difficulties. Explain the problems and why they are problems, and to whom. Incidentally, words and terms such as 'downside', 'bottom line' and even 'upside' have crept into everyday use. 'Upside' doesn't make sense — but it's there. It's probably best to avoid them if you can — at least, in essays or reports. And I become apoplectic when I read statements such as 'the firm will lose out' or, worse, 'loose out'. Don't use slang or 'baby language'. And save your street talk for the street.

Despite these advantages, many small firms face significant problems. Because they are small, such firms rely heavily on their staff, particularly the more experienced members. If these employees leave, or the owner falls ill, then the firm can quickly succumb. Equally, such firms often rely on one product or a limited range of products, so in times of trouble they cannot diversify their activities as can large-scale enterprises. They may have difficulties in attracting and paying for highly qualified staff with specialist skills, such as accountants, marketing experts and engineering craftspeople, and in providing them with fringe benefits. Whereas large, well-organised enterprises can usually afford both good line management and specialist staff, small business managers are relatively isolated individuals, dealing with company policy and operational problems simultaneously despite their personal limitations. The amount of information that such managers have at their disposal may be limited in both quality and quantity.

Their inability to enjoy economies of scale may be significant. As a firm grows, its average cost per unit tends to fall to an optimum point, fixed costs can be spread over a greater number of units, it can buy in greater bulk and enjoy purchasing discounts, and it may be able to obtain loan finance at a preferential rate. Small firms may face difficulties in finding finance for start-up, growth and survival because they will probably have short track records, minimal fixed assets that could be used as security to support a loan, and a limited amount of finance provided by the owners. However, the Alternative Investment Market (the AIM), which opened in June 1995, is an attempt by the Stock Exchange to provide a stock market for smaller companies without it costing too much. Companies coming to the AIM are comparatively small and more speculative than those on the main stock market. Occasionally, they are start-up companies. The AIM is intended to be a cheap and easy way for smaller companies to raise risk capital. Nonetheless, many would argue that there does remain, in effect, a 'financing gap'. There has been, since the 1940s, an increasing number of initiatives, both private and public, to provide industry with adequate funding.

This is quite new, and certainly worth a mention as a source of finance. It shows you're on the ball. But don't go too deeply into the actual mechanics of the AIM unless you're asked to — and in this question you're not asked to!

Of particular note since 1979 is the emergence of 'venture capital', provided by members of the British Venture Capital Association. Since 1984 some £15.6 billion has been invested by British venture capitalists in British firms. The evidence to date suggests that venture-backed companies tend to achieve good results. A number of studies show that investments in smaller companies may offer higher rewards than investments in larger companies. It is argued that it takes a small company less time to develop a product, bring it to the market, and achieve profitability. The amount of cash invested in British companies during 1997 by venture capitalists soared to a massive £2.8 billion — the highest ever recorded in a single year. There is increasing concern, however, that there are fewer investment opportunities in the UK and that more venture capital will end up on the mainland of Europe, where there appear to be greater opportunities.

Over 120 different sources of finance are available to small firms. This plethora of sources can be confusing. It is important, therefore, that the small business first identifies both the type of finance and the amount of finance required. Most financial institutions do not simply provide the money; they also provide a financial package complete with specialist advice to both potential and actual borrowers. Government legislation, rules and regulations do tend to make life difficult for the small business persons. They may be grappling with local authority regulations ranging from fire precautions to pollution control, or with a plethora of paperwork from Health and Safety regulations to employment legislation, from accounts and audit requirements to VAT returns, etc.

A useful way of bringing the answer to a close. A conclusion, yes, but also quite a thoughtful one. It leaves the examiner thinking 'what a wise student...'!

The small business enterprise is a relatively fragile structure with limited resources to overcome its problems. Even minor problems can be a major threat to the company. Yet, paradoxically, it is the very smallness of such companies that often guarantees their success, survival and popularity.

Related questions

1 How structured should a small business be? Suggest what practices it might introduce to compete against larger organisations.

2 Analyse the problems that small businesses face, and suggest how information technology might help them to become both more effective and more efficient.

3 What effect might the prospect of inflation have on a small business tendering for a local authority contract?

4 How might a small business acquire additional finance and what are the likely resource limitations to expansion? How could a small firm protect itself from acquisition?

Question 7

What do you understand by the terms 'capital' and 'capitalism'? Consider the role of the business person and of the government in a mixed economy, and suggest how each contributes to wealth creation and the economic growth of a community.

Tackling the question

This question is quite profound. Capitalism is at the root of British business, so it is quite reasonable to expect candidates to know something about it and, of course, the nature of mixed economies. But you do not need to go into fiery arguments about the wickedness of capitalism or the perils of socialism. A comparison of economic models or systems is required, and some evidence of how and why businesses flourish within those various systems. It might be useful to consider the subject area within a more political framework — politics is about power and its use, and that applies also to any organisation. Alternatively, a more economic approach could be adopted.

Answer

Guidance notes

Capital can be defined as consisting of all those resources that help production or all those goods existing at a particular time that can be used in any way to satisfy wants in the future. Capital consists essentially of those goods (materials, machinery equipment, etc.) that are not wanted as goods to be consumed now, but which are to be used to produce goods and services for consumption tomorrow. The firm's property is called real capital to distinguish it from money capital — that is, the money available to purchase or hire the real capital. In the UK we live within a capitalist, mixed economic system, in which the means of production and distribution are owned, in theory, by a relatively small section of society that runs them at its own discretion for private profit.

The economic growth of a country is not dissimilar to the economic growth of a company. A company can increase its net worth only if it produces and sells more, makes bigger profits and/or ploughs back those profits into the business in the form of more fixed assets, more and better training, and more research and development. These, in turn, will increase productivity, resulting in lower unit costs and making improved products even more price competitive.

If a company makes more real profits and creates more wealth, the firm's employees can enjoy better fringe benefits, higher wages and greater security of employment; shareholders can reap the harvest of improved dividends; the government and the community can benefit from the increased yield from corporation taxes. In short, as a company's prospects and profitability improve, so too can the standards of living of all those associated with that company, and the economic growth of the country can be enhanced yet further. Most people contribute to a capitalist economy and most are indirect beneficiaries of such a system through insurance and pension funds, as well as by directly holding shares in companies. The state significantly intervenes in, and regulates the actions of, business for the apparent good of the whole community. Firms must operate within a legal framework. We live and operate in a mixed economy, i.e. there is an element of free market forces and an element of central government intervention and control.

This is where we must be a little careful. We are not arguing the merits of political systems — communism, socialism, capitalism — and we certainly shouldn't be making an inflammatory political speech! Simply explain the basic philosophy of those opposed to capitalism. We know it's all far more profound than this, but the subject is business studies not politics. Many would argue, of course, that the two are inseparable. Many would argue that business is all about politics — but you shouldn't; not in this answer anyway.

Capitalism tends to be opposed by those who believe in socialism because, it is argued, capitalism leads to economic inequality and the exploitation of labour and the consuming public. It is argued that public welfare rather than private profit should be society's objective and it is this concern that should motivate the economic system. It is also argued that capitalism leads to recurring economic crises — the booms and slumps of economic activity — which can be eliminated by careful central government control and direction of what to produce and when to produce it. In a mixed and predominantly capitalist society, however, if consumers want more of a product at a price that covers its costs of production, the additional supply will be forthcoming sooner under private enterprise. There is a rapid response of supply to effective demand. Nonetheless, in capitalist economies, there have certainly been booms and depressions. Although the growth of wealth in a capitalist economy is often rapid, it is often irregular too.

Here we begin to see some of the forces that act on a business, and how the climate is created in which the business must attempt to operate. The environmental, political and economic forces are, of course, very powerful ones.

There are two popular arguments in favour of private enterprise: that it disperses economic power and acts as a counterweight to the power of the state; and that it is the least expensive way of producing and distributing the individual goods used in the economy and of rewarding people for the economic services that they perform. On the other hand, it would be naïve to believe that the ends pursued by businesses always coincide with the public interest. So, in the background — even in a capitalist society — remains the government of the day, vigilant in its role as a crude regulator of aggregate demand and supply in the economy to achieve its macroeconomic objectives. These include stable prices, low unemployment, balance of payments equilibrium, the redistribution of wealth and economic growth. In effect, the government (and overseas events) sets the climate for entrepreneurial activity. 'Sunrise industries', such as micro-electronics, have had significant encouragement from a number of quarters; while others — the 'sunset industries', such as shipbuilding — have, in the light of worldwide excess capacity, found it extremely difficult to diversify, and closures and massive unemployment have resulted.

In a more or less free market economy, change not only occurs in many ways but it tends to occur at great speed and with bewildering frequency. The factors of production will increase the wealth of a society only when they are mixed with a suitable catalyst. In a mixed economy it is entrepreneurs and managers who decide how the resources are to be utilised in the most effective and efficient manner. Productivity can be increased by more and better-quality investment — fewer goods for consumption now, in favour of capital goods. Firms, however, will invest only when there appear to be profitable opportunities to do so. The relationship between businesses and central government is very sensitive and often very difficult because of the diverging short-term objectives of each. Productivity may also be increased through research and development (R&D) and through technological progress that may yield new products and new production methods. There is, therefore, a strong argument for government funding more technological (rather than military) research than it currently does.

Productivity, and attempts to increase it by all sorts of means, seems to run through everything in business and economics. This is justifiable because productivity isn't just about getting more — that's simply an increase in production. Productivity is about getting lower average unit costs, and that means greater competitiveness, more sales, more contribution, more profit and higher standards of living — eventually.

If the standard of living of the population, as a whole, is to rise consistently then the wealth or net worth of the country must also rise consistently. However, the calculation of these figures is no easy matter and the figures released must be treated with some caution. They may show the country's monetary wealth increasing, but they do not reflect the quality of life and the social costs of that wealth creation, such as pollution, congestion and other environmental hazards; the figures say little about the quality of housing, the infant mortality rate and the condition of the infrastructure. Finally, they tell us little about the 'black' economy — the so-called hidden economy. By definition, the hidden economy is difficult to quantify, but recent estimates suggest that 10–12% of transactions are not recorded in the official statistics, and that the volume of the hidden economy is growing. Estimates of lost tax revenue vary from £4.5 billion to £7.5 billion.

Here are some specific examples of how the government supports business, in all its many forms. You might think: why should government support business anyway? It's not the government's job. Some people believe that. On the other hand, it is the government's responsibility to stimulate economic growth — but I'm not going to get involved in party politics!

Governments do support businesses directly. In the UK alone, approximately 300 separate aid schemes are thought to exist. Such schemes range from the more general and those applicable to a whole industry to the highly specific, such as the Inland Waterways Freight Facilities Grant. The major scheme for supporting capital investment in the UK is Regional Selective Assistance (RSA). One of the prime objectives of RSA is the creation and safeguarding of jobs. Most UK government incentives are in the form of grants, but 'soft loans' are available from the European Union.

The fundamental prerequisite for a successful mixed economy, therefore, must be a fruitful and responsive partnership between central government, including European Union institutions, and the business community.

Related questions

1   What are the broad objectives of government macroeconomic policy and how might they be achieved?

2   Does the division of labour have more advantages for the individual employee or for the firm? Suggest how the division of labour might, or might not, help to fulfil the government's employment policies.

3   It could be argued that the services of the rail industry should be a social service in the national interest, and be subsidised no less than the education or health services. How far do you agree with this statement? Show how such subsidies might benefit the business community.

4   'Privatisation of public utilities may bring economic advantages; it also causes greater social deprivation.' Consider this statement and suggest why it might be true.

Human Relations and Organisational Theory

Question 8

'As organisations grow, they tend to become less flexible and more bureaucratic.' Discuss this assertion and suggest what measures, if any, should be taken to avoid it happening.

Tackling the question

The way in which companies are structured and organised has a major impact on their success. This question is about organisational structure, management styles and organisational theory. Different examining boards may call it different things, but it is important to know about communications, the internal structure of the firm and management structures. Some exam boards even use the correct term: 'the theory of organisations'. Much of it is to do with what some would call 'industrial sociology' with just a touch of 'industrial psychology'. Drucker's difference between efficiency ('doing things right') and effectiveness ('doing the right thing') would be a valuable theme to follow.

Answer

Guidance notes

When an organisation is conceived, the small numbers of dynamic and enthusiastic members usually have few rules and procedures, and there is little specialisation of roles. The organisation tends to be very organic. It is highly responsive and adaptable to changing environmental circumstances and pressures, e.g. market forces and competition. However, commercial success invariably leads to growth of the company and, to control and co-ordinate the activities of the individual members, more specialist roles and duties are agreed. In addition, an individual's freedom begins to be constrained as pressures grow to institutionalise procedures and routines. The firm begins to become more mechanistic. Its ability to respond quickly is reduced, even though its efficiency may have increased. As the organisation becomes larger and more complex, there tends to be an increasing division and specialisation of labour. In addition:

- There is an increasing number of rules and regulations to achieve not only standardisation of the products, but also standardisation of individual behaviour, i.e. conformity and compliance.

- Employees tend to occupy predetermined slots in the organisational chart and there is an apparently clear avenue of decision making. People are placed in charge of others and the organisational structure begins to grow and become increasingly hierarchical as tier after tier of management is added.

- Each layer of the structure is prescribed a defined amount of authority to take decisions. The structure evolves from being comparatively flat and amorphous to a taller, pyramidal and clearly defined shape. Accountability flows upwards and responsibility flows downwards.

- Spans of control become smaller and tighter; there is greater emphasis on such control.

- There is less individual freedom as members are required to become subordinate and submissive to the demands of the organisation.

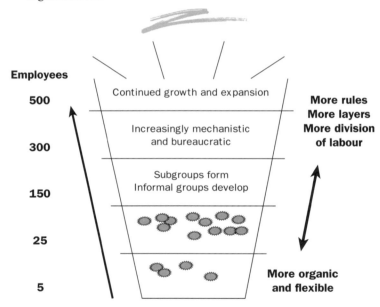

Figure 2 The growth of an organisation

Many people use the term 'bureaucracy', but I wonder how many actually understand what the true meaning is. In everyday language we tend to use it in a pejorative sense — almost insultingly. In the language of industrial sociology, it certainly doesn't mean that.

Such a structure is, in effect, becoming increasingly bureaucratic — a state of affairs that becomes accepted through the passage of time. But the concept of bureaucracy is not meant in a pejorative sense. It describes a set of social relationships first described by the German economist and sociologist Max Weber, who considered a bureaucracy to be the most efficient form of organisation. In a bureaucracy there are four main characteristics:

- Specialisation. The terms of reference of the job holder are clearly defined, usually through the increased use of job descriptions and job specifications, which not only list what employees are required to do, but implicitly define what they cannot do. In many ways, they act as a constraint on their input, but, it is argued, they allow for continuity when incumbents change jobs.

- Hierarchy of authority. There is always someone to whom a member of the organisation can appeal. The amount of authority at each stratum or layer of the organisation is clearly defined. This authority is perceived to be both rational and legal by the organisational members.
- Rules and procedures. A mechanistic approach to control and co-ordination develops, which tends to introduce inflexibility. The rules tend to proliferate over time so that the organisation can deal with new contingencies and still retain control and induce conformity.
- Impersonality. The bureaucracy is impersonal both to those within the organisation and to those with whom it deals outside the enterprise — including customers and suppliers. The rules tend to determine appropriate responses and reactions, to ensure equitable treatment, conformity and control. There is, in theory, no favouritism.

Bureaucracies were a nineteenth-century invention that promised rationality and order, but in describing them Weber placed a great deal of emphasis on the nature of power, authority and influence. The most frequent charges made against this idea of bureaucracy are that it ignores the informal structure and subsystems that develop in any organisation, and that it tends to suppress initiatives and innovation. Rules become ends in themselves, i.e. employees 'go by the book'. The system has no feeling as it becomes increasingly constricted and constrained by 'red tape'. Some writers suggest that this indictment tends to lay too much emphasis on the model of bureaucracy and that it pays little attention to the rich complexities that develop, particularly in action, when patterns of indulgence do begin to emerge. People can alter situations that they perceive to be significant for them. In practice, the rigid enforcement required by the model of bureaucracy tends to be significantly diluted and relaxed.

Clever, these people! They bend the rules, or get round them, often just to make the system work more effectively. It may not improve efficiency, but it does great things for effectiveness.

Weber recognised that no pure bureaucracy existed or probably would exist in ideal form. However, he believed that the closer the organisation came to this ideal form, the more efficient it would be. Many have argued that, while the organisation is moving towards this 'super efficiency', its commercial effectiveness is being sacrificed. It may be 'efficient', but is it 'effec-

Here's an interesting concept that is more than just academic rhetoric: the difference between 'efficiency' and 'effectiveness'. A company can be very efficient, but not very effective. In fact, it can be so efficient that its very efficiency prevents it from becoming more effective. People may become so preoccupied with doing things 'right' and 'by the book' — especially if there's an atmosphere of fear — that the customer or client may not be best served.

tive'? And efficiency, under capitalism, always means efficiency in terms of profit.

To overcome the inherent inflexibility and mechanistic style of bureaucratic management, the larger businesses attempt to decentralise decision making. Regional or product managers are afforded considerable discretion and autonomy, so that they might respond swiftly to changing market conditions and take advantage of such conditions. In addition, many talk of 'the global workshop'. Instant, cheap and easy communications mean that, despite the persistence of regional and local tastes, consumer tastes in many parts of the world are converging. Nonetheless, consumer demands for variety and instantaneity place increasing demands on companies which, in turn, must develop flexibility with the introduction of new methods, including just-in-time management and flexible manufacturing systems.

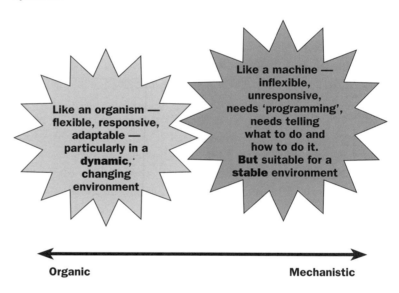

Organic   Mechanistic

Figure 3 Organic versus mechanistic structures

We seem unable to escape the tremendous influence that something called 'the environment' has on a business. But businesses are, of course, part of that environment. In a major sense, businesses do influence and affect the environment, and vice versa. They have to live together, or else someone — the government, the public — will do something about it.

It is argued that in a stable and comparatively unchanging environment, in which risks and uncertainty are minimal and events can be predicted with some degree of accuracy, a bureaucratic model and style of management are appropriate. However, in a dynamic and highly unpredictable environment, in which flexibility and speed of response are becoming key competitive factors, such a structure simply will not possess the adaptability to change promptly as market forces, competition and macroeconomic events dictate. Under these circumstances any organisation, but particularly a commercial one, must possess an ability to revert to an organic style of management that, like any living creature, not only seeks out relevant information, but acts punctually on such information to ensure that it survives and can take advantage of opportunities that present themselves. Evidence shows that businesses do not work effectively if they are held in the grip of a large, remote and omnipotent head office.

And if the evidence does show that — and it does — why do we still have large, bureaucratic, insensitive, inflexible organisations?

Related questions

1 Draw an organisational structure for a light engineering company employing 250 people, and outline the differences between a functional structure and a federal structure.

2 Distinguish between formal and informal chains of communication within a large company. Explain which system appears to be the more successful for the individual employee, and why.

3 'A bureaucratic, mechanistic organisation simply cannot respond to a dynamic market place.' What measures would you suggest to your senior management to improve the company's organisational structure?

4 'The division of labour and specialisation of jobs increases both efficiency and productivity, but it is at a cost to human dignity and creativity.' Do you think this premise has any validity?

Question 9

'Organisational conflict may be regarded as inevitable.' Discuss the phenomenon of conflict and its likely consequences for a business organisation. Suggest reasons why it might occur and what measures might be taken to reduce or resolve it.

Tackling the question

This is another key concept in organisational theory and management style. The plain fact is that conflict exists in all organisations, and there are many different kinds of conflict. We should attempt to understand it, which is what this question is searching for in the first instance. The answer should refer to a variety of views and look at the issue from a number of angles, including the implications for management policies. It is quite a profound question, but the subject cannot be avoided. The most significant aspects are the role of the individual and of groups, diverging objectives within the organisation and how compromises are made — or not.

Answer

Business management is about people — either as employees or as customers, or as both. And wherever people are gathered together, the plain fact is there will be conflict. The key point is not only about minimising it, but about handling it and turning it to the firm's advantage. At work, what is it that gets people angry and irritated? Why doesn't 'management' do something about it?

Conflict is a process that is neither good nor bad, but which has outcomes that can be judged favourably or unfavourably by those who are parties to that conflict. There are many different types of organisational conflict, but the stereotypical impression of conflict tends to be almost exclusively between the management and the workforce, or the trade unions acting on the workers' behalf. The terms 'management' and 'workers' tend, in themselves, to be evocative, and imply a division of purpose that in many cases is simply fallacious, since conflict is just as likely between individuals of similar status as between superiors and subordinates. In addition, intra- and inter-group conflict and tension may arise from the demands of the job, diverging objectives and limited resources. Conflict may be defined as any perceived divergence of interests between groups and/or individuals. However, such a simple definition does not reveal the complex tapestry of conflict in its many forms.

There tend to be three basic attitudes to conflict, one or more of which may be absorbed by managers. They can be categorised rather conveniently as the traditional view, the behavioural view and the endemic view.

- The traditional view sees conflict as something evil: counter-productive for the organisation and ultimately leading to increased inefficiency within the firm. Managers perceive that their objectives for the enterprise are threatened by the irrational non-participation and apathetic withdrawal (in Marxist terms, 'alienation') of the workers. Often, the workers are seen as being simply 'bloody minded' and uncooperative. Managers, on the other hand, may be seen as tyrants and bullies.
- The behavioural view regards conflict as being inevitable in any company because of the cosmopolitan nature of the inhabitants, and their diverging values, beliefs and attitudes.
- The endemic view tends to be rather similar to the behavioural view, in that it considers that conflict will always be present. It is in the resolution of that conflict that the approaches differ.

These last two approaches to conflict draw attention to the manager's fundamental task of managing conflict whenever it occurs and whatever its causes.

Conflict may have a variety of causes. First, there may be a difference between individuals' and corporate goals. Individuals have their own sets of goals, and these are likely to be different from those of the firm, and from those expressed by other individuals, especially those who are at a higher level in the hierarchical structure and who possess greater authority and greater access to information. Conflict also arises between different groups and subgroups within the system. For example, one group may have completely different interests from another and each group will identify priorities according to its own objectives. Group conflict may also occur when groups have to compete for similar roles and resources within the organisation.

If the formal system fails to satisfy the individual members or to resolve the conflict, an informal system may seem the best alternative. This informal system, with its own status, control mechanisms and communication networks, may channel the energies and commitment of the employees, thereby weakening the formal system and making it less effective. Conflict may occur between individuals and their jobs: for example, when there is a demand for an individual to complete a task as quickly and as cheaply as possible. In order to achieve economies of scale and cheaper unit costs, many firms have introduced mass production systems that, in turn, have led to the de-skilling of

Here I begin to explain the various kinds of conflict and how they might arise. These explanations do show evidence of deeper reading, but it's of little use quoting the theory or some nice, cosy thesis; the key point is 'so what?' What does it mean for management and the shop floor — and what, if anything, can be done about it?

many craft jobs. The new job may offer little opportunity for creativity and originality. Suppression of these qualities may lead to feelings of frustration and negativism. Conversely, however, role overload may occur when the individual is not up to the demands of the job. Another type of conflict may occur when individuals are unable or unwilling to form satisfactory relationships. The reasons may include competition for involvement, some specific area of dissatisfaction with status positions and simple personality clashes. If this type of conflict is allowed to escalate, it may reach a point where an individual's contribution and effectiveness are severely reduced.

> We can't treat or handle a condition unless we can recognise and identify the signs and symptoms. The symptoms may affect the whole organisation, a small group within the company or, of course, just one or two individuals within a department. Sometimes the conflict can be harnessed for the firm's benefit, but sometimes minor or even major surgery may be required.

The symptoms of conflict are varied, but they often include poor morale among the personnel, and this general disaffection may lead to increasing tension and a reduction in productivity; effective communication may be reduced; hostility between individuals and/or groups may increase; latent (or hidden) conflict may escalate into felt conflict, which, in turn, may lead to a hardening of attitudes and open, manifest conflict; by which time, the chances of resolving the conflict are considerably diminished. Not all conflict is harmful — open and controlled conflict may be catalytic; it may spawn new ideas and innovative methods. It may reveal clearly irrational views, on either side, which can be analysed and discussed. It may also pinpoint inadequacies within the system, which management may be able to resolve simply because it is now aware of those inadequacies. However, latent and uncontrolled conflict can be positively harmful.

It is foolish to deny the existence of conflict in its many guises, which occurs in all business organisations. Some observers say negotiate, others say bargain, yet others suggest a consensus approach. There are even those who suggest that conflict should be suppressed. Primitive suppression is still what many of us (and companies) tend to do when faced with a conflict situation. For most people, conflict is something to be avoided: it increases tension; it makes people feel uncomfortable and uneasy. Animals, including humans, are tension-reducing creatures.

> This is a useful point, isn't it? On the one hand, we are brought up not to be too 'pushy'. On the other, we're told that we should be assertive and speak up for ourselves and for others. Bit of a dilemma really! Think about that.

There also seems — at least in the UK — to be a social contradiction. While society educates us to be assertive, to speak up and to exercise individual rights, it seems reluctant to teach the value of confronting others on fundamental issues. Many people seem to be most vocal on trivia and seem to avoid asking embarrassing questions about major issues. Indeed, an unwillingness to communicate and a tendency to bury feelings may, more often than not, actually contribute to the conflict and make it worse. Yet change cannot be initiated and conflict cannot be resolved unless individuals are able to communicate effectively and openly. It is, of course, management's task to control and analyse conflict. Although management may attempt to suppress conflict at its source, it does have other options. Much can be done to harness the conflict to productive ends.

Related questions

1 'There is no such thing as bad management or good management; it is either incompetent or indifferent.' Discuss.

2 What are the advantages and disadvantages of management by objectives? How might a poorly administered system lead to frustration and conflict?

3 What are the likely consequences of a mismatch between delegated responsibility and authority? What should be done in this situation?

4 During the 1950s some companies, particularly in the USA, attempted to foster the idea that the company was 'one big happy family'. How true do you think this concept is in reality, and is such a state desirable or attainable?

Question 10

The importance of group dynamics was revealed by the Hawthorne investigations and the work of Elton Mayo. What is the nature of group dynamics and what factors tend to influence and contribute to the development of groups? Comment on their significance for business management.

Higher management courses spend a great deal of time examining this subject, and some massive tomes have been written about it. In a company, most people tend to work with other people, in departments, sections or divisions — that is, in groups. In fact, an opportunity to be with people and work with people is often given as one of the many reasons why people go to work — perhaps after the need to earn a living. How the people in these groups get on with each other can seriously affect the performance of the firm. Group dynamics might be examined from the standpoint of any of the participants. The works of Pondy, and Cartwright and Zander are particularly important in understanding the nature of group dynamics.

Answer

The Hawthorne experiments are one of the corner stones of business management. The fact is that you need to know about them — and rightly so, for this work was fundamental to much of what followed subsequently.

The Hawthorne experiments, which were carried out at the Western Electric Company in Chicago by Elton Mayo and his associates, demonstrated that both formal and informal groups, particularly the informal ones, may have a significant influence on the working and productivity of an organisation. Through a series of field studies, Mayo and his associates discovered the following:

- The amount of work that a worker actually does is determined not only by the worker's physical capacity, but by his or her social relationships within the firm.
- Non-monetary rewards play a central role in determining the motivation of the employee.
- Developing employees with a high degree of micro expertise and a high level of specialisation is not necessarily the most efficient form of the division of labour.

- Employees do not respond to management dictates and norms entirely as individuals, but also as members of an informal group.

Groups are essential to people, for it is in groups that people form their attitudes and aspirations, and develop their knowledge. Groups also provide people with security, set social norms and allow opportunities for education, emotional development and the satisfaction of needs, and for the fulfilment of individual as well as group goals. The study of groups is concerned both with the effect of the presence of others on individual behaviour and with the effect of the presence of groups on other groups. Individuals in a group are members of that group because they believe that they will be able to satisfy certain of their needs. When people join a group, they have seen that the group may have certain advantages. People are not, of course, members of only one group; they are members of many groups — family, friends, workmates, clubs, associations. In other words, people are multigroup members.

> Why do we spend so much time with others? What do we — and the others — gain from that association? What, in effect, are the benefits of belonging to any group?

Groups may be termed formal or informal, or at any point along a formal/informal dimension. At the one end of the spectrum, there is spontaneous association, and at the other, the highly formal and structured groups imposed by, say, the management of an organisation. Included along this dimension at any point are primary groups. These are the most influential for their members, since it is in these groups that people form their attitudes, values and opinions, and identify their personal goals. Examples of primary groups are the family, work colleagues and close friends. Primary groups are also important because they exercise a significant influence in social control and order. Marketing people, in particular, have long realised that the greatest influence on individuals' behaviour is the primary group. Hence it is at this group that their promotional campaigns are often directed.

> In understanding how and why groups do or don't work, an appreciation of the difference between formal groups and informal groups is very important. It is the latter that Mayo eventually spent so much time studying.

Groups that exist over time develop norms that consist of the accepted normal behaviour or standards for the group and its members. In the group context, norms may come from the group itself or be imposed from the outside. Infringement of a group's norms by an individual may result in action being taken against that individual, such as was witnessed during the Hawthorne experiments when 'Chisellers' and 'Rate Busters' were penalised by the other members of the group. Such penalties may include sanctions of one form or another. Solomon Asch demonstrated that there exists a strong compulsion to conform to group norms.

> This is an interesting point because it brings in the commercial or marketing aspects of group dynamics and how groups — both within and particularly outside the company — influence consumer buying behaviour. We may think we're immune and that we're our own person, but just think how powerful and influential 'peer group pressure' can be in your everyday life.

Groups satisfy two significant needs. First, they satisfy organisational needs, in that they provide the means whereby individuals work together so that the organisation's objectives may be met. Normally, groups are established for a particular purpose, but it should be realised that individuals may be members of several groups simultaneously, each of which is performing a different function from the others. Groups are an important means of achieving control over organisational activity, and their use as part of the formal organisation is consistent with the more participative approach to management, whereby individuals are more fully involved in the processes of consultation and decision making.

Second, groups satisfy a range of individual needs related to social and emotional fulfilment. The need for affiliation — to belong — is important for many individuals and may manifest itself in such a way as to reject behaviour that carries with it the possibility of exclusion. Groups, however, may have negative effects for both members and the organisation. As we have seen, there is a great pressure to conform to the ideals and norms of behaviour of the group. Personal stress can result from a mismatch between the group's norms and a person's norms or objectives. Problems may arise when formal organisational and informal group needs do not coincide.

The idea of a group norm suggests a shared belief in something that binds individuals together and to which all members are expected to subscribe. Clearly, individuals bring both knowledge and skills to group membership and this is the basic justification for membership within business organisations. The availability of technical knowledge and the willingness of individuals to make their contribution is important, but it will only go part of the way to ensuring that the group is able to discharge its task adequately.

This adds another dimension: the role and influence of the leader and/or manager. They needn't be the same person and very often they aren't. 'He' may be the appointed manager, but 'she' is the actual leader of the group. The manager has authority, but the leader has influence. Every team needs a leader — and every leader needs followers or, at least, a team. Clearly, the one will have an effect on the other, but the key question is whether it's for better or worse.

The effectiveness of the group is influenced significantly by the perceived and actual managerial and leadership ability of its key members. In many instances, managerial effectiveness may depend on the manager's ability to combine tasks and social skills successfully, so that the needs of the group and the individual are balanced to some degree. The existence of synergy is important to group effectiveness. As information is given and received, each participant builds upon a growing body of knowledge that, in turn, triggers better understanding, creativity and the release of additional information, which would not have occurred without the dynamics of the interaction process. Evidence shows that participative and consultative decision-making processes are more successful and effective than unilateral and autocratic processes.

Informal groups exercise a significant influence on individual behaviour. Groups can and do restrict output, contrary to management's expectations and demands. It is argued by the critics that any organisation is a complex, social unit in which there are many social groups and in which, and between which, there are many interactions. Most of these groups will share a similar interest and often pursue the same objectives — such as the continued viability and survival of the firm — but they will also have other interests and goals that diverge and that are basically incompatible. A company is a maelstrom of continuous power struggles between groups and among groups with conflicting values as well as shared ones.

Do remember that for every benefit, disadvantages or criticisms can usually be found, and you wouldn't be presenting a balanced view if you didn't present those criticisms.

Related questions

1   Discuss the major features and findings of the Hawthorne research. Do the findings continue to have any relevance today? Explain your reasoning.

2   Some people argue that most people work only for themselves and care little for others with whom they work. How far do you think this is true, and what conditions may lead to such a work environment?

3   Informal groups satisfy strong affiliation needs, it is argued, but should management take any notice of these needs of the individual employees?

4   If managers have little time to consider the implications of 'the Hawthorne effect', how might employees be made to feel they are doing a useful job, and how can alienation be minimised?

Question 11

What is job evaluation? Comment on the various methods and show briefly how it might be undertaken.

Tackling the question

This is a fairly straightforward question and the first part can be quite descriptive. But the second part of the question draws attention to the implications, and is therefore looking for a deeper appreciation and understanding of payment systems generally. It is asking you to examine the consequences for the business and, of course, for the employees. New systems will always be viewed with suspicion and may even be resisted. Part of the answer could include an understanding and examination of 'change'. A greater emphasis might also be placed on industrial relations.

Answer

The problems of defining and fixing suitable wage relationships between groups of jobs and workers are of considerable importance in both the theory and practice of wage determination. In the process of collective bargaining, employers and trade unions often base their position on comparisons with wages or wage changes in other firms and industries, and it is not uncommon for arbitration awards and decisions of minimum-wage-fixing authorities to refer to wage adjustments in other parts of the economy as an important factor in determining a proper or fair wage adjustment for the workers concerned.

Not everyone agrees with job evaluation. In fact, there's a great deal of business management practice and theory that someone, somewhere will disagree with — but that's no bad thing, for it stimulates discussion and develops ideas. Many firms don't use job evaluation in the formal sense of the term, but they almost certainly

The technique of job evaluation is often applied to deal with problems of comparative equity in wage determination, mainly, but not exclusively, at the level of the individual firm or plant. Its aim is to provide a means of establishing a wage structure that is acceptable to labour and management, and that, as far as possible, is fair in the sense of ensuring equal pay for jobs demanding broadly equivalent sacrifices from their incumbents. It also attempts to reward the greater efforts and hardships involved in some jobs as compared with others. In this way, the method is believed to be helpful in reducing dissatisfaction that may arise from existing wage differentials. Job evaluation is, therefore, the systematic comparison of the value of a range of jobs, so that ultimately a fair wages or salaries payment scale can be produced. In the past, job evaluation has largely been used for manual/shop-floor workers, but it is being used more and more for clerical and managerial staff.

There are four main types of job evaluation scheme, based on four different methods: the factor comparison method; the point rating method; the ranking method; the grade or classification method. The first two are usually referred to as 'quantitative', while the latter are known as 'non-analytical' methods. Underlying particular systems are certain broad common principles. First, it is necessary to be quite clear as to the criteria to be applied. Under all methods, except the simple ranking method, it is necessary to define either 'grades', in which jobs will be placed, or 'factors', in terms of which they will be evaluated. These criteria must be defined in a clear and unambiguous way. The next step consists of a more or less thorough examination and description of each job to be assessed, in terms permitting them to be evaluated according to the grade or factor descriptions established for the purpose. This examination has to be more detailed when an analytical method is applied than when a non-analytical system is used. Then the jobs have to be compared with each other, or with some other jobs. Finally, the jobs have to be arranged in a certain order, or 'ranked'. Each step involved in the introduction and the administration of a job evaluation system can be fitted into the framework of joint consultation and collective bargaining.

- *The factor comparison method.* In this method, the main job factors are utilised to compare 10 key jobs in the organisation, so that a company-wide basis for job evaluation is established. The main job factors included are usually: education and training, job skill, effort, responsibility, working conditions, physical requirements. All company positions are ranked in the same way, using 10 key jobs as markers or guidelines of the process. The factor comparison method is less refined than point rating systems and it is rather complicated in practice. For this reason, and others, it is not widely used.
- *The point rating method.* This system has proved to be the most popular job evaluation method, particularly when shop-floor evaluations have been carried out. A committee, including representatives of the company management, lists what it considers to be the job factors that can be used to

do use it in some form or another, on a very informal and unstructured basis.

There are many variations on the theme, but here are the basic methods of job evaluation, with a brief explanation of what each entails. However, this is quite a complicated area, particularly when we get into the details, and the question does say 'show briefly'.

Always, always present the disadvantages or limitations of every and any theory or technique, unless the question says otherwise. It's of little use being evangelical about a new drug if we find it has serious side-effects when used the wrong way! Some techniques and theories have serious side-effects and we should be aware of them.

evaluate any job. Point weighting is then given to each factor, depending upon its decided relative importance. All jobs, therefore, have wages or salaries in proportion to the job evaluation points allocated to them, plus a base rate. Current rates of pay are established by giving each point a monetary value. The wage rate equals the points gained (the monetary value of each point) plus the base rate. The principal advantage of the points method, compared with the factor comparison method, is that it uses points and not money values. This enables job evaluation and wage fixing to be kept separate. However, the method has also been said to suffer from lack of flexibility, in that it does not enable economic changes to be reflected in a changing wage structure.

- *The ranking method.* This is the simplest method of job evaluation. From job descriptions, each member of the job evaluation team takes the range of jobs that is done in one department and ranks them in order of importance. It is usual to rank pairs of jobs, matching and rematching pairs until the whole of the department has been ranked. The jobs in different departments are then considered and integrated by matching pairs. Alternatively, each member of the job evaluation team may award a number of points to all the jobs in the department, depending on how important they consider the jobs to be. When these scores are graphed on to a bar chart, the relative importance of the jobs becomes apparent.

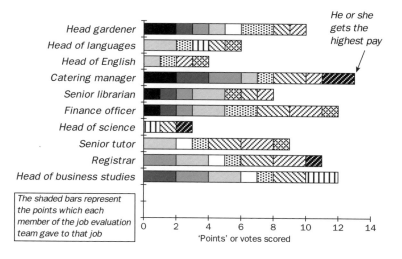

Figure 4 Ranking chart of relative importance

- *The grade method.* Grades often need to be established to make the points system usable. Grade and pay rates need to overlap, so providing flexibility in making merit and long-service rewards.

- *Time span discretion.* This has some bearing on the pattern of establishing fair wage rates. Elliott Jacques, in 1956, suggested that the length of time during which job-holders could carry out their jobs, and particularly make decisions without correction, was the crucial factor in determining wage rate. The longer the discretionary period, it was suggested, the higher the rate of pay for the job should be. This bold statement obviously requires many qualifications.

Job evaluation does have its limitations. Although there are many ways of applying job evaluation in a flexible manner, rapid changes in technology and in the supply of and demand for particular skills raise problems of adjustment that may need further study. In any case, job evaluation does not provide a complete answer to the wage problem. It has nothing to say about the absolute wage level and little about the absolute size of the wage differentials appropriate to the evaluated job structure. It is not concerned with questions of rewarding loyalty, seniority or merit, and its consistent application may be very difficult in cases where payment by results is applied. In this regard, employees' representatives will also wish to make a major contribution. Finally, job evaluation may take a long time and be quite costly to install, and may require specialised technical personnel. It should not be undertaken lightly.

This gives the opportunity to consider not only the monetary rewards, but the other factors involved in a 'rewarding' system. Some jobs provide a reward in themselves: the pleasure of doing the job (teaching, for example!). We should also consider the fact that it may be very difficult to produce a 'standardised', scientifically designed and mathematically precise payment system. For example, how does one build in 'performance-related pay' for the teaching profession, where 'education' is much more than just about passing exams?

Related questions

1   What advantages does a piece rate method of payment have over other payment systems?

2   'Profit sharing and performance-related pay should not be introduced into a company without performance appraisal systems.' Do you agree with this statement?

3   'Job evaluation simply increases the bureaucracy of an organisation and is quite unnecessary. There should be a going rate for a job, negotiated at national level.' How valid is such an argument?

4   'Job evaluation is a management tool that gives the company an opportunity to rationalise the salary structure to the benefit of all.' How far do you agree with this statement?

Question 12

Consider the implications for a business which decides to remunerate its manual employees on the basis of time rates alone rather than another payment system.

Tackling the question

The underlying theme of any payment system is, of course, about getting value for money — increasing productivity and reducing costs — and understandably so. It is also about promotion prospects and the recruitment and retention of personnel. Salaries and wages are by far the greatest part of a company's costs. A knowledge of payment systems is therefore important, but so too is an appreciation of the consequences in terms of human relations and developing commitment, trade union involvement and the fairness of the system. In economic terms, it would be valuable to consider wages and unemployment, inter-firm comparisons, income elasticity, tax disincentives and disposable income.

Answer

Over 50% of all industrial disputes are about pay and awards. In this regard, the government has the biggest headache of all, for it employs more people than anyone else. Many different systems have been tried — pay review bodies, negotiation, arbitration — and sooner or later the systems have been found wanting. Can there be anyone in the country who believes they are getting a fair wage, especially considering the sums awarded to some of the 'captains of industry'? Tricky subject, pay!

At its simplest there are two basic methods of payment: by time and by results. Payment by time rewards employees for the number of hours that they are at work and relies on supervision, group pressure and custom to maintain the required level of effort. Payment by results attempts to maintain the employees' level of effort by rewarding them according to their output. Whatever the method of payment, the desire to work is strongly linked with the desire for financial reward, and the degree of influence that financial incentives have on output depends on a number of factors, such as the relative wealth of the individual employee, the level of pay already being received and the influence of social factors, whether real or perceived. If wages are already high, a further increase may produce only marginal increases in productivity and commitment. It is facile and naïve to link effort only to financial rewards, for although such rewards do satisfy certain social and economic needs, there comes a point when the intrinsic qualities of work are at least as important as the purely economic factors. Attempts to motivate only through financial incentives are, in the end, doomed to failure, for as the effect of one pay rise wears off, the motivational influence disappears and another financial injection becomes necessary.

Money has been described by various writers as an 'anxiety reducer' and as a 'conditional reinforcer'. It is considered to be one of Herzberg's 'hygiene factors', which will cause job dissatisfaction if it is not present in sufficient quantity, but will not lead to job satisfaction if it is. There is some evidence to suggest that piece rate systems, either on an individual or a group basis, may lead to fewer symptoms of boredom. However, if the job itself is disliked by the worker or if there is no inherent reward in doing that task, even monetary rewards are unlikely to stimulate commitment. On the other hand, it must be recognised that job satisfaction, job enrichment, job rotation, job enlargement and many other well-used phrases and their varied connotations also have limited success. The whole arena of motivation and appropriate remuneration is a complex, often frustrating, aspect of company management. Payment is one comparatively small but essential ingredient of the motivational package.

Any payment system must be accepted by the workforce and must be perceived as being fair. The employees must have confidence in its operation and possess a complete understanding of the system, and, to this end, both shop stewards and supervisors can play a vital role in communicating and explaining the details of any proposed change in the payment system. The type of system installed depends partly on the nature of the work undertaken. It might be difficult to pay Members of Parliament on a piece rate system, but quite appropriate to pay them on time rates alone, for time work is suitable where standardisation of work is difficult and where the quality of completed work is very important. It is also used when it is not considered economic to introduce an incentive scheme or when output is not governed by the operator. Strong leadership and supervision are needed to compensate for the lack of financial incentive. However, with less pressure to complete the work, there is usually a commensurate increase in safety and quality standards. There are many variations of time rates, including measured day work (in which a flat rate is provided, but performance is also measured and used to assess the payment of annual increments); graded day work (in which the payment is based on a graded structure according to ability); and graded level day work (a yet more sophisticated scheme, utilising work measurement).

Measured day work provides earnings that do not fluctuate from week to week, where management has a greater degree of control. On the other hand, it does require a great deal of management supervision, and it may be difficult to maintain

Well, that's true. If you haven't got any, that's a real anxiety. But when does one have 'enough' money? And if, as an employee, I think I'm not getting enough, what am I going to do about it — and what, then, will be the implications, and costs, for the company?

the system as an incentive scheme. The 'banding' may become the norm from which to start the next round of pay negotiations. It also requires good management–union relationships, with a high degree of trust and openness.

An important point. Firms get a good reputation too, don't they? You can probably think of a company near you that is well known for the way it looks after its employees — and still makes a reasonable profit — and other firms that don't seem to care quite so much. So what?

Whatever payment system is introduced, its success will be determined significantly by the history and the nature of industrial relations prevalent within the company and of the relationships between management and employees. Nonetheless, if employees feel that they are trusted and that their financial rewards are secure, there is likely to be an increase in co-operation and a willingness to investigate new and improved production practices that may, in turn, lead to increased productivity. Individuals have an image of themselves and put a value on themselves. With this self-image and self-value is a level of aspiration, which may or may not be a conscious feeling, of what the person wants to do or become. These aspirations may have no foundation in financial security. Most employees want some security of earnings: they do not particularly want their pay levels to fluctuate widely from week to week, or month to month.

Many would argue that any time-based system of payment should carry with it a performance appraisal system. Some medium-sized and large organisations have introduced structured performance appraisal schemes but, all too frequently, the reality tends to be very different from the stated objectives and policies. Very often, regular appraisals do not take place — managers are too busy, the demands of the market place take precedence, operational matters become more important. If the appraisal does take place then very often no conclusions are drawn, and little use is made of the appraisal in determining staff development, training requirements, promotions and pay rises.

Appraisal reports and performance-related pay are all the rage these days. They are, in a sense, a way of measuring an employee's commitment as well as productivity — especially if that person is producing baked beans or chocolate frogs. But just how does one formally 'appraise' a nurse or a soldier or a social worker?

Appraisal reports and reward mechanisms are — or should be — linked. In addition, sensible performance appraisal commences with well-established organisational and departmental goals. To introduce any scheme, however, will certainly require the co-operation and commitment not only of the line managers but also of the employees' representatives. The whole concept of appraisal must be fully accepted and supported by all personnel, if it is to function satisfactorily. To this end, any payment scheme, whatever its basis, will require periodic updating and review.

Related questions

1 Despite moves towards harmonisation, there remain major differences between wages and salaries. How important is it to rationalise a company's payment structure?

2 What are the main elements of a payment package, and what part do you think an incentive payments scheme should play?

3 The idea that incremental salary systems keep the total salaries stable around the midpoint of scales is seldom correct when there is low staff turnover. Explain why this might be so and what the company can do about it.

4 If incremental scales cease to be self-financing through lack of labour market movement, what advantage is there to the employer in keeping them?

Question 13

Evaluate the various theories of leadership, and consider whether there is any difference between a 'leader' and a 'manager'.

Tackling the question

Many have written about 'leadership'. The problem is not so much what to include, but what to leave out. Fiedler is often quoted, for example, and his 'contingency model of leadership effectiveness'. Certainly reference should be made to recent models of leadership. The key point is that the terms 'leadership' and 'management' are not synonymous. So, in any essay of this kind there is a need to be selective. Select whatever models you think make the point and, of course, help you to answer the question. An additional or alternative approach might be an examination of power and influence. As usual, it is of little use writing simply about the theories; the implications for management and management development also need to be presented.

Answer

I've tried to keep this essay fairly straightforward, but not superficial. I cover some of the leading and more well-known theories, but I appreciate that I have been selective; that's my judgement, just as it will be yours in the exam.

The early views of leadership considered that leaders were born not made. Often — although there are notable exceptions — this innate attribute was linked with class or social position. This system should not be ignored. It still exists, but with diminishing influence. It may well have been appropriate to a rigid class and status system, such as existed in Britain at the turn of the century, in which the born right of the few to control the many was accepted by the majority. This fact underlines one of the problems in defining leadership — the style of leadership that is successful is the one appropriate to the social system and environment in which it operates. To develop a generalised theory of leadership, therefore, it is necessary to recognise the need for style flexibility. As the autocratic methods of motivation (e.g. fear of dismissal) decline in the face of better education, more leisure, increasing prosperity, better welfare and job security, managers increasingly manage with the consent of the workforce, rather than by the authority vested in them by the company. Without followers, there can be no leaders!

Exam Success Guide

Maslow argued that over time people's motivations will change from basic survival needs towards self-expression and self-fulfilment. In the western economic world, with a workforce rapidly moving into the last two or three stages of Maslow's hierarchy, autocratic styles and born rights to manage are no longer appropriate or sufficient to gain the consent of the managed. Rather, it is necessary for the manager to exhibit the leadership skills that can gain this consent. Katz and Kahn see every act of influence in an organisation as an act of leadership. Again the need for leadership flexibility is important. The organisational structure and the leadership styles are contingent on the tasks that have to be done, the technology involved and what is going on in the environment. What might be right today may be inappropriate tomorrow. This sounds like common sense, but it has given rise to a modified school of management thought known as the contingency approach. The contingency approach holds that there is no one best way of organising, but that all the theories that have been put forward should be used only as they apply to a particular situation. For example, it may be possible to use one type of organisation in some parts of the company, but a different type of organisation in other parts of the same company. However, such flexibility will be possible only in a co-operative climate, and this climate will develop only if the workforce has given its consent to the leadership roles.

> Here we are dealing with leadership in the practical, 'managerial' sense, not the more abstract or esoteric. Practitioner 'academics', such as Katz and Kahn, have made a major contribution to leadership in a management or commercial environment. So, for me, their ideas are important.

R. Blake and J. Mouton attempted to define managerial styles on a grid system that relates concern for people with concern

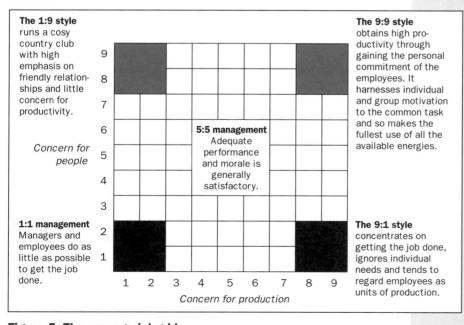

The 1:9 style runs a cosy country club with high emphasis on friendly relationships and little concern for productivity.

Concern for people

1:1 management Managers and employees do as little as possible to get the job done.

5:5 management Adequate performance and morale is generally satisfactory.

The 9:9 style obtains high productivity through gaining the personal commitment of the employees. It harnesses individual and group motivation to the common task and so makes the fullest use of all the available energies.

The 9:1 style concentrates on getting the job done, ignores individual needs and tends to regard employees as units of production.

Concern for production

Figure 5 The managerial grid

The point comes across time and time again. It seems so obvious to me. Yet it is astonishing how many managers will not adopt this approach. On the other hand, perhaps it isn't astonishing. You might like to think why it is that so many managers can be and are autocratic.

for the task and getting the job done. The managerial grid is a useful aid for managers when considering their own organising performance, in their own department or subsystem, but it has tended to fall out of favour, since it shows *what* should be done, but not *how*. It is also necessary to remember that no single style is universally ideal and that style flexibility is imperative. Tannenbaum and Schmidt recognised the need for flexibility in relation to a situation and developed a model of leadership based on delegation and decision making. The successful leaders tend to use a style that works towards the 'consultative/participative'. Such leaders are thus allowing opportunities for the employees' self-expression — assuming, of course, that the organisational culture actually encourages such self-expression.

It is becoming increasingly clear that people are motivated by challenge and responsibility, rather than tight controls and implicit threats of punishment. The suppression of feelings by an individual is dysfunctional. There is no doubt that the involvement of employees enhances the prospects of successful change and diminishes the resistance to change. It seems unreasonable to provide people with a boring, repetitious or unchallenging task and then expect them to put forth maximum effort in carrying it out. Highly structured, bureaucratic organisations often lead to tasks that people find uninteresting and unchallenging. They may leave the company or, if they stay, place increased emphasis on material rewards and conditions surrounding their tasks.

Rensis Likert undertook a number of studies, during which he examined management and leadership styles in such industries as insurance, railways, car manufacturing and chemicals. A number of significant features emerged:

- There is a marked difference in the leadership patterns of the supervisors of high-producing groups and of low-producing groups. The former tend to be employee-centred and aim to build up effective work groups. The latter type of group is led by a supervisor who is more task or production oriented.
- The freedom — within acceptable and defined limits — of employees to set their own pace (or for the group to set its pace) appears to be directly related to the level of productivity. High-performance managers give less specific direction, and put forward general goals with higher involvement from the workforce.
- An effective interaction–influence system is required for high performance; in essence, the amount of influence that superiors have with their subordinates depends on the degree to which they can influence them.

Efficiency in industry and commerce depends on the optimisation of the resources available — financial, technological and human. The most important and the most problematical is the optimisation of human resources which, at its best, amounts to effective leadership. Financial and technological resources are 'managed'; people are 'led'. Leadership is fundamentally different from management and the two should not be confused. If managers can be leaders and leaders can be managers that is a bonus. Evidence shows that the approach of high-achieving managers is to examine their own behaviour and determine what they must do to enable them to release employees' energy in the pursuit of common goals. In other words, there is a shift from the command and control style of traditional management to one where the leader creates the conditions under which ambitions can be achieved and within which people can find meaning in their work. Effectively, management is about using institutional authority; leadership, however, is about vision, exerting influence and providing a clear sense of purpose.

I like this point, which is why I have difficulty with the term 'human resources management'. For me, such a term makes employees no more important than a piece of machinery or any other resource, such as a piece of land or an empty building. It takes the personal out of personnel. People — employees — are the most important asset in most organisations. They aren't — or, at least, should not be — inanimate objects to be deployed or dispensed with at the whim of management. Should they?

Related questions

1   Are there any limitations on achieving job satisfaction for all employees? Does it really matter as long as they are getting a reasonable pay?

2   Many would argue that 'leadership' is something within an individual. How useful and successful do you think 'leadership development and training' is?

3   How flexible should managers be in their relationship with their subordinates?

4   Consider the factors that might lead to effective teamwork and discuss the role of the manager in achieving that teamwork.

Question 14

There are many theories of motivation. With reference to the main findings, suggest what use, if any, they might be to a practising manager.

Tackling the question

Theories of motivation are abundant and most, if not all, theorists have been criticised. It would be useful to explore some of those criticisms. However, this kind of question really does produce some quite irrelevant answers and lots of rhetoric; it seems that anyone who has ever written anything about 'motivation' — and many have — is included in the answers of some students. Of course, you need to know some of the theories, and the main findings, but the key point must be 'so what?' How can such ideas be applied to the shop floor and translated into practical reality? That, of course, is the thrust behind the second part of the question. It seems perfectly rational that an understanding of human behaviour in the workplace — industrial psychology — should be a prerequisite for any manager at any level in any department. In fact, a departmental approach might also be appropriate.

Answer

The persistent theme that runs through all the writings and research on motivation is the requirement to satisfy a need of some kind. A need, of which the subject may even be unaware, begins a motivational sequence. Motivation is only one of the many determinants of behaviour, but it is a highly influential one.

A fundamental problem that commercial organisations face is not only getting people to work for them, but making employees give more commitment once they are on the pay-roll. Increasing an employee's motivation is about increasing commitment, which is about increasing productivity. While many companies manage to engender commitment from their employees, many more companies fail to do so. The more successful firms — in terms of sales revenue, profits, employee satisfaction, reduced labour turnover, customer goodwill, etc. — effectively provide the conditions within which, and through which, the employees give consistently of their best. Such employees are motivated to work harder and for longer periods, and to achieve some kind of self-fulfilment in the process. Empirical evidence shows decisively that most people have a positive self-image. They tend to think of themselves as 'winners'. Evidence also shows that the more successful companies constantly strive to reinforce this notion. However, if people carry a negative image of themselves — 'losers' — they will in due course begin to act like losers. This concept, clearly, has implications for any company in areas such as sales quotas or production levels. Targets that are set consistently high by management and that are rarely achieved by individual employees (or departments) have a pernicious and demoralising effect, whereas when the employees make and achieve their own targets in consultation with their line manager, there is an enormous feeling of self-satisfaction.

Yes, everyone wants everyone to be 'happy' at work! It's like apple pie and home cooking. But there's little or no correlation between being happy at work and working harder. Happiness simply doesn't equate with higher productivity. I can be very happy being very lazy! Being quite cynical, one might say that the reason why 'motivation' and related subjects are popular areas of study is that they may lead to decreases in absenteeism and labour turnover, to increases in productivity, to lower costs and ultimately to higher profits.

The successes of individuals have a cumulative effect. Past personal successes lead to greater and even more persistent attempts to succeed again, and to keep on succeeding. Although the behavioural scientist B.F. Skinner has been criticised, an important and undisputed factor emerges from his work: namely, the concept of positive reinforcement; of suitable rewards for a job well done. The significance of this point is that people who are punished for a poor job are not simply less inclined to behave in a proscribed way; they may just learn, over time and with experience, how to avoid the punishment and sanctions. Positive reinforcement not only teaches positively, but has the decided advantage that it enhances the person's self-image. A study of school teachers showed that when they had high expectations of their students, that alone was enough to cause an increase of 15 points in the students' IQ scores. Despite the evidence, research shows that astonishingly few managers know of positive reinforcement, even by any other name. Of those who do, few are inclined to use it. However, it is important to realise that reinforcement that is frequent and regular begins to lose its impact, mainly because it comes to be expected. Intermittent and unpredictable reinforcement is more effective, and small rewards, almost of a symbolic nature, are frequently more effective than large ones. Other researchers have shown that any job must also provide for intrinsic motivation, i.e. the employees must believe that the job is inherently worthwhile, if they are to be committed to it.

Motivation and related areas are all subjects within the study of psychology, and here we're concerned particularly with industrial psychology (and consumer psychology, of course) — with what turns people on at work, and when consumers buy, or don't.

A study of the work of 20 behavioural scientists has shown that the concept of 'self-actualisation' or 'self-fulfilment' appears to feature prominently in people's hierarchy of needs. Maslow described other factors — esteem of others, status, survival needs. Herzberg talks of hygiene factors ('why work here?') and

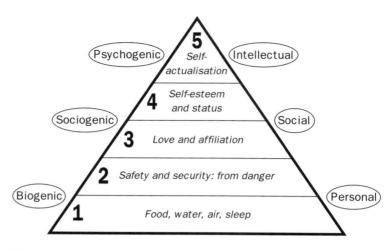

Figure 6 Maslow's hierarchy of needs

motivational factors ('why work harder?'), and developed his ideas of job enrichment. McLelland emphasises three important needs of power, achievement and affiliation, which he describes as nPow, nAch and nAff, where 'n' is an indeterminate amount. The expectancy theory of Vroom explains how people are motivated. Vroom argues that the strength of the motivational force is a function of how much people want to achieve a particular objective and what probability they give to actually achieving it. It may be comparatively easy to provide the conditions leading to successful motivation of those employees who already enjoy a high level of discretion and autonomy; it may not be quite so easy to do this for those employees engaged in routine and tedious tasks. With these kinds of job, management's ingenuity will be taxed in finding a less tedious way of doing an inherently tedious task. Many firms have introduced job enrichment, job rotation and autonomous work groups.

Now we can start to consider the impact and importance of motivation studies on the workplace, and how such studies can be implemented there. But we should also give examples of good working practices and those firms that have had some success or, at least, have been innovative and enlightened in this area.

The benefits associated with quality circles, in which individual employees are encouraged to comment on the product's design and quality, or on the production process itself, are also becoming more widely recognised. While, in the short term, the introduction of job enrichment, quality circles and greater individual freedom may be marginally more expensive, in the long term there appears to be a significant increase in productivity and employee morale. Inevitably, management style and receptiveness will influence the success rate. Likert demonstrates clearly that worker participation in decision making, and a reduction in management autocracy, leads to increased productivity. Any management style or organisational structure that recognises the individuality of the employees, that allows for greater recognition of the total attributes that an employee brings to a firm, and that allows for such employees to satisfy needs, other than the purely biogenic and economic ones, is more likely to create the ambience and conditions that will encourage the commitment of the workforce.

While economic rewards do have some motivational influence, their use and marginal utility tend to decline in importance over time. A financial injection in the form of higher wages may produce an immediate response, but its effects will be short lived; it will not be long before another injection is necessary as the effects of the first one begin to wear off. Increasingly, the purely biogenic needs assume less significance as they are achieved and satisfied, and the psychogenic needs begin to dominate. Motivation is an innermost force and a personal quality. No company or manager can motivate an employee in the long term; all that can be done is to provide the environment in which individuals can attempt to satisfy their own needs. If the company is unable to satisfy those needs, the employees may seek satisfaction and challenge elsewhere. In effect, employees need to be treated as more than agents to be manipulated with carrots and sticks. Theories of motivation that ignore the emotional and psychological aspects of motivation, and which rely almost exclusively on the logical and rational argument of financial incentives, have consistently encountered difficulties. Effective managers recognise that, as far as personnel are concerned, management is more a psychological business than a logical one.

> This a very relevant point. It leads inevitably to that well-known and over-used business studies question: 'Money is not the only motivator.' Discuss.

Related questions

1 In what ways, other than by changing the payment system, do you think the motivation of the employees of a light engineering company might be improved? How far is it true that satisfied workers will be more productive employees?

2 If a person wants something badly enough — such as money — he or she will work hard whatever the job. On the other hand, some people think that money is not the only motivator. What do you think? Give examples in support of your conclusions.

3 How far do you think Maslow's theories provide an adequate explanation of motivation at work?

4 What would be the most appropriate methods of identifying the training needs of (a) shop-floor operatives and (b) a newly appointed sales manager?

Question 15

'Industrial democracy and worker participation are obsolete concepts. There is no place in management for the shop-floor workers.' Consider this statement and evaluate the arguments for and against worker participation.

Tackling the question

This is not, perhaps, quite the popular or topical question that once it was but as new, in vogue ideas, such as 'empowerment', emerge the concept of worker or employee participation is never far below the surface of labour relations. Of course, for those who are actively involved in labour relations the issue is still a real and pressing one and you should say why. Similarly, you should draw attention to employee participation, managerial styles, and increases in productivity; in fact, that's what it's all about: productivity improvements and lower average unit costs. Mention them. The question starts off in a deliberately provocative way. That does not mean you have to agree or disagree with it, but it does mean you have to present a balanced and rational argument.

Answer

Industrial democracy challenges the legitimacy of decision making by management alone. Worker participation consists of any set of social or institutional devices by which subordinate employees, either individually or collectively, become involved in one or more aspects of organisational decision making. Industrial democracy can take several forms, but basically it involves the participation of employees in board-room decision making, either in influencing or in taking such decisions. In other words, it means that employees gain access to, and influence over, the strategic direction of the company.

In many European countries, employees have the right to be represented at some level of company management decision making. Companies in Germany with a workforce greater than 2,000 must ensure that half of the board members are employee representatives. Similar practices operate in France, the Netherlands, Luxembourg, Denmark, Sweden and Belgium.

In the UK proposals for establishing the legal right of employees to participate in corporate decision making have been a major political and industrial relations issue since the early 1970s, but the history of the movement can be traced back to the early nineteenth century. While there has been significant reform for the working class during the past 150 years, there is still no legal right for employees to participate in company decision making. The traditional view is that managers are accountable to the shareholders. Any shared power that employees have achieved has happened largely through the intervention and insistence of the trade union movement and through collective bargaining.

Some history — a brief history — is often useful in setting the subject in context. But don't go too deeply into it.

The report of the Bullock Committee, with majority and minority versions, was published in 1977. It proposed that in companies of over 2,000 employees the board of directors should consist of equal numbers of shareholder and employee representatives, plus a smaller group of co-opted independent members — the $2x + y$ formula. In the event, no Bill went through Parliament. However, the Companies Act of 1985, in particular, does require firms with more than 250 employees to provide them with relevant information and to make employees aware of the financial and economic factors affecting the performance of the company. The 1982 Employment Act also requires companies with more than 200 employees to include in their annual report a statement of action taken to introduce or develop arrangements for employee participation. A survey in 1981 showed that at least 42% of manufacturing plants had joint management and employee consultative committees.

Some companies have deliberately embarked on a policy of involving their employees, e.g. ICI, Philips, Volvo, the John Lewis Partnership, and have developed autonomous and semi-autonomous work groups that meet to discuss such issues as production scheduling, shift planning, quality circle issues, and health and safety matters. However, in the absence of board-level representation, there is no doubt that some trade unionists find it very difficult to influence corporate decision making. Other companies, such as Polaroid, have taken the concept one step further. Polaroid employs about 14,000 people, and employee representatives sit on committees that represent employees with complaints in a hearing before management. Researchers claim that many management decisions have been overturned in this process. If employees are not satisfied, they are free to submit their case to an outside arbitrator.

This shows that you're familiar with the latest thinking in this area. It's probably too early to decide whether it's a 'good' thing or a 'bad' thing; the fact is that it has arrived and we should be aware of it. That, of course, is true of many aspects of business management. The theory of business management — if there is one, or ever was — is never static; it's a dynamic and evolving subject and you should keep up to date with the latest thinking by reading relevant magazines and journals.

It is argued that employee participation will bring:

- personal development of the employee;
- greater industrial democracy, with workers having some say in their own future and corporate destiny;
- improved and improving industrial relations;
- increased industrial efficiency;
- corporate cohesiveness and *esprit de corps*;
- shared corporate objectives, and a greater determination to achieve them, for the benefit of all.

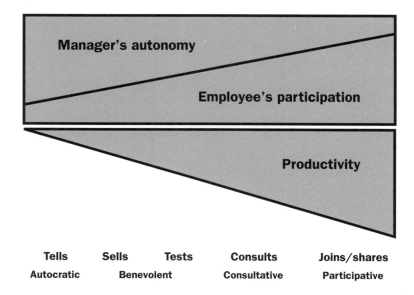

Figure 7 Participation and productivity

Nonetheless, the arguments against employee participation in decision making are also quite compelling:

- Some employees take the view that it is not their responsibility to take decisions; that is what the managers get paid for.
- Employees may not have the skills, technical knowledge and education to handle complex organisational and/or financial issues.
- Employees may feel socially ill at ease, daunted and apprehensive at sitting on the same board as their bosses.
- Managers must take a medium- and long-term view; employees may not have the same perspective.
- Employees' representatives may be very reluctant to support decisions that might adversely affect some members of the workforce, e.g. redundancies and plant shutdowns.

Inevitably, such arguments are countered by those in favour of greater industrial democracy for the following reasons:

- It acknowledges employees' aspirations to have a greater say in events that affect their work.
- It increases the degree of job satisfaction achieved.
- Far too many company decisions are taken at levels remote from the shop floor, inevitably resulting in some degree of alienation for the employees.
- It increases the degree of employee motivation and commitment.
- It reduces the possibility of conflict, or rejection of company decisions, because the employees have been instrumental in formulating those decisions.
- It uses the employees' skills, knowledge and experiences.
- Modern education and training no longer produce 'drones'; young people are encouraged to think and to question. Their latent abilities should be fully utilised.

A deceptively simple idea that is gathering momentum is that of empowerment. Empowerment entails giving individual employees some 'ownership' and control over their job; it gives them the authority to make decisions within a limited sphere, arguing that employees are responsible for their own actions and should be trusted to do those jobs. Evidence suggests that empowered employees are more productive and effective employees. It many ways, it has the same meaning as 'delegation', but it goes much further. Given the right environment, it is argued, most employees will flourish and grow.

The deep recession of the early 1980s, and particularly its effects on the manufacturing base, allowed managers to wrest control from the unions, which had dominated the industrial relations scene of the 1960s and 1970s. It must therefore be considered unlikely that management will now give up its perceived, traditional right to manage. Moreover, extensive research during the 1980s suggested that employees actually had little interest in making decisions without management involvement. Twice as many people wanted involvement only in matters concerning their own work and conditions as those who wanted involvement in issues concerning the company as a whole. Clearly, therefore, empowerment is a move in the right direction.

An intriguing area to consider is 'motives'. What have managers and employees got to lose if there is greater involvement of employees in decision making? More importantly, what do they both stand to gain?

I wonder what this says — if anything — about the non-managerial employees?

Related questions

1   Are there any advantages to employees owning shares in the company in which they work? Do you think that a 'share-owning democracy' is likely to improve the wealth of the country?

2   What do you understand by the term 'collective bargaining'? Does it still have a place in pay negotiations today?

3   Why is the role of the workplace representative or shop steward important in employee relations?

4   Research suggests that managers tend to favour forms of participation that emphasise communication and consultation, whereas trade union officials favour extensions to the range of items subject to collective bargaining. Why do you think this should be so?

Question 16

Why might change be resisted? Consider what measures, if any, management might take to minimise such resistance.

Tackling the question

Clearly you need to give reasons why change might be resisted and, if possible, consider the consequences of such resistance both for the employees and for the business itself. But the real depth comes in the second part of the question — how to minimise change or harness it to good effect for the benefit of all sections of the company and the community in which it operates. The three Cs are important: communication, consultation, collaboration... and, therefore, management and leadership styles. 'Autocratic' is all about fear; 'democratic' is more to do with trust. Consider the qualities which all employees bring — experience, training, skills. How are they to be harnessed? Quality circles and brain-storming sessions are relevant here.

Answer

Change is inevitable. The dynamic environment in which the firm exists and operates may necessitate frequent reappraisal of existing organisational techniques, methods, product suitability, service delivery and even philosophy — in response to a shifting demand curve, a shift in the public's spending habits, the introduction of competing services or products, the identification of new market opportunities, technological innovation, government legislation, and changes in society's beliefs and expectations. A viable organisation is one that is compatible with the environment. The essence of corporate survival, therefore, is to bend with the winds of environmental change. There can be no movement without friction, but the friction can be minimised.

Change of any kind — in job design, salary and wage structure, working practices and routines — can be very difficult to implement. People become comfortable with what they know; they have learned, through experience, to overcome the inadequacies and peculiarities of their existing organisation, and its methods and styles. Change brings uncertainty, doubt and the unknown. Change disturbs an individual's equilibrium, and

Guidance notes

The world, the environment, the communities in which businesses operate are never static. If businesses want to stay in business, they must not only detect those changes, but change themselves in order to cope with the wider changes. This may bring new and additional problems.

interferes with traditional practices and working relationships. Not everyone is going to welcome change with open arms. Many will have a preference for the status quo. Proposals to introduce change will bring many reactions and some of these will be positive, but many will be negative, unless the management has policies and procedures for minimising and dealing with resistance.

The major reasons for change resistance and increased friction include:

- fear of the unknown, which is probably the most powerful driving force of resistance;
- apprehension about loss of status, privileges and benefits;
- fear of loss of earnings and possible redundancy;
- fear of the possibility of a downgrading of expensively acquired skills;
- an increased awareness of one's own inadequacies, and a feeling of helplessness;
- the uncertainties of working with new technology;
- fears of increased exploitation;
- fears of intensified supervision and control;
- a possibility of increased accountability;
- possible loss of influence and/or power.

The evidence in favour of consultation with subordinates, before taking a decision, is so overwhelmingly in support of democratic supervisors and so overwhelmingly against autocratic managers (at least in most companies in the UK) that a manager would be foolish and/or insensitive to ignore its conclusions. It seems fairly obvious that if employees have had a hand in the decision making — if they have been instrumental in the architecture of a decision — then those employees are much more likely to want it to succeed. They will take a proprietorial interest in the outcome. They may assume ownership of the decision. Neither they, nor the manager, want to be associated with failure. Consultation, collaboration and participation are the key factors in implementing any change process, for the following reasons:

- Consultation helps to alleviate the fears of the employees.
- The process may in fact be a positive source of motivation towards change.
- It provides a better understanding of all that is entailed.
- It spreads a general awareness of the need for change.
- It brings employees closer to the planning stage.

I see nothing wrong with giving lists like these in business studies answers; they are precise and concise. Do avoid waffle and don't take six pages to say what you could have said in one. But it is an absolute imperative to amplify and explain; so you'll forgive me if I remind you of the need to DEEE — define, explain, expand, exemplify!

You've heard of the four (or five) Ps of marketing. Here are the four Cs of change management: collaboration, consultation, communication, cogitation — not necessarily in that order!

- It allows employees to express their views and reservations, and to suggest new ideas.
- Management will be more in tune with the values and aspirations of the employees.
- It reduces the risk of potential conflict and resistance to change.
- It allows management the opportunity to rethink its proposals if there is clear and overt opposition.
- It enhances the possibility of shared organisational goals and norms.
- Consultation and participation are economically effective and humanitarian.

There is a great deal of evidence to support this approach. Michael Argyle undertook a study of 90 foremen in eight different factories. The foremen who had the best productivity record were those who exercised general rather than close supervision, were more democratic and rarely resorted to punishments. R. Katz and D. Kahn found that, in an insurance company, the supervisors of the high-producing groups were those where the section heads were given a great deal of freedom by their superiors; the supervisors, in turn, exercised a democratic watching brief over their section, rather than close supervision, and invited the comments and observations of their subordinates.

You can see (and read) just how often this idea comes through.

Despite these findings, and many others, there are those who conclude that it is still not clear how likely, or under what circumstances, participation will improve employee satisfaction, increase productivity or stimulate organisational innovation. Management consultant Tom Peters argues that excellent companies have a bias for action, encourage innovation, are prepared to risk failures in some areas, are obsessively responsive to the customer, and believe in productivity through people. Few of these characteristics can be achieved unless the company is willing to change.

However, in some companies — or countries — the prevailing culture may actually prevent or seriously impede a transition from autocratic to participative leadership. Employees who, for years, have been used to doing what they are told may have some difficulty in adapting to a change of management style. In addition, some employees do not want responsibility — even shared responsibility — thrust upon them. Nonetheless, while working leadership (i.e. functional leadership) is important in bringing about change, there is growing emphasis on what leaders do rather than on what they know. Increasingly, a leader is a facilitator of change, not an order-giver.

It's perfectly acceptable, indeed advised, to draw in and paraphrase leading writers. It's a practice used by most (thorough) textbooks: 'Smith and Weston (1997) found that...'.

I think this is an important point. You will often hear people say 'It's not what it was...'. Of course not. Societies change, cultures change (slowly) and organisations change; they have to or they're unlikely to survive.

Organisational structures continue to evolve — to change. Roles and jobs within the company change and evolve for many reasons, not least because of pressures from information technology, changing customer requirements and patterns of demand, total quality management, just-in-time management, and so on. Many factors may act as a change force — new technology, macroeconomic variables, a shift in the behaviour of competitors, new legislation, etc. If the company does not react to these forces, it may well suffer a decline in its market share, total sales or profits. Different situations, therefore, require different change approaches. Essentially, however, and depending on the change force, the company must undertake four phases to make the change happen successfully: prepare the organisation for change (some call this 'unfreezing' the organisation); implement the change; follow up, monitor and modify the change; prepare for the next change.

Companies that have been opened up by change are much more able to accept future changes and are more responsive to the dynamic market place; indeed, many Japanese companies support and encourage appropriate and relevant change through a philosophy of *kaizen* — the continuous search for improvements. The management of change is recognised as one of the fundamental tasks facing a modern business, yet some managers fail to match up to its imperatives and their organisations suffer in consequence. It has been suggested that the most successful change agents — i.e. those who can manage change — are those who are prepared to change themselves. Managers and other employees need reassurance and a compelling vision of change: not just of why such change is good for the company, but of why it is good for themselves, and of what benefits they are going to get from the changes.

Perhaps an obvious conclusion, but one that needs to be said, anyhow. Do try to draw your ideas together in your conclusion. It gives your essay an air of finality that tells the examiner you've finished.

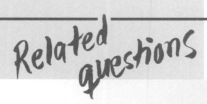

Related questions

1   Change brings uncertainty and doubt. What can management do to allay the fears of the employees?

2   How much should employees or their representatives be involved in the planning of any major change that a company may be contemplating?

3   'Consultation and communication take time and slow down change.' 'Democracy is time consuming.' Consider these statements in relation to the organisation, and suggest how true they might be.

4   What organisational and behavioural problems of implementation may be experienced by a company that is proposing to install a new computer-based stock control system?

Question 17

Consider the work of Douglas McGregor and Frederick Herzberg on management style and job design. What conclusions did these two behavioural scientists come to, and what might be the implications for today's management?

 Tackling the question

McGregor and Herzberg are two leading theorists who are quoted by everyone. But it's surprising how often these two authors, and others, are misquoted and their ideas misused. Here's an opportunity to set the record straight. The format of the question is predictable. First, present the theories and the ideas, and then illustrate what they mean for management and how they can be applied in practice. Any study of how to use personnel more effectively must include consideration of how a company might use the total skills and experiences of its employees. So you might want to include discussion of delegation and empowerment. It could be argued that most jobs can be tedious. The key question is how to make them less tedious, more meaningful, more challenging. But not everyone wants a challenge, so there are balances to be struck. The answer might also include elements of specialisation, role overload, responsibility and accountability.

Answer

McGregor divided management styles into two extreme groups, behind each of which is an assumption about the nature of people. He called the two sets of assumptions: Theory X and Theory Y. Theory X managers believe that:

- People are inherently lazy and have a natural dislike of work. They will avoid it whenever possible.
- Most people need to be coerced, controlled, directed or even threatened with punishment to get them to put in adequate effort towards achieving the organisation's goals.
- Most people prefer to be directed; they wish to avoid responsibility and they have relatively little ambition.

On the other hand, Theory Y managers believe that:

- External control and the threat of punishment are not the only means of directing effort to achieve goals.
- People learn not only to accept responsibility, but actively to seek it.
- Psychological rewards (ego satisfaction, etc.) are associated with meeting the organisation's goals.
- Work is a source of satisfaction and will be voluntarily performed.
- Under the conditions of modern industrial life, the intellectual potentialities of the average human being are only partially utilised.

These two 'theories' represent extremes on a continuum of management style — Theory X at one end, and Theory Y at the other; most managers fit somewhere in between. Effective managers are able to have many of the needs of the workforce met in the workplace; they are both leaders and managers. One of the most profound truths about human behaviour is that expectations of human behaviour often become a self-fulfilling prophecy. If we treat people as fools, we should not be surprised when, eventually, they begin to act like fools! If the validity of Theory X is accepted as a management style, in time our assumptions about the workforce are justified because the employees respond negatively which, in turn, requires the supervisor to exercise even greater control, and crack the whip even harder. A vicious and unproductive circle of negative behaviour is established. Theory Y assumptions, however, require managers

When we are talking about people behaving in any way, in any situation, we are, of course, discussing and presenting theories of psychology. However, this is a very profound subject, not completely understood even by those who are experts in the field. Inevitably, therefore, we can only skim the surface.

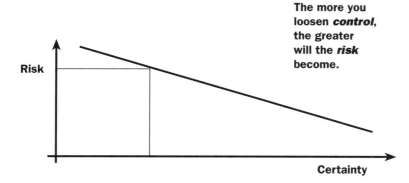

The more you loosen *control*, the greater will the *risk* become.

On the one hand
the organisation needs to standardise, optimise control, restrict 'behaviour' and make outcomes more certain.

On the other
individuals don't want telling what to do, how to do it and when to do it. They want a degree of autonomy.

Figure 8 The risk/certainty dilemma

to recognise that organisational and individual goals are not mutually exclusive; they are, in fact, complementary.

This seems to be a very reasonable and practical question to ask.

Herzberg developed two sets of factors to explain motivation: hygiene and motivator factors. The hygiene factors address the question: 'Why work here?' They include good pay, job security, fringe benefits, considerate supervision and pleasant working conditions. However, although good hygiene in the home may prevent disease, such hygiene will not cure the disease. To cure and eliminate a disease requires more than just keeping the place clean. One has to introduce other measures. So, although the hygiene factors may prevent lack of motivation, they will not cure lack of motivation and commitment where they exist.

And so does this.

The motivator factors answer the question: 'Why work harder?' They include:

- opportunities to achieve;
- recognition and status;
- the value of the work itself;
- additional responsibilities;
- opportunities for advancement;
- level of self-esteem;
- the esteem of others.

Herzberg's work has had considerable influence. A result of this has been the concept of 'job enrichment'. A survey in the 1970s revealed widespread agreement on the desirability of greater autonomy — in particular, the formation of autonomous work groups and achieving individual job enrichment.

Many maintained that traditional methods of work organisation inevitably create boredom, and a sense of frustration and alienation. The better the education of the employees involved, the greater is the sense of frustration. In any case, most workers are no longer willing to accept autocratic management styles and Theory X management practices. Although there are slight differences of opinion between the various schools of thought, both schools conclude that the way to use their findings at the workplace is through the design of work itself.

In a sense, this is what it's all about as far as 'good' industrial relations are concerned. It's not so easy, of course, to put it into practice. But do note that the topic is first introduced, then explained,

The principal ingredients of good job design include:

- provision for learning, advancement and recognition. The job should have variety rather than routine; it should be demanding not only in the physical sense, but also in terms of the mental processes involved, so that it is worthy of a certain degree of respect in the work community. The employee should be trusted to get on with the job. Today this practice is given the term 'empowerment'.

- achievement possibilities. Work should be organised such that the worker or the group can clearly identify with what has been accomplished. There should be regular feedback to let the employees know how they are getting on.
- group jobs, with an opportunity for the group members to rotate between the various tasks.

Many of these ingredients can be achieved using some or all the following:

- *Job rotation*. This is used to denote the situation where a worker spends a certain time working at task A, then moves on to task B for a time, then to task C, and so on. The aim of job rotation is to provide variety and to give opportunities for learning and advancement.
- *Job enlargement*. This refers to the redesigning of jobs in such a way that the employees do more of the same kind of work than they did before: in other words, they become responsible for a greater part of the work. For example, if one worker carries out operation A, and another worker does operation B, the job could be enlarged by combining both operations into a single worker's task. So instead of perhaps producing 100 units of A, 50 units of A and B are

and then expanded. The same applies to the key elements below.

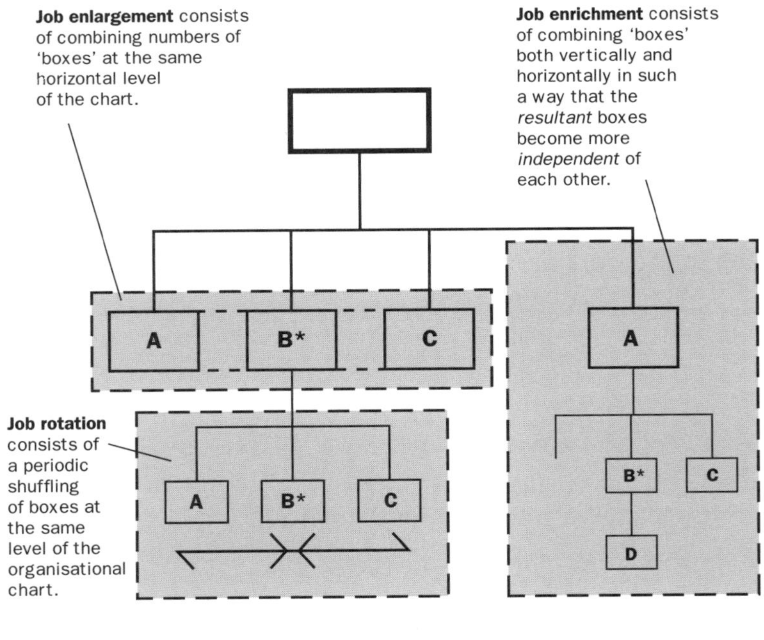

Job enlargement consists of combining numbers of 'boxes' at the same horizontal level of the chart.

Job enrichment consists of combining 'boxes' both vertically and horizontally in such a way that the *resultant* boxes become more *independent* of each other.

Job rotation consists of a periodic shuffling of boxes at the same level of the organisational chart.

Figure 9 Job rotation, job enlargement and job enrichment

now produced. Again this system provides greater variety for the employee and gives a greater sense of wholeness to the job.

- *Job enrichment.* This is probably the most useful yet the most difficult way of applying motivational theory to the design of workers' jobs. What it means, in effect, is that individual workers (or a group of workers) have much greater discretion in what is done, and how. They are given greater autonomy. A group, given such autonomy, would carry out all the operations directly associated with the manufacture of the finished article, and might even be responsible for the maintenance of the machinery and filling in the necessary paperwork that goes with the task.

No such essay would be complete without a clear demonstration of how the theories can be translated into practical reality. Here are quite a few practical examples, and you may be able to think of several more. Again, take the opportunity to cite companies where such changes have been made. It's perhaps even more important to illustrate where they have, or have not, been successful. Not all change is successful — sometimes a company needs to go back to the drawing board — but that is important if the company is to learn from its mistakes.

When restructuring work, pay and other tangible benefits must also be considered. Conditions of employment may need to be changed to reflect the new organisation. In addition, the design of new plant, or the purchase of new equipment, often provides an especially good opportunity to introduce new working practices. Job rotation is very desirable for a group if it is to become truly autonomous, and managers should leave sufficient room within a job for job holders to have plenty of scope for determining their own work pace and methods.

Regular two-way communication must be established and managers must be committed to change. 'Insincerity, like leadership, permeates throughout the enterprise.' Job structuring will normally give rise to fears concerning security of earnings or of employment. An honest statement of intent at the beginning of the exercise is essential, and management must be prepared for a dip in performance while employees learn new jobs and get to grips with the new structure. Group assembly plants, with job rotation and participation in local decision making through works councils and employee directors, appear to have significant potential in moving towards a more satisfactory relationship in the workplace.

Related questions

1 How might job enrichment lead to higher productivity? Explain the difference between job enrichment and job enlargement.

2 'Motivation of subordinates is a manager's task.' Do you think this statement is true? Suggest what factors might motivate employees to be more committed to the company for which they work?

3 Discuss the difficulties that might be encountered in attempting to redesign jobs and make them more interesting.

4 Briefly comment on Theories X and Y, and comment on some of their practical applications to the management of a large production department.

Production Management

Question 18

A large firm acquires a smaller one as part of its strategy of horizontal integration. Examine the differences in production management if the larger firm is engaged in flow production and the smaller company employs batch production techniques.

If you're doing a modular course, not all syllabuses include production as a compulsory unit. Nonetheless, there are many aspects of production within the core areas. Do remember that all organisations produce something. It may not be a tangible object — a washing machine or bar of chocolate — but something must emerge from the other end of the 'firm', whether it's better singing from the church choir, better medicine from a team of doctors or better chemicals from ICI. That's the whole basis of the systems approach. In this question, we are concerned with the production of tangible outputs.

One potential area of conflict, at least in bigger companies, relates to the line and staff structure. Given that the production department is so specialised, the introduction of this concept could be quite useful. The batch producing company is unlikely to have many, if any, staff managers. Another key point is the co-ordination and planning of resources. Failure to optimise stock control, as well as other resources, can have serious production, financial and, subsequently, marketing implications. Of course, just-in-time inventory management is important, but probably within a framework of total quality management (and *kaizen*), which would also give an opportunity to examine BS 5750 and ISO 9000.

Answer

Guidance notes

Production management is concerned with the organisation and control of the production function, and specifically the conversion of inputs — raw materials and component parts — into outputs of a higher value that can be sold. It is concerned with adding value at all stages of this conversion. It must ensure that finished goods are made according to the requisite quality standards and specification, in the right quantities, at the right times and at minimal cost. The scope and nature of the production manager's job are influenced primarily by the nature of the production system. However, modern manufacturers must aim to produce at low cost, deliver rapidly and frequently, and be highly responsive to customer demands if they are to remain competitive. While price is always important to a final customer, non-price differentials are frequently an equally important consideration.

In this question, the major firm is involved in a flow process production system, while the subsidiary is involved in a batch process production system. In consequence, the methods, attitudes and approaches to production management are different and different problem areas may exist within each type of system. It is necessary first, however, to consider the wider implications of production management. Production management may be divided into three main branches:

- production (industrial) engineering: methods, assessment of rates and standards, work study;
- production planning: construction of a schedule by which products will be made in the correct quantities and in the times available;
- production control: the implementation of production planning decisions, involving monitoring and adjustments of the operational plans.

These three factors are the primary ones to be considered when establishing a production process. In addition to these, however, two equally important factors emerge: namely personnel relationships and the co-ordination of the team effort and activities. In the production function, there are two major problem areas: the design and construction of the production system itself, and the operation, performances and running of that production system.

With a flow system of production, attention must be painstakingly paid to the design of the flow line, so the pre-planning phase is of paramount importance. Accuracy and timing are fundamental to efficient mass production; minor errors in quantity or timing may result in expensive hold-ups and significant and costly loss of production. Essentially, this system has little flexibility. There is minimal scope for adjustment or manoeuvre once the production line is installed.

The production managers of the larger parent company will therefore have, as their immediate problems, the size of the production unit and the possible lack of contact between the higher management and the operatives (although, with good communications and a reasonable degree of democracy in the

---

This is fairly straightforward, but it does need some definitions as well as explanations later on.

The question invites you to write about the differences between batch and flow production, but more than just a list of the differences is required. Consider the implications.

Here are some of the implications; the key element is the human one. How are the employees going to feel about it? Resistance to change; worries for their job; fear of the

factory, these problems can be alleviated). Perhaps their most important problem area, however, is production control, in that the machines (being purpose-built and automated) may cause jobs to be de-skilled and result in a reduction of interest among the operators. Boredom and alienation (first described by Karl Marx in the mid-nineteenth century) become almost a by-product of mass production. Disaffection may lead to poor industrial relations, lack of employee commitment, an emphasis on financial rewards, and conflict for apparently trivial reasons.

In flow production, major management decisions must be medium to long term because the plant, being specialised and comparatively inflexible, allows little room for alternative deployment. In addition, the customer lead time (i.e. the time between receipt of order and delivery of product to the customer) may be less than the production lead time (i.e. the time between receipt of order and delivery of product to finished stock). In other words, the customer is most likely to be supplied direct from finished stock, which is continually replenished according to a production plan based on forecast demand and market research, on which considerable emphasis is placed. There must be planned preventative maintenance of the plant and full utilisation of equipment and labour.

In contrast, the subsidiary firm, producing batch goods, will possess a more flexible system and organisation. The equipment and plant will tend to be more general-purpose than specific, and a higher degree of skill and craftsmanship will be required. Production controls tend to be more difficult to secure. In order to meet customer demands, the practice of reverse scheduling might be employed. This requires the subtraction of operation and idle or waiting times from the completion date to produce a fairly accurate assessment of customer lead time.

An important consideration for the production control team, in both parent and subsidiary companies, will be to minimise the total costs of establishing the production facilities while also minimising the stockholding — in other words, estimating the economic production batch quantity (EBQ). However, the essential prerequisite for all production planning is a statement of demand — known, expressed or expected. In flow production, the demand is likely to be an expected or forecast one, while in batch production, the demand is probably known or at least expressed.

In the flow system, optimising plant utilisation is of considerable importance; high fixed costs and plant inflexibility necessitate a steady or increasing demand for the product. Advertising and brand image will, therefore, play a great part in stimulating that demand and maintaining a reasonably busy production

unknown and of what the future is going to bring. The production managers can sort out the machines fairly quickly; but what's going to happen to the people who operate them?

Any production process must be about optimising the resources. I have an aversion to the use of the word 'maximise' — how does one 'maximise' anything? And rarely, if ever, can data be complete, so how do you know when you have 'maximised' it? You can maximise to your heart's content in an economic model. It doesn't go anywhere. Once it's been drawn, it stays where it is. The best that can be achieved in any business is 'optimisation' — the best under the prevailing circumstances.

system. In batch processing, producing a more diverse range of goods, and with greater inherent flexibility, skilled personnel and a more general-purpose plant, a fall in the demand for one product may be counteracted and compensated by the production of another, more profitable or saleable product.

Both types of production system — flow production and batch production — require appropriate measures of effectiveness to be installed. Such measures of production effectiveness include:

- the incidence of obsolete inventories;
- customer complaints about delivery and quality;
- the size of inventory levels;
- the internal rates of waste, reworking, and spoilt products and rejects;
- the percentage of products delivered on time;
- throughput time.

It can be seen, therefore, that while the best practices of production management must prevail in both companies, the operational aspects — including the scheduling of the work and its control — are likely to be quite different, with different pressures. It is probable, of course, that management and production expertise from one system will cross-pollinate the other to their mutual advantage.

Related questions

1 Some firms tend to grow very quickly; others grow more slowly. Why should this be so? Explain the problems likely to be found in a company that is rapidly expanding.

2 Suggest why a manufacturing company might decide to integrate vertically. What advantages would it be looking for and how might such a venture help its marketing strategy?

3 There is a danger in integrating too far, either backwards or forwards. Comment on those potential dangers and discuss how the firm should deal with them.

4 Asset stripping is seen by some to be morally indefensible; others see it as a perfectly legitimate commercial practice. Consider this practice and discuss its merits or otherwise.

Question 19

Why is it so important to control stock levels? Suggest what factors should be taken into consideration by a company when it is seeking to control and optimise its stockholding.

Tackling the question

This is a very popular question, along with methods of stock valuation. Quite properly it tends to be part of the production element of the course, although it would clearly sit comfortably somewhere within the finance and management accountancy module. The key point is that failure to optimise stock control can have serious production and financial, and subsequently marketing, implications. Of course, much is made of 'just-in-time' stock management and much of the answer could focus on that possibility. Remember that JIT is not the panacea for all the production or stock control ills of all companies. But *mura, muri* and *muda* are no bad thing in anyone's language!

Answer

Guidance notes

Stock control systems aim to minimise both the costs of holding stock and the costs of ordering stock, while ensuring that sufficient stock is held to satisfy the demands of the manufacturing department and customers' orders. Stock-outs may lead not only to loss of sales, but also to loss of customer goodwill. In addition, adequate stock must be held to guarantee uninterrupted production runs and a minimum of operator and machine down-time. Stock is a major element of working capital. Typically, stock can be 50–60% of current assets and 30–35% of total assets. Hence, its control is fundamental to the financial health of an enterprise. Which kind of stock — raw materials and component parts, work in progress or finished goods — is the most important will depend on the kind of business the company is in, the nature of its products and the characteristics of its markets. In essence, then, stock control ensures that the optimum amount of stock is held by a company, so that its internal and external demand requirements can be met economically.

The question does require you to point out the benefits of introducing an effective and an efficient stock control system, but it's difficult to do that without first determining just what the firm's priorities are. There's a basic dilemma for the company and the key word is 'compromise' — a trade-off between competing objectives.

There are three basic types of inventory in manufacturing industry. Stocks of finished items are held to act as a buffer against fluctuations in demand for the product. It is not easy to alter production schedules to accommodate these fluctuations, particularly in flow or process production methods. It is easier to control the level of stocks. Finished goods are also held to provide a quicker service and to reduce the risk of stock short-fall associated with production stoppages because of break-downs, industrial action, raw material shortages, etc. They are held to increase sales, sales revenue and, ultimately, profitability. Increased stocks may give rise to better sales for two main reasons: diversification (a wider range of goods) and better service (increased customer satisfaction).

If diagrams add to your answer, use them. But you don't need to spend a great deal of time drawing them to very high standards, or include lots of whistles and bells.

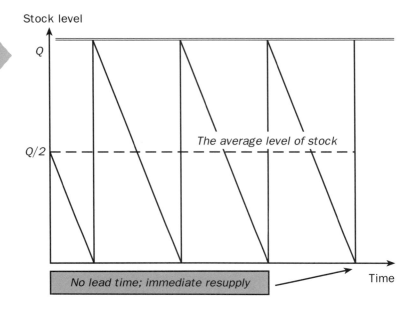

Figure 10 The simple stock control model

The second type of stock is work in progress, which needs to be valued periodically. Raw materials, purchased items and component parts are the third type of manufacturing stock. A company would acquire these to take advantage of bulk buying, purchase discounts and special offers, and to reduce the risks associated with delays or late deliveries. The firm might also require spare parts, tools, jigs and consumable items that are used in the process itself, or which are necessary to keep the plant going. Where a large amount of stock comprises a wide variety of materials and components, some classification of stock, according to its relative value, is necessary. Analysis usually shows that a small percentage of item types (e.g. 20%) accounts for a high proportion of the annual usage value (e.g. 80%). This has led to the classification of stock into three groups:

- Class 'A': high-value items;
- Class 'B': medium-value items;
- Class 'C': low-value items.

Class 'A' items require tight control. The establishment of trends of usage or sales on a routine basis and frequent assessment of control levels will be required. For Class 'B' items, which usually include the bulk of the stock file, slightly less control can be applied.

There may be a point beyond which further increases in stock will not give rise to sufficient additional sales and gross profit, to justify the additional stockholding costs involved. Such holding costs include the opportunity costs of capital and the costs of obsolescence, deterioration and pilferage. The dilemma of stock control, which faces the production department immediately, but which will have a 'knock-on' effect on the other departments, is whether to have large orders delivered infrequently, or small orders delivered frequently.

Factors in favour of large orders delivered infrequently are:

- economies of purchasing;
- security of supply in case of delivery difficulties and a reduction in the probability of shortages;
- flexibility of production;
- immediate availability of goods for sale, with a reduction in customer disaffection;
- ability to gain from price increases;
- reduction in ordering and administrative costs.

Factors in favour of small orders delivered frequently are:

- less cash (consider the opportunity costs involved) tied up in stock;
- less warehouse space, air conditioning, heating, etc., and less store-housekeeper time and inventory control required;
- lower insurance premiums;
- less chance of fashion or technological obsolescence;
- less possibility of deterioration, depreciation or spoilage;
- reduced likelihood of pilfering.

Many of these policies and decisions will be influenced by the company's service policies. The service level to customers, the extent to which finished stock can be supplied to them 'off the shelf' and the level of stock-outs that the firm is prepared to accept will be set by the senior management. Such a policy will, of course, be influenced by the level and nature of the competition, the type of product, the availability of substitutes, and so on.

It is necessary, therefore, to establish a policy on how much buffer or safety stock should be carried. This constitutes the excess of the reorder level over the expected demand during the lead time. Second, there should be a policy on the extent to which back-ordering is permitted, i.e. accepting orders when no actual stock remains; thus, in effect, allowing negative stock (or dues) to build up. The appropriate quantity of stock to order each time is that which minimises the sum of the delivery cost and the stockholding cost. This is known as the economic batch quantity (EBQ). No stock control system can guarantee that the company will never be out of stock, but to reduce the likelihood, owing to fluctuating demand and uncertain delivery times, a safety stock (or buffer stock) level should be built into the system for each item of stock held. More and more companies are employing purchasing specialists or materials controllers, particularly when there is a wide variety of stock items or the value of many items of the stock is high.

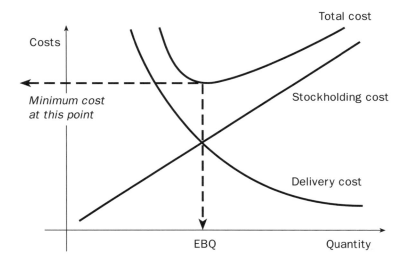

Figure 11 The cost minimisation model

The increasing use of information technology is important, particularly in automated stock-ordering systems. When the stock falls to a pre-set, minimum level, the computer automatically generates a reorder. The use of EPOS, for example, in retail outlets has made

Computerised stock records are being increasingly employed, particularly where standard costing procedures are also used. Their speed of operation, recall and immediate valuation of stock at any given moment, together with their accuracy (assuming the data input is correct), make manual systems of stock control look very primitive indeed. In addition, just-in-time stock control management is being adopted by more companies in an attempt to control the level of working capital, to reduce wastage and excess stock, and to iron out unevenness in the supply chain; in effect, to improve quality control. Just-in-time stock control, while not appropriate to all companies, often brings the benefits of zero defects at entry, improved productivity and investment savings. Production management is concerned with managing the physical resources necessary to create products in sufficient quantities to meet market requirements. A significant proportion of those physical resources will include stock, in all its various guises. The introduction and maintenance of a comprehensive and exacting stock control system are fundamental to the control of cash flow and improved liquidity, the success of the production department and ultimately the satisfaction of customers' requirements.

stock control much easier and faster.

Related questions

1   What factors might you consider when setting up a reordering system for a large supermarket? How far do you think the store manager should rely on this system, given the use of computer technology?

2   What factors need to be taken into account when deciding reorder stock levels?

3   Discuss the difficulties in controlling stock of different value, and suggest what procedures a company might implement to ensure that too many high-value items are not stocked.

4   Just-in-time management has been hailed as something of a panacea for many of industry's problems. Consider, however, why JIT is not suitable for all manufacturing businesses.

What are quality control charts? Explain the concept and statistical techniques behind them, and suggest how the use of such charts might help a manufacturing company to improve its processes.

Tackling the question

Not all business studies syllabuses contain a statistics module or element, but many do. The more numerate candidates may relish getting stuck into a bit of number crunching — and it's not really as daunting as it might first appear. Quality control charts are an absolute necessity in checking the dimensions and specifications of products as they come off the production line. Control charts can also monitor variables such as rates of defects and critical ratios. Clearly, competitors' products will influence the level of quality set, as will consumer expectations and perceptions of value. An important factor that could be developed in this answer is that the best quality level for an output is not always the highest, but should reflect the trade-off between the cost of producing high-quality output and the cost (and frequency) of producing low-quality output with some defects.

Answer

A manufacturing process, no matter how precise, is subject to a large number of random variations, many so small as to be insignificant, but the cumulative effect of these variations may result in products that are unacceptable for the purpose they were intended. The problem is exacerbated when the products must be precision made and tolerances are very limiting. In addition to random causes of variability, there may be other, more obvious, reasons why the manufacturing process deviates from the established mean. Such causes may include human error, variations in the raw materials being used, and variations in the conditions of manufacture.

The variability of the process is indicated by the amount of spread of the results: when the results are clustered around a central figure — usually the arithmetic mean — then there is a low variability. If the results are widely scattered, then the variability is high. Every process has its own characteristic variability. The spread of the variation is distributed between two values, and this spread can be represented by a frequency polygon or histogram. More often than not, this frequency distribution represents a bell-shaped, symmetrical diagram, in which there are just as many variations below the mean as there are above it. The curve that is produced by joining the frequencies of the values is called a Gaussian or normal curve (or normal distribution). The determination of this normal distribution is at the root of much statistical analysis employed in market research and quality control. The normal curve has three important properties:

- It is always bell shaped.
- It is symmetrical about the mean.
- The measures of central tendency (or central values) — the mean, the median and the mode — always lie at the peak of the curve.

In a production process (or any statistical analysis) it is necessary to determine not only the value of the variation from the mean, but also how many articles — what proportion of the articles — are of a particular size. It is necessary to know whether the values are clustered closely around the mean (i.e. there is little variation), or whether the values are well spread out (i.e. widely dispersed). Three main measures are used to express the dispersion of a group of figures: the range, the quartile deviation (semi-quartile range) and the standard deviation. In quality control, the standard deviation is usually of prime importance.

The standard deviation is significant because it allows for further mathematical manipulation and uses every value in the distribution. However, it does have a major disadvantage for, when calculating the standard deviation, more than proportional weight is given to extreme values, because the deviations of all the values are squared during the computation of the standard deviation. Nonetheless, the standard deviation is the most useful of the measures of dispersion. There is a distinct relationship between the standard deviation and the area under the normal curve. If a distribution of values is approximately normal and the mean and the standard deviation are known, then it is possible to calculate the proportion of observations that are likely to fall outside any given limit in the whole population from which the sample distribution was drawn.

Example:
As a result of tests on electric light bulbs, it was found that the lifetime of a particular make was distributed normally with an

The question does ask particularly about the concepts behind the techniques. The most obvious concept, perhaps, is that of the normal curve, which then leads to all sorts of other tricks of the trade. None of the syllabuses — at least at this level — go into deeper statistical methods such as *t*-tail and chi. So you need not go too deep.

Not only do you need to understand the method — here's a simple example to show how it might be used. It is useful to include a numerical example that you've made up, but don't make it too complicated. It just needs to show the examiner that you know what you are talking about.

average life of 2,040 hours and a standard deviation of 60 hours. What proportion of bulbs can be expected to have a life of more than 2,160 hours?

Answer:
Mean 2,040 hours; standard deviation 60 hours.
2,160 – 2,040 = 120 hours
120/60 = 2.0 standard deviations
From tables: the area of the curve occupied by 2.0 standard deviations = 0.4772, or 47.72%.
As the mean bisects the curve, then from 0.4772 to 0.5 = 0.0228 or 2.28%.
(Note: as the normal curve is symmetrical, there will be just as many 'negative' light bulbs. So 2.28% will fail to last 2,040 hours – 2 standard deviations (120 hours), i.e. they will last *less than* 1,920 hours.)

However, during a manufacturing process, it is possible for the mean and the variability to change. If they do change, it is important to know of the change as soon as possible, otherwise a significant number of rejects may occur, with a resulting increase in costs and a shortfall in production quantities. This defect may be because of assignable variations. It was to detect such a change that Shewhart, in 1931, proposed a system of quality control based on regular recordings of sample results on control charts. The basic format of these charts has changed little since they were first proposed. The procedure is to take frequent and regular random samples of the product and to calculate the mean value and the standard deviation of each sample. An important point about control charts is that the information must be acted on immediately by the production

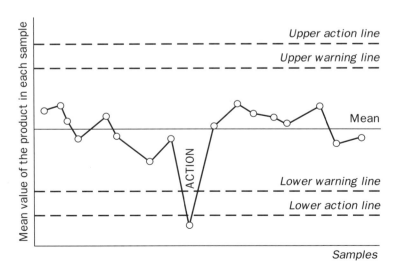

Figure 12 Quality control chart

department. The two main uses of control charts are, first, to record the average level at which the process is running and, second, to record the residual, as well as the assignable, variability, which is produced over a period of time.

Most products will have degrees of tolerance built in, e.g. 10 mm ± 0.5 mm, i.e. the customer will accept the product if it measures between 9.5 mm and 10.5 mm. Anything above or below these measurements is 'intolerable'. It is highly probable, particularly in precision engineering, that the customers will also undertake random sampling of the batches that they receive. It is usual, therefore, to undertake production in identifiable batches. Rejected batches may then be used for lower quality requirements, or may be offered at a lower price. Whichever scheme of batch sampling is introduced, the important factors to be considered are the cost of the sampling and inspection scheme, the cost of rejecting a batch that is good, and the cost of accepting a batch that is defective. If a bad batch of components is passed to production, it may be possible to calculate the losses due to rejection later in the production line. If a bad batch of articles is sold to a customer, the losses may vary from only having to replace that batch to losing the customer's goodwill and the manufacturing firm's reputation. The key to the Japanese approach to quality is that the responsibility for quality rests with the makers of the parts; in effect, the responsibility, and any associated defect cost, is shifted to the supplier of the components.

> Here are some of the implications; in this case, costs. There's no need to list the implications. If you can, just weave and thread them throughout your answer — but in a relevant manner, of course.

The virtues of control charts are that they give a good visual display and they are easy to interpret and operate by systematising the sampling and recording procedures. Quality may slip for a number of reasons — operator boredom, tool wear, weather, fatigue, poor maintenance. The purpose of quality control is to detect defects and to ensure that during design, manufacturing and servicing both work and materials are within limits that will produce the desired product. Effective quality control is, therefore, a fundamental requirement for any organisation.

Related questions

1 Discuss how different payments systems may sometimes clash with quality control requirements. How might such clashes be avoided?

2 How would you assess an existing system of quality control within a company? Suggest what alterations you might recommend to improve the system.

3 'A commitment to total quality management (TQM) would eliminate many of the product reworking problems that manufacturers experience.' What is TQM and how far do you agree with this statement?

4 How would you generate and implement teamwork for quality management and control, and ensure that individuals accepted responsibility?

uestion 21

There are several different types of production system. Explain briefly the production function within a manufacturing company and, with examples, consider the different types of production. Suggest what factors determine which system is likely to emerge.

Tackling the question

This is a good, meaty question because it gives you lots of scope to write a great deal about the production function, and why and how such production systems develop. The danger is that you might get too carried away if this area is your particular forté. So you must break down the question into its component parts, and make sure you answer each of them. It's always a good idea to make an essay plan, even if it consists of just a few headings and key points. That way you discipline yourself and structure your response. In addition to the points covered in the essay below, you might include plant layout — especially layout by process, with its emphasis on flexibility and the individuality of each station, and layout by product, with its emphasis on minimisation of through-put time. Inherent within all of this is the importance of materials handling and physical distribution management (PDM). If time and space permit, it would be useful to give examples of each in some detail.

Answer

Production management is concerned with managing the physical resources necessary to create products in sufficient quantities to meet market requirements. Every manufacturer is looking for a competitive edge. It might be better quality, additional product features, lower costs or improved technology. Perhaps the most important feature is product differentiation and having a unique selling proposition (USP), for otherwise the company is competing mainly on price. However, any competitive advantage that a manufacturer might achieve is likely to be quickly eroded as competitors follow suit. The adoption of total quality management, by many leading manufacturers, almost guarantees standardised products of consistently high quality. What is clear, therefore, is that companies must have a faster rate of improvement than their competitors — from supplies in, to final product delivery. In manufacturing organisations, much of the workforce and a high proportion of the capital investment will be devoted to the production function. However, the techniques and methods that have been developed by production functions are being adopted increasingly by the growing number of service industries.

> This is a good opportunity to bring in the importance of adding value at every stage of the process, whether the firm is producing washing machines or chocolate bars.

The way in which products are manufactured depends to a large extent on what those products are, what they are to be used for, who the customers are, how predictable the demand is, how significant the competition is, and what resources are available. Production is concerned primarily with the supply functions of the business, whereas marketing tends to address the demand side. Production management is concerned with the conversion of inputs into outputs of a higher value. Any production process — any business — is concerned with adding value at all stages of this conversion. Production management is also concerned with the decision making necessary to ensure that goods are made according to requisite and pre-determined quality standards, in the right quantities, at the right time and at minimal cost.

> The production methods or types of production can be broken down into discrete blocks; well, they can in theory. In practice, a firm may use several of these different types of production, depending on what is actually being produced and whom it's for.

The scope and the nature of the production manager's job are influenced by many factors. Chief among them, however, is the nature and complexity of the production system, which will depend on the demand and volume required and the nature of the product. There are several types of production system:

Jobbing (or unique jobs)
Examples of jobbing are fulfilling printing/design orders or completing civil engineering projects. With this system there tends to be one product, designed and produced to the customer's specification, and only one person or a small team, composed of specialists, is involved; sometimes the job passes from one person to another. For the larger jobs, many hundreds of people may, of course, be needed. For these huge tasks, which may take many months or even years, the overall technique is enshrined in project management, which plans and controls the whole project using techniques such as network planning and progress control. A high degree of skill and flexibility may, therefore, be required. The plant and tools must be versatile and a wide range of tools may be required. However, not a great deal of time is spent setting up a machine or tool for a particular job, unless the job is so specialised that it might even require specialised machinery — such as the construction of the Channel tunnel. The cost per unit or project is invariably high because it is a 'one-off'. Because of the high degree of

involvement, a great deal of worker satisfaction is usually associated with the completed task.

Batch production
Examples are producing a batch of cream doughnuts, a batch of ladies' cardigans or a batch of brown leather shoes. Batches are passed through successive machines, or each skill section, which reduces the amount of time needed to set up the machines and therefore tends to lower unit costs. This is known as layout by process: facilities of a similar type or purpose are grouped together, and products move between the groups of equipment according to the order of operations required to be performed on the product. However, some degree of specialisation of plant and labour is required to produce the range of products. The system requires greater production control, and stock and sales management, although it tends to be a reasonably flexible system that can be easily adapted should there be a production hold-up in one section. A development of the batch production system is known as flexible manufacturing systems.

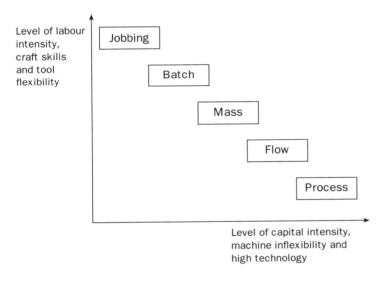

Figure 13 Types of production

Flow (or mass) production
Examples are the manufacture of motor cars, Mars bars, cameras, washing machines and computers — assembly-line operations. Flow production is used where there is a regular and consistent demand. It requires continuity of operation and constant output. The products are standardised as the products move by conveyor belt from one worker to the next, who adds another component. It requires a high degree of planning of materials and component parts, all of which must be standardised and identical, and in-bound raw materials and component parts may need to be checked, assayed and verified against a

The increasing use of computer-aided production systems is never far away. That isn't what the question is asking for, but you'll have to mention it somewhere. Information technology is in the syllabus. How can you study business management and not know something about IT in business?

pre-determined specification. The company must undertake routine preventative maintenance of plant and equipment, usually during the night or at weekends. Increasingly, many flow production systems also employ computer-integrated manufacturing techniques (CIM), which use information technology to integrate the various processes. CIM is the ultimate development of CAD/CAM systems, linking them through to manufacturing with computerised production planning and control systems. Ideally, a comprehensive CIM system would involve the complete automation of the factory, with all process planning and control functions under digital control.

A flow or mass production system produces a high volume of goods at a comparatively low cost per unit because of the economies of scale that can be achieved. It invariably utilises the techniques of scientific management, e.g. work study, and requires significant synchronisation and balancing of personnel, materials and machinery. Both labour and machinery tend to be highly specialised in one particular, micro and specific task; for the employees, the work tends to be repetitive and tedious. Part-finished products pass directly from one operation to another throughout the production sequence. The outflow of one machine becomes the input of the next machine. Therefore, the output at every operation must match that of the preceding and the succeeding operations. This is known as layout by product and it is comparatively inflexible because the arrangement of facilities is dictated by the way in which the product is to be manufactured. Clearly, the initial capital costs in setting up the production lines are extremely high.

Process production
Examples of this are the refining of oil, the production of chemicals, and brewing. Process production is similar in many regards to flow production, but production is normally in bulk rather than in discrete items. It is the continuous production of large quantities of materials, such as plastics, chemicals and cement. The capital costs are very significant as much of the process is carried out in closed tanks and vessels, with few employees required, other than those necessary to operate the (usually) computer-controlled machinery and cycle of events.

However, many companies do not have a single type of production system; there may be various permutations depending on the variety and range of products that the company manufactures.

Related questions

1   'Planned preventative maintenance is better than responsive maintenance and repair.' What is the difference? Explain why this assertion is usually true.

2   Discuss why time and motion studies might be viewed with suspicion by the employees. Suggest how their anxieties might be allayed.

3   What key factors will determine whether a firm should use batch production or mass production? If a firm changes from one to the other, what might be the implications for the workforce?

Question 22

Consider the tasks of the production manager and, with several examples of your own choice, describe how project and production control techniques might be used in order to optimise control, increase certainty and minimise risk.

Tackling the question

This question focuses less on the production system, as such, and much more on what might be expected of a production manager. So we need to consider what production managers actually do. They aren't just engineers or technicians; the emphasis is on what they do as managers of a specific department and, just as important, how they link in with other subsystems within the company. Very often, the exam question may ask you to consider the relationship between, say, production and marketing especially.

Answer

Sampling and statistical analysis techniques, such as the use of standard deviation, Poisson and binomial probability, are commonly used by production managers, particularly for quality control purposes. However, production is one of the core activities of any business; inevitably, therefore, it interfaces with all other departments of the company. Production management can be divided into three identifiable phases:

1. *Production control.* This consists of planning and monitoring:
(a) the sequencing and the processing of jobs;
(b) the updating of production schedules;
(c) a comprehensive stock control system;
(d) quality control and inspection;
(e) the maintenance and replacement of production machinery and equipment.

2. *Before production*
(a) the location of plant;
(b) the design and layout of the production unit and the design of tools;

(c) the identification of appropriate machinery and equipment and the installation of equipment and plant;

(d) the design of flow systems for materials handling;

(e) work measurement and method study.

3. *Before, during and after production*

(a) product innovation and development of new versions in collaboration with R&D;

(b) product screening for technical viability and materials testing;

(c) the development of payment systems and work schedules in collaboration with the personnel department and trade union representatives;

(d) the acquisition of raw materials and component parts; decisions about which are to be 'bought-out' and which manufactured in-house.

A job must be planned before it can be controlled. Many techniques of production planning have been developed in the past, most of which have been variations on a time bar chart. The Gantt chart consists of bars drawn to a time scale representing the total duration of a job, in turn broken up into a series of events to be achieved in completing the overall task. In effect, it is a graphical method of depicting work or task schedules. Such charts have stood the test of time, and are still used, particularly as multiple activity charts in method study.

Gantt charts began to give way to flow process charts, particularly after the successes associated with the introduction of work study techniques. The use of networks specifically for planning and scheduling purposes was first introduced into the UK in about 1955 when the CEGB used critical path methods for the planning of nuclear power stations. In each of these techniques a 'network' of activities is drawn that shows the relationship of each activity to all the other activities making up the network. Such network analysis is useful for almost any kind of project — the launch of a new product, the manufacture of a new product, the commissioning of a new factory or a production unit, building and construction projects, civil engineering, shipbuilding and aircraft construction. The critical path method of network analysis assumes that the time required to complete an activity can be predicted accurately, identifies the critical path and calculates the total time along that path.

The techniques employed today can be very sophisticated and complex. The use of information technology facilitates their completion. In addition to the basic time factor variable, such networks can also introduce and handle cost factors, probabilities and resource allocation.

A manager's role — any manager's role — is to minimise risk and increase certainty. The use of number-crunching techniques — operational research, statistical analysis — helps to do that, of course, although it doesn't remove the need for judgement, intuition and flair. However, you certainly need to mention some of the techniques, for the question asks you to do that.

A technique that may be used to optimise the use of scarce resources and customer service is queuing theory. A queue in production or retailing may be expensive — in terms of delays, resource downtime, loss of sales and interruptions to supply. Time is being wasted. There may be a slower turn-round of lorries or aircraft, ships may have to pay increased port charges, and work in progress may be held up. Queues, therefore, should be minimised. In operational terms, a queue consists of people or products awaiting some sort of service or processing. Obvious examples are queues of shoppers at supermarket check-outs, incoming calls at a telephone exchange, aircraft waiting to land or takeoff, and cows in a milking parlour.

Of course, the queues can probably be eliminated by simply installing more services, more machines and more staff, but to do so will increase capital costs and the revenue costs. This might be practical if a permanent increase in the number of 'customers' could be guaranteed, but sometimes there may be no queue. The arrival of customers (or part-finished products), and how long they actually take to get served, is variable. So a balance needs to be struck to optimise the expenditure against the customer's inconvenience.

Queuing theory, which uses mathematical techniques based on probability theory and statistics, has been developed to handle these types of problem. Queues can be simulated by inserting different inputs (e.g. arrivals and service points) and different outputs (e.g. numbers in the queue). In many situations the numbers involved vary in a random manner, and this randomness can also be simulated. Probabilities can be assigned to the random elements. Simulation provides a trial and error approach that is relatively cheap and easy to apply. In carrying out the simulation, unforeseen problems may be detected, which can then be avoided or corrected if the simulation is translated into reality.

The question is fairly loose, in that it asks for 'several' techniques; it doesn't specify how many to include or which ones, so you have to make a judgement as to whether you have answered the question as fully as you might. The question doesn't ask for detailed examples. It's trying to determine whether or not you understand some the more obvious operational research techniques, and if you know how to use them.

Finally, decision trees may be utilised. These are a pictorial method of showing a sequence of interrelated decisions and outcomes, which assists in the clarification of complex decision-making situations. They are particularly useful when a sequence of decisions has to be taken and when the decisions to take alternative courses of action are dependent on the decisions and actions taken earlier. This whole series of decisions and likely outcomes can be viewed conceptually as a decision tree. Management decision making consists of a sequence of decisions, actions and outcomes. Given one outcome, managers have to decide on which alternative courses of action to take next, and they have to have some idea of what the likely consequences of those actions will be. Complex decision problems have a sequential structure to them, and this can be represented by diagrams that show the probabilities, the likely consequences and the expected monetary values of a course of action.

Each decision tree is individual, constructed and tailored to meet a unique problem, so there is no universal model. There are, however, some common features: the probabilities associated with each outcome are based on someone's experience, opinions or best calculations. If necessary, the probabilities must be guesstimated — divided into an optimistic outcome, a realistic outcome and a pessimistic outcome.

> Models and number-crunching techniques help us to understand, predict, contemplate, analyse and so on. But they are simply and only models. We must use them carefully and judiciously.

Decision trees are not the 'be all and end all' of decision making. Like all models, they are used to guide, to indicate, to inform and to reduce uncertainty. If probabilities cannot be assigned to some particular set of outcomes, this means that the company is in a situation where it is about to launch into the future with no idea of what is likely to happen. This is not impractical management theory; it is bad management practice.

> Planning and control for operations requires an estimate of the demand for the product that an organisation expects to provide in the future. This answer could, therefore, have explored the importance of demand forecasting as an operational research tool.

Related questions

1   Using a linear programming method, show all the relevant constraints on a graph in order to optimise the output, given the quantities involved, and calculate the contribution that might be expected from each product at that optimum level of production.

2   Consider how a house-builder might use network analysis to assist in the planning and development of a new housing estate.

3   How far do you think mathematical models of operational problems can assist corporate decision making? How much notice should be taken of the proposed solutions?

4   'Any model produced by management experts is merely a static representation of a very dynamic situation and has little relevance to management problems.' Is this a fair statement?

Financial and Accountancy Management

Question 23

What factors should a firm consider when contemplating the acquisition of finance, and what will be the effect of gearing on the firm's profitability? Explain the advantages of using internal sources of finance.

Tackling the question

One of the first areas to be tackled in the finance module is, of course, where the firm can get its money from. So this really is foundation material: namely, sources and types of funding. But the type of funding used may affect the management of the company as well as restrict what it can do, and what risks it can take. Similarly, a high level of gearing may be great when demand is high, when there's little competition, and when the market is growing. Under other conditions, however, high gearing could spell disaster — remember what happened to Laker Airways. Two important points are the cost of capital and the return on investment opportunities. Like many other resources, capital is limited and there is a cost involved in choosing which source or method of finance to use. The key element, from a commercial point of view, is whether the capital we decide to use increases or maintains the firm's profitability and earns a satisfactory return for the shareholders. If the cost of capital is high, the investment opportunities will be limited.

Answer

There are three fundamental requirements of corporate finance:

- venture capital, i.e. initial finance with which to launch the firm and set up the business;
- working capital, i.e. continuation finance for the day-to-day running of the enterprise and to pay costs as they become due;
- investment capital, i.e. finance with which to acquire new resources and fixed assets, and for research and development purposes.

One of the major factors that the firm should consider in acquiring any kind of capital is the timing of the financial

Guidance notes

This is a good, solid introduction to the answer. We are really asking: what is the money needed for; what is the firm going to do with it, if it gets it? The answers to these questions will influence the type of funding that it might be best to use.

injection. To determine its level of finance, perhaps through a series of timed injections, the firm must prepare budgets and cash flow projections. The types of finance will fall into two main categories. First, debt finance includes short-term loans (such as bank overdrafts), medium-term loans (i.e. bank loans) and long-term finance in the form of debentures or preference shares. Second, equity finance includes retained profits, revenue and capital reserves, which belong to the owners of the company (i.e. the ordinary shareholders). Further equity finance may be raised from new issues and rights issues of ordinary shares.

This is a comprehensive list, but it emphasises the many areas that must be considered before the firm gets the additional finance. Not all of them will apply to every firm, every time, but most will.

Many factors must be considered when deciding on the type of capital to be raised. The most important are:

- the cost of money, i.e. the prevailing interest rates and how they are likely to change in both the short term and the long term;
- repayment periods. The maxim of borrow long and lend short is significant for firms, depending on the purpose of the capital required. In times of high inflation, even with high interest rates, the longer the loan period, the cheaper the net cost of borrowing.
- reward payment dates. In its cash flow analysis, the firm must consider when interest or dividend payments will become due because, whereas dividend payments may be deferred or may be paid on equity capital only if circumstances allow, interest on borrowed finance must be paid on due dates that may cause acute liquidity problems.
- control. Issuing new capital may change the ultimate control of the organisation, which may affect managerial style and current organisational objectives.
- risk. The riskier a venture is, the more nervous a lender will be and, not unnaturally, the higher the interest rates that will be demanded in compensation. A risk venture should be funded from equity capital rather than debt capital because, in the event of the latter, debt payments will have to be made even if the venture collapses.

The launch of a new issue of shares is not only complicated but very expensive. The success of the launch depends also on its timing: a bull market will be more receptive, but there may not be one when the shares are ready to be sold. So the basic questions to be asked concern the appropriateness of equity capital versus debt capital and, if debt finance, whether it should be short-, medium- or long-term funding. The sources of finance may be divided into two main categories:

Internal sources	External sources
(a) Retained profit	(a) Trade creditors
(b) Depreciation provision	(b) Bank overdrafts
(c) Tax provision	(c) Bank loans
(d) Reduction of current assets	(d) Factoring
	(e) Debentures and mortgages
	(f) Hire purchase
	(g) Leasing
	(h) Sale/leaseback
	(i) Share issues: new issue or rights issue

Internal sources of finance should always be examined before considering external borrowings or share issues because significant advantages may be obtained:

- No repayment is (usually) necessary. However, the opportunity costs involved must be examined.
- There are no interest payments to meet on a regular basis, which would become an on-going fixed cost for the duration of the loan.
- It is not necessary to negotiate suitable finance, and the associated setting-up costs are avoided.
- It may result in a more financially fit business that comes close to maximising the efficient and effective use of its own resources.

An enterprise can frequently provide itself with a steady source of finance by the simple act of ploughing back some of its profits. Current tax legislation is designed to encourage the retention of profits, since undistributed profits remain free of tax, whereas, paid as dividends, they are subject to income tax. However, the disadvantage of using retained profit is, of course, the absence of dividends. Making a depreciation provision results in reducing the stated profit without cash actually being paid out, i.e. cash is retained by the company above the normal undistributed profit. Depending on the capital nature of the organisation, this sum may be very significant. Of course, in a stable business such cash will be required to replace fully depreciated fixed assets. Corporation tax is not payable until one year or so after the end of the company's trading year. If current assets can be reduced, funds will be released for use elsewhere. Often stocks creep to unnecessarily high levels and debtors'

Before a firm turns to the outside world for finance, it really should stop and ask itself whether it can generate some of the finance from its own resources. Can it do anything to release monies tied up, sitting idle, not contributing a great deal? Or could it use the finance set aside for one project for another one, at least in the short term? A firm shouldn't dash to the nearest money lender. There's always a catch — not least that borrowing someone else's money is never cheap. Of course, if the firm uses its own finance, it should consider the opportunity cost of doing so.

payments are allowed to fall behind unless there is an effective credit control system within the organisation. Any obsolete stock or equipment should be sold for whatever it can fetch — its net realisable value (NRV).

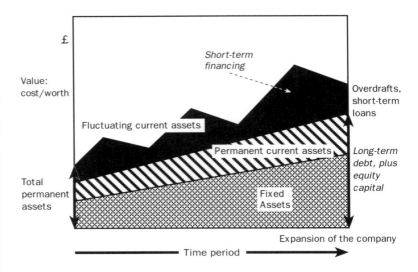

Figure 14 Fluctuating versus permanent assets, and financing

Another important consideration in the generation of cash and the improvement of liquidity is the control of debtors. Inevitably, most companies will experience bad debts and most will make appropriate provision based on experience and historical evidence. Effective credit control, nonetheless, is a prerequisite of financial control. Debt collectors may be called in to handle old, often individual, debts. One method of collecting invoice debts is by factoring. Factoring companies buy the company's debts as they arise and before the settlement date of the invoice. Adequate liquidity is especially important to small and medium-sized firms to fund the next working cycle. In effect, therefore, the factoring firm provides immediate finance of up to 80% of the value secured on the outstanding invoices of the company, with the balance, less fee, paid later. It is estimated that, at any one time, there are more than £57 billion of payments due to small businesses and tied up in unpaid invoices; and that, on average, companies are having to wait 75 days before being paid.

The final influences on the firm's decision to obtain finance are the financial structure of the company and the effect of gearing, which is the ratio of debt to equity capital, i.e. high gearing means large amounts of debt (interest-bearing) capital. Changes in gearing result in changes in the levels of return. In a time of good profits, shareholders obtain an exceptionally high reward

Remember that firms don't dash to the stock market either. Whenever this kind of question is asked, many say 'The firm can sell shares.' It can't — at least, it can't very easily. And even if it could, it's

in a high-geared company, since debt capital is rewarded by fixed interest payments that, once paid, leave the remaining profit for distribution to a relatively small number of shareholders. However, when profits are low the payment of fixed interest on high debt capital may absorb most of the profit, leaving little or none for subsequent distribution or for ploughing back into the company.

The appropriate level of gearing for any company depends on the riskiness and other characteristics of the industry, the firm's markets, its dependency on exports and foreign exchange rates, anticipated changes in interest rates and whether they are fixed or variable. There are, however, distinct advantages in the careful use of debt capital. In the first place, its judicious use will increase the earnings per ordinary share and, second, given that interest charges are tax deductible against profits, the net cost of borrowing may be relatively low. Generally, a company will use debentures and/or mortgages and long-term loan capital to finance non-risk, secure investments (such as land and buildings) which may then be used as collateral for the loan.

expensive to do so, even if it's proposing a rights issue. Usually, but not always, a firm issues shares, perhaps at a premium price, to raise initial capital. But when it comes to subsequent capital, shares are not usually the first option.

Related questions

1   If you were a member of one of the following groups, would you prefer your company to be high geared or low geared: an employee; a shareholder; a creditor; a customer?

2   What factors would a firm take into account when deciding between equity capital and debt capital?

3   A company is considering the launch of a new product in a niche market, but needs the capital to fund the project. What advice would you give? Explain the importance of such advice.

4   A firm operating in a very dynamic market is keen to maintain the confidence of its shareholders, but needs to acquire more modern machinery to improve productivity. Consider the financial dilemma the company faces and suggest an appropriate compromise plan of action.

Discuss the use and limitations of management accountancy ratios in determining and measuring the performance and financial health of a company.

Tackling the question

This is what I call 'a banker'. It is a perennial favourite, and understandably so, for it requires both analysis of accounts — trading documents — and, perhaps even more importantly, interpretation. I've analysed the accounts — so what? What do they mean? What does the analysis reveal? Ratios act as a 'red flag' to signal potential problems and provide a starting point for both investigation and control purposes. It would not be inappropriate to indicate in the answer why different groups might be interested in different ratios and for what purpose. There are four main groups of ratios: liquidity, activity, debt and profitability. Clearly, each of these will be of greater or lesser importance to whoever is interested in the company and its accounts. But note that accountancy ratios will not always reveal what is wrong. As with every other technique, we have to be aware of their limitations.

Answer

The purpose of interpreting company accounts is to assess the company's past performance to obtain some idea of how well the company is likely to do in the future, and to decide what corrective action it needs to take to achieve that success. However, to determine whether the performance is satisfactory requires some yardstick to be provided. There must be a standard. The basis for comparison may be last year's (or the previous period's) results (trend analysis), the competitor's performance, an industrial norm or average, or a calculated norm (such as an optimum stock ratio). The comparisons used are the accounting ratios. They are, in effect, a short-hand way of showing relationships between figures in financial statements.

The data contained within the trading documents must reflect the firm's true financial condition. The basic sources of information for subsequent analysis are the company's balance sheets, fund and cash flow statements, and profit and loss or income statements. However, to analyse a single set of accounts will not be very useful; in fact, it could be very misleading. A number of periods' accounts are required.

A useful mnemonic in remembering ratio analysis is GAPS — gearing, activity, performance, solvency. The essential, financial criteria of the successful operation of a company are profitability and liquidity (or short-term cash flow), which enables the company to continue operating and, in due course, achieve its long-term cash flow.

The analysis and determination of the ratios are straightforward; it is the interpretation of the ratios that is more problematical. Ratio analysis does not simply involve the application of a formula to financial data in order to calculate a given ratio. Far more important, assuming the data and calculations are correct, is the interpretation of the ratio value. Financial ratios need not be expressed as ratios in the mathematical sense, but can be in any form that conveys information to the interest group concerned. The interested parties may not be looking for the same aspects, since their motives may be very different.

Ratio analysis is undertaken for two main reasons:

- to determine and establish trends, both intra-firm and inter-firm;
- for comparative analysis, both intra-firm and inter-firm.

Those who scrutinise company accounts and financial data are generally looking for one or more of four main factors: company earnings and earnings potential; operational success (which is not the same as profit, but is more a reflection of the effectiveness of management); stability (some companies are very stable and achieve steady sales, but may not be very profitable, while other companies may be affected by seasonal or cyclical sales); and liquidity (the speed with which an asset can be converted into cash and the firm's ability to meet its short-term debts).

The same ratio may be expressed in a number of ways.

Example:
An organisation's sales in one year are £200,000 and the average value of its finished stock is £50,000. This relationship can be expressed as:

- ratio of sales to stock 4:1;
- percentage of stock to sales: 50,000/200,000 × 100 = 25%;
- number of days' sales held in stock: 50,000/200,000 × 365 = 91 days;

This is where the higher-grade candidates begin to score highly. These are the kind of comments for which the marks come tumbling in because they show a much deeper understanding of the technique: they show the need for evaluation, and they illustrate the technique's limitations and the need for caution.

- number of times stocks are turned over in one year: 200,000/50,000 = 4 times;
- annual sales per £1 of stock held = £4.

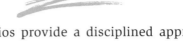

There's something of a medical parallel here. Doctors may be able to detect the signs and symptoms, but they may not be able to diagnose the actual condition of the patient until they undertake further tests. So, too, with a company 'doctor'. Be careful not to treat the 'patient' until you're quite certain you know what's wrong. More tests and analysis may be needed. Of course, if the company is in a really bad way, you might have to introduce 'life-saving' measures.

However, while ratios provide a disciplined approach to the analysis of accounts, there are limitations inherent in the use of such ratios. It will almost certainly be necessary to supplement the ratio analysis with additional information for a number of reasons:

- Ratios are a measure of past performance and there is no guarantee that what happened in the past, even with trend analysis and comprehensive forecasting techniques, is likely to be repeated in the future.
- Accounting statements present only a limited picture of the business. They do not cover all aspects of the business (e.g. they would not show qualitative data, such as employee morale, although this in itself may be reflected in the productivity figures, which, in turn, may affect unit costs, prices, etc.).
- Many of the figures used are calculated according to accounting procedures and conventions. Companies may treat these figures differently (e.g. depreciation), and may operate different financial policies, or firms may value assets differently. There is room for considerable differences between companies.
- External analysis of the balances can be misleading because the picture, at that particular moment, may not be representative of the year as a whole. For example, companies may stock-take when their stocks are at the lowest level.
- The liquidity ratios are based on a static view of the company. They provide little or no information on funds or cash flow.
- A change in a ratio may require careful consideration of both the numerator and the denominator.
- Ratios provide no information on important changes that may affect future company performance, such as a change of management or the emergence of strong competition.
- In general, it is incorrect to compare small firms with large firms. Many of the general industrial analyses of ratios are overall averages and are, therefore, not strictly comparable.
- Many companies have seasonal or cyclical patterns of production or sales; ratios calculated at different points in the cycle may vary.
- The analysis of financial information can only be as good as the accuracy of that information.

Ratios tend to be more diagnostic in their use than in providing definitive answers to problems. In other words, they may reveal that all is not well with a company, but they will be unlikely to tell the management what remedial action to take. When a ratio has been calculated, it is still necessary to consider what message the value should convey. Undue importance must not be given to any single ratio, for its value is limited and it must be seen in the context of the firm's objectives. A single ratio does not generally provide sufficient information from which to judge the overall performance of the firm. Only when a group of ratios is used can reasonable judgements be made.

When determining ratios, it is vital to compare like with like. For example, when discussing 'profit', is the reference to gross profit or net profit or retained profit or operating profit? Operating profit is normally used in the calculations. Each industry has different 'acceptable' levels for its ratios. They may even vary by geographical region. Published industry averages can provide quite a useful comparison, but must not be used in isolation.

For any company the key ratio is profit/capital employed. This is used to evaluate the performance and the efficiency of the management of a company, or a unit within a company. It is of particular use within a group of companies, as the underlying information can have the same basis.

The primary ratio, turnover/capital employed, affords a measure of the use of capital at the disposal of the management. When multiplied by the other primary ratio, profit/turnover, which indicates the profit margin, the key ratio is obtained. Any change in the key ratio will be due to changes in the primary ratios. For example, a reduction in the rate of return on capital employed can be due to a reduction in the profit margins and/or a low rate of asset turnover.

Once a particular aspect of company performance has been identified, most of the relevant information can be determined from one or two ratios. Thus five ratios may contain about 80% of the information available from a set of 40 or more ratios. By summarising a large number of ratios, the financial analyst, or other interested party, can assess many aspects of the firm's activities to isolate key areas of responsibility.

I don't think you need to go into the micro detail of the ratios — the question does not ask you to do so. Just give the key ones, so the examiner knows what you're talking about. Of course, if you're presented with a balance sheet and a P&L account, that's a different matter; you may well have to go into considerable detail with your analysis and interpretation.

Related questions

1 Why should a balance sheet not be taken at its face value? Explain which entries may require further analysis and investigation, and comment on the kind of information that is not usually in the trading documents but which, nonetheless, might be of interest to others.

2 Consider and discuss the following statement: 'The balance sheet is the dead past; it is of little relevance to today or the future.'

3 Explain why ratio analysis may be useful, but should be viewed with some caution. How can the findings be made more credible?

4 Many financial statements are biased or incomplete. If it is a requirement that accounts must be audited and verified, how can this be so? What additional information would you require if you were a shareholder?

What are the basic methods of valuing a business? Discuss the difficulties that might be met when attempting such valuations.

Tackling the question

Valuing a business, particularly one which is ripe for takeover or acquisition, may not be easy. The book value, the actual net worth of the assets — a building, a piece of land, a factory, a warehouse full of stock — may be fairly easy to determine. Simply stated, the value of any asset is the present value of all future cash flows that it is expected to provide over the relevant time period. But what of those elements that once made the business successful or continue to make the business successful — the intangible assets, not least goodwill and branding? And how is 'success' to be measured, and over what period? Even the local fish and chip shop will have generated some customer goodwill, some good relations. How does one put a price on that? In any case, a company might only realise its net realisable value (NRV), which is the best price that can be obtained.

Answer

Guidance notes

Most business people need to have an idea of the value of their business at some time or another. The true return on investment (ROI) cannot be determined without this knowledge, but the need to know what a business is worth arises particularly when considering:

- introducing a new partner or buying out an existing one;
- buying or selling a business (acquisitions and takeovers);
- joining up with another business (mergers).

The value of a business may be one thing to the seller, but quite another to the person considering its purchase. Ultimately, the value of a business, like the value of anything else, is the price negotiated between a willing buyer and a willing seller. There are two basic approaches to valuing a business: the assets basis and the earnings basis.

It's always a good idea to include an example, as it shows the examiner that you can manipulate the concept. There's another well-known mnemonic you may have heard: 'KISS' — keep it simple, stupid! It's a bit crude, but it makes the point.

The assets basis

One way of valuing a business is simply to say that it is worth the assets that it owns. This means its net tangible assets, i.e. assets other than goodwill, patents and trademarks, less all outside liabilities. This is not to say that anyone selling a business would necessarily let the goodwill and other intangibles go for nothing, but these would have to be valued separately.

Example:

The balance sheet of a business is as follows:

	£	£
Fixed assets, less depreciation	10,000	
Goodwill	2,000	
Current assets	20,000	
		32,000
Financed by:		
Share capital and reserves	17,000	
Loan	5,000	
Current liabilities	10,000	32,000

Taking the balance sheet figures at their face value, the business has net tangible assets of £15,000.

However, it would be unwise to rely solely on the book figures; a more realistic view of what the assets are worth is required. What they are worth depends on whether it is intended to use them or sell them off. This may often amount to the same thing, but not necessarily so, particularly where specialised plant is concerned. If specialised plant (bought with the intention of using it) is worth what it would cost to purchase it then, because of its special nature, this might be a considerable amount. On the other hand, if there was no use for it, it might be worth only a small amount as scrap.

The earnings basis

This basis for valuing a business follows from the view that the worth of a business depends on what it can earn. If a return of 5% per annum from an investment can be expected, then a business that earns £1,000 a year has a capital value of

$$100/5 \times £1,000 = £20,000$$

Use of this method depends upon determining the maintainable earnings of the business and deciding a fair rate of return for the particular type of business.

Currently maintainable earnings (profits)

If a business is being purchased for what it is capable of earning, it is current and future profits that will be of interest. Past profits, or earnings, which can be determined from the latest profit and loss accounts, serve only as a guide to what the business might be expected to earn. As with balance sheets, profit and loss account figures should not be taken at their face value. Items often requiring adjustment are depreciation, remuneration of the proprietors, stock values, provisions for doubtful debts, exceptional items and taxation.

Fair rate of return

Deciding what is a fair rate of return for a business is a highly subjective matter. One may start with the current rate of interest and say that, because of the risk attaching to business, a fair rate of return for the business should be something greater than this. There are also capital investment appraisal techniques that may help to reduce uncertainty. Ideally, comparison with a similar business in the same locality should be used. Often, a standard may be determined by using the published figures of earning and share prices of public companies.

Goodwill

As a going and profitable concern, a business will be worth much more than the book value of its net tangible assets. It has an established reputation and trade connections, and may have other real advantages, such as its management and technical knowledge. Together, these intangibles comprise goodwill. The problem is to put a figure on this goodwill. There is no scientific way of measuring goodwill, but some of the 'rules of thumb' methods appear more reasonable than others. The goodwill element in acquisitions and takeovers has become a much more significant factor in recent years. In 1978 the average large UK company had a stock market value that was about £74 for each £100 of book equity. The acquirer who paid a typical 30% premium to acquire control of a company was thus buying its assets at around the book value. However, the rise in stock market prices around the world caused companies to revalue their worth relative to the book value of the company's assets. There was a consequent growth in the value of goodwill. By 1988 the same company was trading at £168, so the acquirer would pay around £210 for a company with a book equity of £100.

There are two main ways of valuing goodwill: purchase of profits; and the difference between earnings-based valuation and assets-based valuation.

So here are two fairly simple methods of valuation based on profits and asset valuation, but they don't handle the concept of 'goodwill' very well.

Now we can launch into the more difficult areas: goodwill and branding. Both areas give you an opportunity to show off — and so you should — but keep your eye on the question. It's about valuing a business, not the merits or otherwise of branding as a marketing/promotion strategy.

Purchase of profits

Goodwill is often valued at so many years of past average profits. The particular number of years is often a matter of tradition. Three to five years is quite common.

Example:

	Profit for the past 5 years (£)
Year 1	1,000
Year 2	1,200
Year 3	900
Year 4	1,000
Year 5	1,400
Total	5,500

Average profit:	£1,100
Goodwill at 3 years' purchase:	£3,300

This method is not looked upon with favour for several reasons:

- If profit is very small in relation to the value of assets employed, it is doubtful that any goodwill exists at all, but this method would nevertheless give it a value. It would therefore take no account of potential.
- The fact that profits were made in the past is no guarantee that they will continue.
- In an environment of rising prices, profits can be overstated and the values distorted.

The difference between earnings-based valuation and assets-based valuation

Example:
The current maintainable earnings of a business are £5,000 p.a. A fair and comparable rate of return for the business is 10% p.a. It has net tangible assets of £40,000.

Value on an earnings basis 100/10 × £5,000	50,000
Net tangible assets	40,000
Goodwill	10,000

Any exercise in valuing a business should take account of the assets that the firm owns and its past and projected earnings. It is usual to look at earnings after tax because some businesses have distinct tax advantages over others. Any assets should be valued as realistically as possible. Past profit figures should be adjusted if necessary to serve as an indication of future trends.

I have given several examples here. Any conscientious business studies student will get into the habit of browsing through the business sections of the quality press just to keep aware of what's going on. And if a particularly useful titbit catches your eye, make a note of it for future use. In fact, it may be no bad thing to develop your own bank of useful anecdotes and examples.

An estimate of future profits should be made and the realism of this should be checked against the technical and commercial background. However, if the respective managements involved in the bargaining have to live with one another in the future, it is as well not to let the negotiations get too acrimonious. When considering the acquisition of an overseas company, even within the European Union, the problem of valuation becomes even more acute. Different legal systems, capital-raising mechanisms and tax systems are among the explanations for the failure of the EU to harmonise the reporting of profits.

Another area difficult to evaluate when considering the total value of a business is the worth of a brand. In the last decade the importance of valuing brands has become even more dominant, for many argue that stock markets have failed to recognise the true economic value of firms that possess a strong portfolio of brands. The problem for brokers has been how to build a premium into a share price for an intangible asset such as a brand name. The investment required to establish a strong brand is considerable. Clearly that value should be represented somewhere, since if balance sheets show little more than debits and credits, they are probably meaningless. The increased prominence given to the role of brands in mergers and acquisitions means that the concept of brand valuation is much more acceptable, if still problematical, to the financial markets.

Related questions

1   What precautions might an acquiring company take when contemplating the takeover of another company in times of rising inflation?

2   'It is a sensible business strategy to acquire ailing companies with a view to asset stripping and releasing the capital within the business.' Discuss the merits and disadvantages of such a philosophy.

3   Regulation of accountancy practice is clearly desirable, but are the regulations and requirements too restrictive and severe, particularly when considering intangible assets?

4   How assets are accounted for can dramatically affect a company's financial profile. Explain, with examples, how and why this might be so.

Question 26

What is depreciation? Consider the practical problems associated with this concept and the implications for the financial reporting of a company.

Tackling the question

Some people find the concept of depreciation quite difficult to understand: it may not be too simple, but it really is an important idea. You simply must know how to deal with depreciation and the effects that it has on the profit and loss account (which some call 'the income statement'), the balance sheet and profits. Depreciation involves matching the historic costs of a fixed asset with the revenues that the asset generates. It is the systematic charging of a portion of the costs of fixed assets against annual profits over time. But remember that depreciation does not involve the movement of cash. Stress this point. It is merely an accounting procedure; a book transfer.

Answer

Depreciation is measured at any given date as a drop in the price or value of an object, from a previous date. However, price and value are not the same: price is cost (and therefore factual) whereas value is relative (and therefore judgemental). Depreciation is a process of allocating the cost of plant and equipment, including the cost of installation, over the accounting periods included in the life of that plant. It is an essential component of cost build-up in product costing. Depreciation and amortisation, of course, assume greater importance in those businesses that tend to be capital intensive. (Amortisation is similar to depreciation, but usually refers to the reducing life of natural assets such as mines, quarries and oil fields.)

This is a very relevant point. It stands to reason that the more a company has invested in plant and machinery and other capital goods, the greater will be its levels of

Companies are permitted to charge systematically a portion of the capital costs of fixed assets against annual revenues. Fixed assets are those items of equipment that are bought by the company for continued use in earning profit and are not going to be sold off in the normal course of the business. They are called 'fixed' assets because the money invested in them is 'fixed'. They include everything that the company uses, ranging from computers and photocopiers to petroleum-refining plant and agricultural machinery. The purpose of depreciation as a business concept is the matching of revenue against expenses during the same time period. The process attempts to amortise the cost invested in the plant during its useful life. An asset's useful life is limited mainly by wear and tear over a period of time, and by its technical obsolescence.

Methods of calculating depreciation attempt to achieve the following objectives:

- to account for the loss in value of the asset;
- to allocate the cost of that asset;
- to amortise the cost (although 'amortisation' is usually applied to the depreciation of intangible assets);
- to provide a fund for asset replacement, although a fund, as such, is not actually created.

Depreciation is a cost of service, not a separately managed cash fund earmarked for asset acquisition. In so far as accumulated depreciation expenses reduce the income available for dividend distribution, it can be viewed as conserving and retaining a part of the shareholders' investment. Depreciation begins from the day the construction, installation or purchase of a unit of property is completed and placed in service. Ideally the depreciation accruals, collected over the asset's useful life, should equal its cost, plus or minus the cost of retirement and salvage realised from the disposal of the entire asset. Annual depreciation charged to operations is a non-cash expense and the accumulated depreciation is a reduction of assets on the asset side of the balance sheet. The cost of depreciation is no less a cost than the cost of labour or materials. If depreciation is omitted or distorted, the company's net profit will also be distorted.

The total accumulated depreciation, including that shown as a provision in the current profit and loss account, appears in the balance sheet, where it represents an amount held back from profit for use in replacing those fixed assets on which it was originally charged. The measurement of depreciation must take into account its causes — physical wear and tear, decay and weathering. The functional causes include obsolescence, inadequacy and changes in technology. Depreciation is a process of estimation; it is judgemental in nature, based on experience. Nonetheless, a systematic measurement must be applied because, particularly with increasing automation, depreciation cost may indeed be higher than material and/or labour costs. Some of the common methods of accounting for depreciation

annual and accumulated depreciation. If you consider and compare two companies both producing the same kind of product, but one of which is labour intensive and the other capital intensive, clearly depreciation is going to affect one firm more than the other. The key question is: with what results or effects?

are straight-line, declining balance, units of production, and hours of service. Such methods are fairly straightforward. However, in utilities such as gas, electricity, railways and the water industries, depreciation accounting is a more complex subject.

A more sophisticated technique, which takes into account the asset's remaining life (particularly useful when the asset's life is revised), is as follows:

$$\text{Depreciation} = \frac{\text{Purchase cost} + \text{Removal cost} - \text{Depreciation to date}}{\text{Asset's remaining life}}$$

You should be aware of the pros and cons of the various methods of depreciation and, more importantly, the effects that each has on the level of profit. Try a small calculation using each different method and see what happens to the final profit figures. Which method is the most advantageous, under what circumstances, and for whom?

The various methods of calculating depreciation aim to charge the net cost of the asset over the expected economic life of that asset, but each method will provide a different pattern of cost allocation. Using the declining balance method, it is argued, will more accurately reflect the true depreciation in the real market value of the asset, because many assets tend to lose significant value in the early years of their use (e.g. a new motor car or van). In other words, the earlier years of an asset's life are weighted more heavily. When comparing two or more companies, therefore, it is important to note the methods of calculating depreciation that each company uses, since different methods will provide different profit and loss figures. When a company buys or disposes of fixed assets, during the accounting year, the value of the asset or the amount of depreciation is expressed as a proportional amount depending on the time remaining to the year end. However, it must be emphasised that depreciation is not a cash movement. It is neither a source nor a use of cash, but merely a bookkeeping provision.

It will be evident that, whatever depreciation accounting system is used, the accuracy of the cost allocations depends to a very great extent on the accuracy of estimate of the asset's average life, and it is very difficult to make such estimates with precision. The importance of depreciation increases in direct proportion to increases in capital investment, much of which is usually funded from undistributed profit or revenue reserves. In addition, depreciation based on historic costs may completely fail to show the cost of replacing the underlying assets in a period of rapid price and cost inflation. However, few firms rarely replace obsolete or worn-out assets with identical equipment.

There is a very strong argument that all companies should be required to depreciate on replacement costs rather than historic costs, and that they should also value fixed assets at replacement costs. If this were to be introduced, stock market valuations and inter-firm comparisons would change considerably.

In an attempt to stimulate corporate investment, successive governments have variously offered companies a number of financial incentives, including increases in the deductions allowed for depreciation for tax purposes. This tax system allows for depreciation to be deducted from gross profits, before determining the final corporate tax liability. Depreciation of assets should, of course, be standardised from year to year, and depreciation allowances for tax purposes may be a subject of negotiation between the company accountant and the Inland Revenue. However, a company's method of calculating depreciation may be ignored by the Inland Revenue inspectors, for they have their own methods of calculation.

Related questions

1 Consider what effect the chosen method of depreciation might have on a company's profits and cash flows.

2 Explain the significance of depreciation and where you would expect to find it on the balance sheet and the profit and loss account. In a manufacturing company, what difference, if any, does it make to the 'cost of goods sold'?

3 Depreciation is simply a book adjustment. It does not involve the payment of any cash. Explain why this is so.

4 Explain the various depreciation methods and, with an example of your choice, demonstrate how the various methods can present a different financial picture of a company.

What capital investment criteria should a firm consider when proposing to embark on a capital project? Show, with examples, what methods of investment appraisal are at its disposal.

Tackling the question

This is a fairly standard question in management accounting. You should know the difference between those methods of capital investment appraisal that consider the time value of money and those that don't — and, of course, the limitations of each. A relevant point to consider is that time value of money techniques are used in personal financial transactions as well as in managerial finance, such as in determining the value of annuities. Capital investment appraisal techniques have to do with assessing long-term investments. Such decisions are, of course, concerned with long-term planning and the achievement of corporate objectives. Ultimately, such calculations are about optimising certainty and minimising risk. Clearly, the extent and depth of your examples will be limited by the time available.

Answer

The selection and the financing of capital projects are undoubtedly two of the most critical decisions that have to be made by any organisation. The amount of capital involved may be considerable; mistakes in this connection can prove costly and sometimes the very future of the organisation may depend on the correctness of the investment decision. For this reason, the appropriate criteria for appraising investment in capital assets are vital, since the decision, once made, commits the organisation for a number of years and is virtually irrevocable.

Usually, a minimum rate of return — based on expected sales volume, pricing strategies and cost factors associated with the project — will be stipulated, which will take into account the potential risks and the probable levels of interest rates. Capital investment appraisal techniques are useful in analysing the potential of a project, but there will be many more considerations, not all of which will be financial. An array of data must be collected that express some arithmetical relationship between the proposed capital expenditure and the forecast increases in 'earnings'. Earnings in this context means either increased income or reduced costs, or a combination of the two.

Ideally, five steps are required in investment analysis:

1. Forecasting the incremental cash involved — both inflows and outflows.
2. Determining the appropriate discount rate or cost of capital (by comparing the rate of return that investors might expect from another investment with a similar risk profile).
3. Calculating the net present value.
4. Deciding whether the project should go ahead.
5. Sensitivity analysis, using break-even analysis and profit: volume:contribution analysis. During this process, the critical variables can be identified and manipulated to see what effects they have.

Different methods will give different answers and may result in a different ranking for investment projects. Of the following methods, the first two may be called the traditionalist approach and have been used for a considerable number of years.

Here are the main methods of capital investment appraisal, together with examples. You should be ready to list the advantages and limitations of each method.

The payback method
This method simply calculates the time taken to recover the initial capital outlay.

Example:
An investment of £100,000 is estimated to increase the company's earnings by £20,000 p.a.

$$\frac{£100,000}{£20,000} = \text{Payback period (5 years)}$$

The earnings figure is usually taken as net of tax and ignores depreciation, since this is only a book entry. However, this system has several fundamental weaknesses:

- No account is taken of the earning life of the investment.
- Where this system is used exclusively, a company could put all of its capital into projects yielding little or nothing after the payback period. Thus, money could be pumped around a system without making anything out of the process.
- No account is taken of the fact that £1 next year is worth less than £1 now.

The method is quick and useful, however, when considering the apparent riskiness of the project.

Rate of return
This is a better criterion and seeks to evaluate the project by the return on the capital remaining invested.

Example:

Investment £95,000	1st year	£45,000
	2nd year	£50,000
	Estimated life	10 years
	Residual value	nil

Year	Profit (£000)	Depreciation (£000)	Book value (£000)	Rate of return (%)
1	0	5	40	—
2	0	10	80	—
3	12	10	75	16
4	15	10	65	23
5	16	10	55	29
6	16	10	45	36
7	16	10	35	46
8	12	10	25	48
9	5	10	15	33
10	1	10	5	20
			Average	25

Remember that if you're producing financial or numerical statements of any kind, it really is helpful to produce them in tabulated form. Apart from anything else, it keeps the numbers neat and tidy, makes the calculations easier, and disciplines your approach to the answer. Try it!

Some companies take a representative year or a long-term and short-term average. Other companies take the average over the whole life of the asset. Though better than the payback method, the rate of return has several weaknesses:

- Since depreciation used in the accounts usually varies from that used for tax purposes, the figure can be misleading.
- No account is taken of the timing of the earnings. Two projects can show the same rate of return, but one could earn the profits in the early years, the other late in the life of the project.
- All money is regarded as of equal value.

Discounted cash flow
To overcome some of the deficiencies outlined in the above methods, the discounted cash flow (DCF) method may be used. The objective in assessing capital projects is the same as any investor might have — to determine the maximum net cash flow after tax. The cash flow must be sufficient to repay the initial outlay and earn an adequate return on the balance outstanding at any time. Therefore, the financial adequacy of the investment will be measured by the average effective rate of interest on the

outstanding balances over the life of the investment. This is what DCF endeavours to do.

The main features of the method are that the life of the project is estimated and the relevant cash flows, both in and out, are forecast for each year of its expected life. Net cash flows comprise the net cash receipts arising from the investment in the project. In this connection, the timing of tax allowances and tax payments is an important factor in the calculation. The cash flow is discounted in relation to the timing of its receipt.

The basic assumption of discounting is that money has a time value.

- £100 invested today at 10% will be worth £110 in one year's time.
- £100 invested today at 10% will be worth £121 in two years' time.
- Thus £121 received in year 2 is worth £100 at year 0.

By the use of discount tables, the present value of the cash flow for the respective years can be obtained. The object is to use a discounting factor that will result in the net amount equalling the original investment. It will be necessary to achieve this by a process of trial and error.

Example:
Suppose an investment of £1,000. Life, 6 years. Residual value, nil.

After applying the discount factors (from tables):
Present value of inflow: at 11% = £1,009; at 12% = £975.

Comparing the two factors, it can be seen that 11% is too low and 12% is too high. The actual factor is somewhere in between. Using linear interpolation, we can calculate the exact rate.

Present value at 11%	£1,009	Present value at 11%	£1,009
Present value at 12%	£975	Actual capital cost	£1,000
	£34		£9

Therefore: $\dfrac{9}{34} \times 1\% = 0.265$

Calculated rate of return: 11 + 0.27 = 11.27%

Thus, management is given information on the true rate of interest that the project is likely to earn. Where a number of projects are competing for the available finance, they can be judged according to their real earning capacity. A standard rate of return on capital can be set and, if a project cannot match up to this standard, it is not considered unless there are safety matters or other considerations to take into account. Capital budgeting is concerned with identifying and valuing potential investment opportunities to enable the management of a company to make sound and rational investment decisions. If access to capital is not limited, the company should accept — on financial grounds — all projects with positive net present values.

Note how the conclusion mentions the importance of 'capital budgeting'. If you're going to write about capital investment appraisal, you need to know about budgeting for capital expenditure.

Related questions

1   Discuss the value of capital investment appraisal, and discounting techniques in particular, in company decision making. Do you think such techniques work in practice?

2   Examine the reasons why companies invest in fixed assets, and discuss the problems that such acquisitions might bring.

3   State some of the limitations of NPV and IRR methods of investment appraisal, and explain what investment appraisal methods you would use under conditions of capital rationing.

4   Explain why the stream of future cash flows used in the capital investment appraisal methods may be highly inaccurate.

Question 28

Compare and contrast absorption and marginal costing methods, and suggest how well such methods fulfil the purposes of cost accounting. With an example of your choice, expand on one of these methods.

The control of costs is perhaps the most basic of all requirements in a firm. Close behind, however, must be an accurate determination of costs for product pricing. Knowing how much a product costs to produce is an essential element in profitability. The standard costing approach is the most precise of all costing methods. However, this presupposes that the cost accounting system of the organisation is itself cost effective. It should make a positive contribution to organisational efficiency. It should also be remembered that some costs behave differently in different circumstances.

Answer

Guidance notes

Costing is not the sole concern of a company accountant: costs affect everyone within an organisation, and it is in everyone's interest to ensure that costs are minimised.

Cost accounting has several purposes:

- It attempts to secure more cost-effective use of limited resources and more efficient operations by comparing actual costs with predetermined, target costs, allowing for any variance to be analysed.
- It allows for product unit costing, which, in turn, allows for logical and rational pricing decisions to be taken.
- It allows for the evaluation of stock for pricing purposes and for current asset valuation.

Internal cost analysis is required to indicate a breakdown of cost per unit of production or service and then comparisons may show the contribution achieved per product, service or activity. This, in turn, will show the responsibility of managers for incurring costs through the efficiency or otherwise of their part of

It would surely be difficult to study business management without coming across 'costing' in all its many forms and methods. However, there's something of a confusion: economists talk of fixed and variable costs, while accountants tend to talk about direct and indirect costs, overheads, expenses and so on. If you're talking about marginal costing, it's probably best to use the economist's language, but for any other type of costing try being an accountant.

With this kind of costing, we are very much in the realms of the accountant rather than the economist. Clearly, you should mention the advantages and limitations of each costing method, and why this method rather than that one might be used. Sometimes, a firm may use a combination of two or more costing methods, depending on what the costing is going to be used for.

the organisation. It will therefore assist in planning, control and review of each of the functions within the organisation.

There are several ways of classifying costs, depending on the purpose for which the information is required. Some items may be identified immediately with a particular cost unit, e.g. the amount of steel used in the construction of a washing machine and the wages of the operative producing it. These are known as the direct costs of the unit of product or service. Other expenses, such as factory lighting, may cover a number of different cost units. These costs are known as the indirect costs, which may be variable or fixed, and can often be identified with specific cost centres. A cost centre is a location, person or item of equipment (or a group of these) concerning which costs may be determined, and then related to cost units passing through that cost centre.

Absorption costing
In the long term, this method relates all costs, both fixed and variable, to products, since both types of cost must be covered by revenue. The overheads are broken down into component parts (such as rent, rates, depreciation, salaries and energy) and then allocated on an equitable pro-rata basis using a consistent yardstick, such as floor area, number of employees or number of radiators within that department or cost centre. This process is known as apportionment. Having charged overheads to cost centres, it remains to charge a share of these overheads to each of the cost units passing through the cost centres. This is called absorption and involves the calculation of an overhead absorption rate (OAR).

This method is more complex than contribution costing or full costing, but it does have particular advantages. Absorption costing can improve budgetary control and allow for the pricing of specific jobs, such as printing orders or vehicle repairs and servicing. It is a particularly useful method of costing because it ensures that, over time, all costs are fully recovered. In summary, the advantages of absorption costing are as follows:

- It provides the detail that is necessary in job quotations.
- It stimulate cost consciousness.
- It allows for better timing and control because it allows target costs to be analysed.

The major disadvantage of absorption costing is that the financial data are nearly always historical and therefore of limited use. While it is of value to be aware of what happened in the past, it is the anticipated future and the interpretation of predicted events that should influence the firm's decisions and actions today. In addition, this method can be particularly complex in large firms with many subdivisions. Nonetheless, absorption costing is very precise in that most production overheads are shared by a number of cost centres and are distributed on an equitable basis.

Marginal costing

While less complex in application than absorption costing, marginal costing is much more useful as a decision-making tool. In this method, costing takes account of the variable or marginal cost of products rather than the full production cost. The marginal approach states that fixed factory overheads are a function of time. Only variable costs are charged to cost units. The fixed costs attributable to a relevant period are written off in full against the total contribution. This method is therefore easy to use, since apportionment is unnecessary. The greatest profit will be earned by optimising the contribution per unit of the factor: for example, labour hours or machine hours. This technique leads on to break-even analysis and the compilation of profit/volume graphs. Marginal costing is preferred in most decision-making situations, particularly those of a short-term or exceptional nature, and is becoming increasingly popular.

Now I begin to develop one of the costing methods — in this case, marginal costing — in some depth. It also allows me to introduce techniques such as break-even analysis and profit/volume charts, both of which are methods of undertaking profit sensitivity analysis.

Break-even analysis

This is a comparatively simple accountancy technique that relates different types of cumulative cost to the revenue obtained by the output of units of production and the subsequent sale of those units. In essence, the technique simplifies the cost/revenue and volume/profit relationships. Graphical or algebraic models assume that the fixed costs and price per unit remain the same over a range of time and output. They further assume a perfectly linear relationship between the two variables, which, while it facilitates decision making, is an unrealistic assumption.

The break-even model can only be as accurate as the information used, and the more complex the model becomes (e.g. by building in changing demand curves) the more difficult it becomes to elicit the relevant information. Nonetheless, the more complex models do permit variations in costs and prices over output levels and over time. The technique is based on the determination of marginal costs and revenues, and therefore is concerned primarily with the calculation of unit and total contribution.

A simple calculation is as follows:

$$\text{Break-even point} = \frac{\text{Total fixed costs } (+ \text{ Desired level of profit})}{\text{Unit selling price} - \text{Unit marginal cost}}$$

Example:

Fixed costs	= £10,000
Profit required	= £2,000
Unit selling price	= £15
Unit marginal cost	= £10
Contribution	= £5
Break-even point in units	= 2,400

$$\frac{10,000 + 2,000}{15 - 10} = \frac{12,000}{5}$$

The assumption that the variables are independent is not always realistic, and the market response to the price charged will not be easy to determine with any degree of accuracy, particularly when the demand is price sensitive or promotionally elastic and if there is significant competition. While an accurate assessment of costs is important, company pricing policy is unlikely to be based solely on costs. Some of these factors can be built into the model, but most are of a judgemental nature and, therefore, difficult to quantify.

The usefulness of break-even analysis is that it indicates approximate profit or loss at different levels of activity with changing variables — sales volume, variable costs, fixed costs, price, etc. The difference between the level of activity at which the firm is currently operating and the break-even point is known as the margin of safety. The anticipated revenue, profit and margin of safety will all be contributing factors to the pricing policy. The model makes no attempt to take stocks into

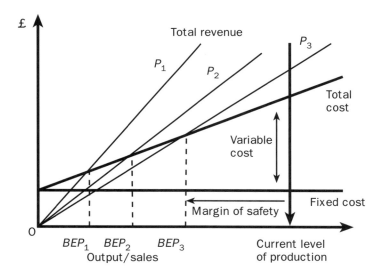

Figure 15 Break-even analysis

account, and the final predicted profit figure may, therefore, be misleading. In addition, as the volume of production and sales increases, it may be possible to achieve economies of scale, as a result of which costs per unit may fall because of administrative, marketing and purchasing economies.

The simple break-even model assumes that the firm can sell its output at any price, and that, of course, is quite unrealistic. Fixed costs (such as rent, depreciation, loan interest and lease charges) may increase as the firm increases its capacity, but these stepped increases can be reflected in the graphical models. It may, however, be difficult to differentiate conveniently between some fixed and variable costs. The break-even model is thus an extremely useful tool in the decision-making arsenal, but its limitations must be recognised.

A useful mnemonic for remembering most of the fixed costs is RIDSINL: 'get rid of sin in hell' — rent, interest charges, depreciation, staff salaries, insurance premiums, national non-domestic rates, leasing charges.

Related questions

1 List and explain the factors that should be taken into account before any company undertakes profit sensitivity analysis and, especially, break-even analysis.

2 'Variance reports attach too much importance to figures and too little importance to reasons.' Discuss.

3 'Costing methods are unnecessarily complicated. It is much easier and more sensible to use the cost-plus approach to pricing.' Discuss the implications of this statement.

4 Which method of costing is most appropriate in decision making? Using an example, show why this is so.

Question 29

What factors may lead to insolvency and liquidation, and how might they be avoided?

This is an opportunity to show that you know something about cash flow, liquidity and control of working capital — it's right at the sharp end, where the day-to-day, operational work is done. But there's an inherent danger: this is not a question on company law, so keep it mainly financial, even if you do occasionally wander off down legal roads. It seems perfectly reasonable, however, to include the consequences of liquidation or insolvency, whether of an individual or of a company. The key point is that businesses usually fail because they have negative or low returns or are unable to pay their liabilities as they become due. It is argued that over 50% of all failures happen because of mismanagement. However, it is seldom remembered that businesses, like products, have a finite life. Some may seem to go on for ever, but if the business does not change fast enough, react promptly to market forces or, better still, anticipate market changes, it may become obsolete.

Answer

The collapse of a firm because of insolvency is seldom sudden. It is usually the result of a number of weaknesses in the company, which together eventually add up to failure.

A temporary lack of cash may not necessarily herald the end of a company's operations; nor may the appointment of a receiver or liquidator. Insolvency refers to the condition in which the company is not able to pay its bills as they fall due. The company may be able to defer payment of bills for quite a long time, but if the creditors insist that their bills are paid and the firm cannot pay, or if the company is in default on mortgage or loan repayments, then the company is considered to be insolvent. This could be the case without any action resulting, but a creditor may take action through the courts to have the company put into liquidation (or wound up) so that the due can be paid.

An excess of liabilities over assets does not necessarily amount to insolvency because it may be possible to find the money to pay each liability as it falls due. Conversely, people whose assets exceed their liabilities might be insolvent because the great part of their assets, say a house or land, cannot immediately be turned into cash, so that they cannot meet their debts. They are thus deemed to be insolvent because an insufficient proportion of their assets is liquid.

The liquidation procedure is the process of selling company assets to raise liquid cash with which to pay the creditors. A liquidator, who is independent of the company, is appointed to supervise the process, which continues until all creditors are paid, or all the assets are exhausted, whichever is the sooner.

The causes of insolvency may be described as controllable and uncontrollable. Examples of uncontrollable causes are illness, injury, the loss of key executives, an abrupt alteration in the law and some other misfortunes that can be insured against. Causes that might be deemed controllable range from inadequate capital and mismanagement (e.g. inadequate costing, poor supervision) to recklessness, fraud or simply extravagant living.

Many people talk of companies being made bankrupt; this simply cannot happen. Companies are not made bankrupt, for the state of bankruptcy applies to individuals. However, directors of a firm who have given personal guarantees may find themselves declared bankrupt as a result of their company's liquidation.

Bankruptcy proceedings are initiated by a petition to the court. The debtors (i.e. the people who owe the money) can take the initiative and file a petition against themselves, if they feel that they must do something to unload their financial burden, and that bankruptcy is the way to do it. Alternatively, as very often happens, one of the creditors may petition the court. Bankrupts are subject to legal restrictions. They cannot be directors of a company, or manage its affairs (unless the court permits), and they cannot trade without disclosing the name under which they were adjudicated. There is usually a minimum period of three years before the bankruptcy can be discharged and the restrictions can be lifted. Preferential rules give priority to three main types of debtor:

This is useful to know and to include, but not in too much detail.

- debenture holders, who have first charge on a company's assets;
- the government, for rates, taxes, social security contributions, VAT, etc.;
- employees, for outstanding pay (within limits) and holiday pay.

These preferential categories enjoy a high degree of priority. However, some in the UK believe that the priorities given to secured creditors are too high and, as a result, companies are too often liquidated when it would be better — not least for the employees — for them to be kept as going concerns.

Remember to include not only the factors that may cause insolvency, but also the reasons why they happen and, implicitly, how they can be avoided.

The factors that lead to insolvency will include the following, but it is arguable that, in essence, all insolvencies are probably the result of poor management.

Over-trading is a common cause of insolvency. In this situation, the company attempts to expand too fast before sales have been translated into hard cash. This often occurs when a sales campaign generates a higher level of sales, for which suppliers have to be paid and overheads, wages and other costs have to be met. The inward cash flow is inadequate to service outward cash flow requirements and a shortage of funds results. Management may consider sales expansion and increased market share important, but may fail to consider the associated costs of such expansion: in effect, managers ignore profit in search of turnover, and ignore cash in search of profit. Simply to expand trade on the same terms will require proportionally more working capital; increased sales will lead to an increased number of debtors and increased holding of stock such as raw materials.

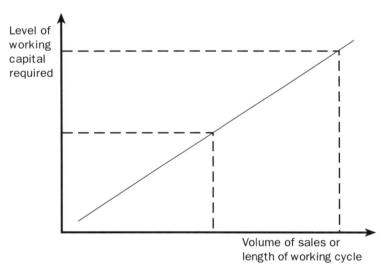

Figure 16 Relationship between sales volume and working capital (net current assets)

All these factors and variables affect the firm's cash flow and, therefore, its liquidity and potential solvency — or insolvency. You have to know about them. They are key concepts.

High gearing, in which the company's funding is provided from a high proportion of fixed-interest-bearing capital rather than equity capital, may be particularly important in times of economic depression, and when domestic monetary growth is being restricted through the mechanisms of high interest rates, so that the cost of capital becomes prohibitive. In such a situation, high gearing presents a particular risk. The proportional effect on net profits is significantly greater with high gearing.

Terms of loans should be matched with the flow of profits. The pattern of the payment periods may conceal danger signs in the same way as the amount of borrowing can. It is important that an attempt is made to predict the type of cash flow requirements that are likely. A loan for repayment in, say, five years may not pose an immediate problem, but repayments of shorter-term borrowings may cause acute financial difficulties.

In the search for expansion it is common to see the eroding effects of over-competitive quoting upon a business. Although increased activity is apparent, so too is the need for increased working capital; simultaneously, however, there are much lower profits available to meet the cash flow requirements.

Companies' attitudes are as important as their actions, and inaction can be as damaging as wrong action. The business that shuns change and resists technological advances may not collapse as quickly as a firm that has all the latest equipment, but it will inevitably drift down the market, with significantly reduced chances of survival in a competitive environment.

Accounting procedures, in particular, must be up-to-date and relevant. This will require the compilation of cash flow statements and sales forecasts. Budgets should be projected in an attempt to predict the likely consequences of current policies and practices, and must be scrutinised very carefully to give an early indication of over-trading and liquidity ratios. Ratio analysis should not be regarded in absolute terms, but be used only for trend analysis and for intra- and inter-company comparisons.

Related questions

1   'Profit is not necessarily cash; and cash is not necessarily profit.' Explain why this is, or is not, true.

2   Discuss the measures that a firm's accountant might introduce in order to improve liquidity and to alert management when a cash flow crisis is looming.

3   Why is the control of working capital of such fundamental importance to a business? Explain why the level of working capital must rise in line with the level of sales volume.

4   Consider, with the aid of diagrams, why working capital must increase with an increase in the volume of sales or with an extension of the working cycle. How can the working cycle be reduced?

Question 30

Comprehensive financial control is a requirement of any business. What do you understand by the concept of financial control with particular regard to working capital? Suggest what part budgets play in this process.

Tackling the question

No matter how brilliant the marketing department is, or the production department or indeed any other department, if someone — especially the manager — does not keep an eye on the finances, a company can soon be in trouble. Explain why and how financial and cost control are not just the responsibility of the firm's accountant. Explain budget holding, cash flow and investment decisions. You should also consider the fundamental role of any manager in any department which is to plan, control and co-ordinate. The finance manager might co-ordinate, but all managers will need to control expenditure and the creditors they create. The key point, however, is the control of working capital — so also consider the components of working capital.

Answer

The essence of financial control is the making of frequent comparisons, not only against previous achievements of the company, and not only against industrial norms and competitors' standards, but against rational, declared and attainable objectives. Four major areas must be considered:

- raising and spending capital;
- control over revenue, income and expenditure;
- assessment of profits;
- use and/or distribution of profits.

The capital of a business comprises fixed and working capital. Fixed capital is the money (or its equivalent) raised to finance fixed assets, such as plant, fixtures and machinery. Working capital is used to finance the day-to-day activities of the firm, including the purchase of raw materials and the payment of wages and short-term creditors. The amount of fixed capital required will vary from one business to another. The most important criterion is how much extra profit (and then cash) will be generated by employing additional fixed assets. In other words, the measurement of success must be the ratio: profit before tax/fixed capital. To assess the likely effect of further investment in fixed assets, capital investment appraisal techniques may be used.

The usual method of control over capital expenditure is by budgets on an annual or perhaps three-year plan. Each department is asked to forecast its future capital expenditure requirements, from which forecasts a master budget is prepared. The objectives of making this budget are to plan for expenditure and to derive a financial plan of action — which is precisely what a budget is.

The control of working capital is important because it affects the firm's immediate liquidity. Working capital (or net current assets) is calculated by deducting the total current liabilities (creditors, tax due, overdrafts) from the total current assets (stock — in all its many forms, such as raw materials and component parts, work in progress, finished goods — debtors and cash). This is known as the current ratio. However, the inadequacy of this ratio is that it includes stock, which is not usually easily liquidated. A more realistic assessment of a company's liquidity is obtained by using the quick (or acid test) ratio, in which the value of stock is omitted.

The amount of finance required is the amount that funds the working capital cycle, i.e. from stocks of raw material received to cash received from customers, through creditors, sales, debtors, cash and yet more stocks. The shorter the cycle, the less working capital that will be required. The cycle can be reduced by minimising the time for which stocks are held, by reducing the amount of credit that the firm gives, by preferring to sell to cash customers rather than creating debtors, and so on.

A common reason for the failure of small businesses, in particular, is the disproportion between sales turnover and the working capital available. Since it takes time for debtors to pay — but, meanwhile, creditors and wages must be paid — the firm may end up insolvent. The situation is known as overtrading. The relationship between sales growth and the need to finance current assets is very close and direct. The management of current assets and working capital has an immediate urgency, and daily or weekly detailed statements, giving an analysis of cash, debtors, creditors and stock, must be made. These figures should be related to the level of sales turnover achieved. The problem of liquidity may be made worse where the company experiences seasonal or cyclical sales. The level of assets

Think about where the money goes, and where it comes from — current assets such as stock; the large capital assets such as buildings, machinery and vehicles; and even the smaller items, from office chairs to shop shelving, and from computers to envelopes. They all tie up money. There are hundreds of ways for firms, or people in firms, to spend money. So who is controlling what? Any tendency to take things for granted could be dangerous!

Question 30

Financial management, and particularly cost control, is the concern of everyone in the company. The key question is: would you spend it if it was your money, or if it was your company?

The control of working capital is critical. If the volume of sales goes up, so too must the working capital — the net current assets. If the firm is going to make and sell more, it will need more stock, incur more labour charges, use more power — so it needs more working capital. It will also need more working capital if it has a longer working cycle. Think of it this way: a taxi driver's working cycle is very short, but a farmer spends a long time preparing, sowing, tending, harvesting, etc. before he or she gets any revenue; meanwhile, what's happening to the farmer's working capital?

required will fluctuate and there is a danger that some fixed assets, in particular, may be idle. However, in most businesses the level of current assets rarely falls to zero.

Permanent assets should be financed with long-term capital, while temporary assets should be financed with short-term credit. The larger the share of funds obtained from long-term sources, the more conservative the firm's working capital policy should be because, in times of company and/or national financial stress, it may be difficult for the firm to renew its short-term credit.

The analysis and subsequent acquisition of current assets are just as important as the thought and deliberation that must be applied to the investment in fixed assets. Whatever decisions are taken, the ultimate measure must be the effects of current or fixed asset acquisition on future profitability. Increasing the firm's current assets, especially cash, while holding constant the expected production and sales may reduce the risk to the company, but it may also reduce the overall return on assets. While fixed and current assets should reflect the level of expected sales, only current assets can be adjusted to the actual sales in the short run. Hence, adjustments to short-run fluctuations in demand lie almost entirely within management's ability to adjust working capital accordingly. The ratio of current assets to sales is a policy matter among other things. If the company decided to operate aggressively, it would hold the minimum of current assets, but such a policy would increase the possibility of running out of cash or stock, or of losing sales and customer goodwill because of stock-outs or an excessively tough credit policy.

The most important variable that influences a firm's financing requirements is the projected profitability and cash value of future sales. An accurate sales forecast is, therefore, a basic prerequisite for forecasting financial requirements. Firms need assets to make sales. If sales are to be increased, assets must also be expanded. All of this requires a careful and rational budgetary policy. Any departure from the budgeted figures — particularly an increase in the forecast expenditure — must be investigated, and corrective action taken if necessary and possible.

Profits are often forecast in the medium to long term. Short-term losses on some products may occur and may even be built into a company's marketing and pricing strategy: for example, in penetration pricing where the company may budget for a loss-leader, to capture a market share. But long-run survival requires the business to deal with possible liquidity problems that may arise in the short term. Clearly, a firm must be concerned with both making a profit and maintaining its solvency. Just as reasonable profitability is a necessity for a business (at least in the long term), so too is the holding of a reasonable proportion of liquid funds. Liquid funds consist of cash 'at bank' and cash 'in hand', and cash equivalents (e.g. investments held as current assets), less bank overdrafts and other borrowings repayable within one year of the accounting date.

If liquid funds are allowed to deteriorate, the business may well find its freedom of action seriously curtailed. However, while a firm must have adequate liquid funds, such funds do not necessarily lead to profit. Too many liquid funds will reduce the rate of return on investment, since too large a proportion of total funds will be tied up in non-profit-making items. Too few liquid funds will pose real problems of survival. All businesses are concerned with striking a balance and holding an appropriate amount of liquid funds. A cash flow forecast — assuming the information on which it is based is as accurate as possible — will identify the periods of potential liquidity crisis when short-term finance, such as overdrafts, may be necessary to finance continuing operations and to supplement working capital requirements.

Budgets allow management to delegate authority and responsibility to departmental managers without losing control and co-ordination of the overall expenditure. In this way, financial and management weaknesses can be revealed very quickly. Zero-base budgeting requires all managers of departments to justify their entire budget each year in detail. In practice, this is difficult to implement and some modification may be necessary, such as prioritising and justifying only the bottom 20 or 30% of items in that budget. Budgets must, therefore, be reasonably flexible. Contingency funding must be available centrally, not least because some costs are very difficult, if not impossible, to foresee and control: for example, when the employees' wages are subject to national agreements.

Occasionally, however, budgets may become too restrictive and lead to a reduction in departmental innovation and initiatives. Complying with the budget requirements may become an end in itself, to the exclusion of almost all other objectives.

Note that to achieve closer control, yearly budgets can be broken down into monthly or quarterly budgets for each department and variances noted. The answer could also consider contribution and SWOT analysis, which will enable planners to select the optimum mix of products, probable sales and anticipated revenues. A closer examination of budgets would consider in more detail the need for flexible budgets and zero-based budgeting, an activity that is very time consuming and requires input from heads of departments.

Related questions

1   What do you think are the possible consequences of using budgets as pressure devices for increased efficiency?

2   'Budgets are simply financial plans of action.' How far do you agree with this statement, and what corrective action might be taken if the plans begin to go wrong?

3   Consider how information technology has made the operation of budgetary systems cheaper and more effective.

4   Distinguish between the motivational and managerial reporting aims of budgetary control. How far should employees be involved in the budgetary process?

The valuation of stock is important for balance sheet purposes and for cost determination when setting prices. Identify which methods of stock valuation are currently in use and comment on their usefulness.

Tackling the question

This is a no-nonsense question. Do you know how to value stock or don't you? And what differences do each of the various methods make? Stock valuation is comparatively easy, once a system has been agreed on. The use of computer data files makes it even easier, provided the data have been accurately entered. It would be reasonable to extend the answer provided, or to examine the question from a different angle, by introducing just-in-time stock control, and the advantages (and the potential disadvantages) that such a system might bring in terms of calculating the cost of goods sold. A key point to emphasise is that different stock valuation methods lead to different reported profits. Whatever scheme a firm adopts it should use consistently, year after year.

Answer

Over a time, a company's purchases of stock items — raw materials, component parts, etc. — will be at a variety of prices. A major problem, particularly in times of rising prices, is the valuation of those stocks. Stock valuation is necessary for two reasons:

- It is necessary to determine the true 'cost of goods sold' which, when deducted from the total sales revenue, gives the gross profit. As new stock comes in and more stock is issued, the true cost of the stock may be difficult to determine.
- It is necessary to value the stocks for balance sheet purposes, bearing in mind that the accounts must reflect a 'true and fair' view of the company's financial stock.

We can see the nature of the problem by considering an example.

Guidance notes

It's important that the production department — or the servicing department of, say, a garage — knows the value of the stock it's using. It is then able to complete accurately the manufacturing account or servicing account, from which comes the 'cost of goods sold' — the second line of the trading account or profit and loss account. (What's the top line of the trading account?)

Example:

The Anciente Rutlande Fabrication Company issues 16,000 widgets to the production department during the year. The company purchases widgets as follows:

1997		Units	Unit cost (£)	Valuation (£)
1 Jan	Opening stock	2,000	10	20,000
31 Jan	Purchases	3,000	11	33,000
14 Apr	Purchases	3,000	10.50	31,500
22 Jul	Purchases	5,000	9	45,000
2 Oct	Purchases	7,000	8	56,000
Total		20,000		185,500

It therefore has 4,000 widgets unused. What value should be put on these?

To determine the cost of sales, it is necessary to know the value of the stock as it was issued and the value of the closing stock.

While it should be easy to calculate the exact quantities issued to, say, the production department, it may be more difficult to determine the real cost of those issues because it is often difficult to separate and to identify similar or identical goods received at different times and with varying prices. It may be possible to issue some stock at the specific identification cost: in that case, the true cost is known and can be charged as a direct cost to the production department. Where the specific identification method is not possible, other costing methods are necessary.

There are three main stock valuation methods:

- first in, first out (FIFO);
- last in, first out (LIFO);
- average cost (AVCO).

The first and last methods are common in the UK; the LIFO method tends to be more popular in the USA.

First in, first out

This basis assumes that the first goods purchased are the first sold. Because of the danger of obsolescence, limited shelf-life and deterioration, it makes sense to issue the oldest stock to production first. However, this may be difficult in practice because new purchases arrive, issues are made and similar stock items get mixed up with each other in the warehouse. The simplest method is where the oldest stock is issued to

Here we come to a comparison of the principal methods of stock valuation. Remember to cover their advantages and disadvantages.

production first, and charged at the old price; the next purchase of that stock item is then issued at the revised, new price, and then the next, and so on. While it is a logical method, the use of FIFO may involve many different prices; the arithmetic, although simple, can be a little laborious and tedious. Nonetheless, the method does have advantages, in that the value of the closing stock is closer to the current economic reality, and the method is acceptable for corporate tax calculations.

Last in, first out

In this method, the latest prices are charged to production. The quantity of the issue is calculated and the latest price paid for the last delivery of that stock item is determined. The stock items issued are then charged out at that price. It assumes that the replacement cost should be charged. The use of the LIFO method can affect the stock valuation of current assets on the balance sheet and in the gross profit figure. Particularly in times of inflation, the gross profit figure will be lower using this method than when using the FIFO method. If prices are falling then the reverse will be true. However, in the UK, the LIFO method of stock valuation is not acceptable for tax purposes, although the actual production costs will be closer to current economic prices. Under LIFO the alleged value of the closing stock may bear little relation to current prices of stock items. Moreover, the LIFO method, while having some degree of logic, is arithmetically tedious.

If these two methods — FIFO and LIFO — are applied to the hundreds of stock items held by a retailer or a manufacturer, it becomes obvious that there will be a significant impact on the gross profit figures and, eventually, the distributed and retained profit.

Average cost of stock

It would seem that neither FIFO or LIFO is entirely satisfactory. A compromise solution is the average cost basis. There are two methods:

- the periodic weighted average cost;
- the continuous weighted average cost.

The cost of goods sold and the year-end stock-level cost are calculated at the average cost of that stock item throughout the accounting period — one month, or one quarter, or even one year. This cost is called the periodic weighted average cost. This method does mean, however, that the cost to the department that receives the stocks, say the production department, cannot be calculated until the end of the time period. The continuous weighted average cost, on the other hand, allows for a new average price to be calculated each time a shipment of stock is received, and so the price charged to other departments can be frequently updated.

Ideally, stock should be costed at the 'specific identification' level, i.e. what the item cost the firm. Often, however, it will not be possible to do this. The accounting rule is that, for balance sheet purposes, stock should be shown either at cost or at the net realisable value (NRV), whichever is the lower. NRV is whatever the firm can get from a buyer for that item of stock.

Related questions

1   Consider the importance of stock valuation in helping to determine the market price of a product, particularly in times of rising inflation.

2   A large manufacturing company may have difficulty valuing its work in progress. Suggest how this might be accurately done by using computer technology and information systems.

3   What difference will the method of stock valuation have on the profit and loss account?

4   What is meant by opening stock and closing stock? Explain the difference between LIFO and FIFO methods of stock valuation.

In recent years there has been a significant increase in the number of acquisitions and mergers. Discuss the nature and advantages of such action and consider how goodwill might affect the venture.

Tackling the question

Just lately, there has been an astonishing number of mergers and acquisitions (you should explain the difference between the two and the consequences) and you should speculate on why that should be — competitive strategies, economies of scale, concentration on what the real business of the company is and divesting itself of peripheral activities — there are many more. So this question is asking why mergers take place and what's in it for whom. But the second part — from both a marketing and financial view — is very important for how an intangible asset such as goodwill is to be judged and costed. You should give some explanation, discussing why it is difficult to price but how it might be done... and how it might affect the balance sheet.

Answer

Guidance notes

It is widely accepted that, in some industries, it is now necessary for optimum operations to reach a minimum critical size. Existing firms may find that, by combining with similar companies, external expansion becomes a more viable proposition and easier to achieve than attempting to grow from within. Not only can merging firms increase their production capacity, but also their share price may increase and, with it, the shareholders' and the stock market's confidence. However, the economic climate and financial markets have to be sympathetic to such activity. Many of the takeovers in the early 1980s were financed by companies issuing shares, particularly rights issues, to fund their bid ambitions. But institutional investors became increasingly reluctant to take up these new share issues. In consequence, acquisitions were possible only if the predator companies were cash rich.

Acquisitions are invariably costly and, in buying a 'package', the acquiring company is not usually able to be selective about the parts of a firm that it wishes to purchase. There is therefore an obligation to manage all that comes with the package. Of course, the company may later divest itself of the unwanted parts: indeed, it may sell some of the acquired fixed assets to improve liquidity.

This answer contains some key 'buzz' words: convergent, divergent, merger, acquisition, takeover, integration, consolidation. They do mean different things and you should be aware of these different meanings.

Convergent acquisitions occur when a company acquires a direct competitor. Divergent acquisitions occur when companies acquire unrelated firms to broaden their profit base. To effect a purchase or amalgamation, the parties must first establish the value of the undertaking's shares. To value the quoted shares, the current Stock Exchange price may be taken as a useful guide. The market capitalisation of a company is given as the current value of the shares multiplied by the number of shares in circulation.

In a takeover bid, the predator company must persuade sufficient shareholders of the target company to relinquish their ownership, which may require a premium to be paid. On average, the value of that premium is about 25% of the pre-bid price of the share. If the bid is contested, the premium tends to rise still further.

A consolidation occurs when both companies — the acquiring one and the acquired one — lose their identity altogether and take on a new and separate identity: Martin Ltd combines with Smith Ltd and becomes known as Brown Ltd. That is consolidation. A new corporation is formed.

The cost of a mutually acceptable merger may be much less than that of a fiercely contested takeover — it's not necessary to pay a premium to shareholders in the target company, in order to persuade them to part with their shares.

A merger is quite similar to a consolidation except that, when two or more firms are merged, the resulting firm maintains the identity of one of the merger firms; usually, the identity of the larger firm in the merger is retained. Sometimes both names are retained, e.g. Cadbury Schweppes.

Many takeover bids are energetically resisted by the target company and negotiations can become exceedingly acrimonious. During the 1980s about one-quarter of takeover bids were contested and, of such bids, only about one-half were eventually successful.

The main reasons for mergers, acquisitions and takeovers are:

- to achieve greater market control and influence over a larger territory;
- to obtain better and improved access to supplies (backward integration) or to the markets (e.g. retailers — forward integration);
- to achieve economies of scale and to produce a synergistic reaction;

- to achieve access to better technology;
- to achieve access to better people/employees/management;
- to achieve access to better assets, such as land, buildings and prime sites;
- to achieve access to cash and improved liquidity;
- to eliminate competitors;
- to fend off potential threats from a third party, i.e. for mutual defence (e.g. through lateral integration);
- as a hedge against declining markets.

However, there are risks in divergent diversification. Invariably, integration results in excess personnel and management, and there may be costly redundancies. In addition, the acquiring company may not have the management and financial skills necessary to manage the newly acquired company in an unrelated business.

Horizontal growth (or integration) occurs when firms in the same line of business are combined. The resultant firm may then achieve economies of scale through bulk purchasing, redundancy/redeployment of some managers, administrative economies, and rationalised transport and distribution networks.

Remember that economies of scale = greater productivity = lower average unit costs. But remember also that there are economies of scale other than bulk purchasing (which everyone quotes). What economies of scale can be obtained in marketing, production and even finance? Think about it.

Vertical growth, backwards or forwards, occurs when a firm grows by acquiring suppliers of its raw materials or purchasers of its finished products, so that it can exert greater control of supplies or retailing. A firm that is totally integrated is one that controls the entire process from the raw material stage to the sale to the final consumer. The value of the business may be one thing to the seller, but another to the person proposing to buy. Ultimately, the value of a business is the price negotiated between a willing buyer and a willing seller. Price is a fact; value is a judgement. It is comparatively easy to value the stock, in all its many forms, and the fixed assets; it is not so easy to value goodwill.

One of the fastest ways for a company to grow — assuming it can afford the expense — is to acquire and/or merge. This paragraph gives an opportunity to introduce and discuss integration and the various forms of integration — forward, backward, vertical, lateral...

Goodwill (in accounting) is a term that describes a slightly vague and nebulous concept. It has been described as the acquisition of a benefit that will arise in the future. It is the projection into the future of something built up in the past, but the past is used only as a basis on which to assess the future benefit. In other words, it is that part of the value of a business attributable to its reputation and standing in the market place, and above the book value of its assets. As a going concern, a business is usually worth more than simply the value of its net tangible assets. The owners will have taken great care and will have spent time and money in establishing a good reputation, making connections, developing trading relationships, training employees and management, and developing a bank of technical knowledge and information. To develop good corporate and public relations takes time, commitment and money. When such relations are positive and productive, more effective business can be undertaken. The sums of all these non-cash assets add up to the goodwill of a company. In a sense, goodwill is the lubricant that oils the relationship between the corporate machinery and its external environment.

The problem in evaluating goodwill (and a portfolio of brands) is in the determination of its financial worth. There is no precise mathematical way of measuring goodwill. However, some of the rule-of-thumb methods appear just as reasonable as any other. Here are two such methods:

- *The purchase of profits*. This method does not find much favour because, if profit is very small in relation to the value of the assets employed, it is doubtful if any goodwill exists at all. So, although this method would give a value, it would give little indication of potential, and the fact that profits were made in the past is no guarantee that such profits will continue.

- *The difference between an earnings-based valuation and an asset-based evaluation*. All sorts of peculiar figures can arise from this method, but it does seem rational that any exercise in valuing a business takes account of the assets that the business owns, and its past, current and future earnings. It is usual to look at earnings after tax because some businesses may have distinct tax advantages over others. Any assets should be valued realistically. Past profit figures must be adjusted if necessary, to serve as an indication of future trends. To this end, an estimate of future profits will have to be made and the realism of this figure must then be checked against the technical and commercial background of the industry concerned. However, the value of a business is what someone is willing to pay for it at a particular time. Any potential seller — willing or unwilling — of a business should be more than a little interested to know why someone would wish to buy the company.

Related questions

1 The management of ABC Ltd is considering a merger with a company in a different field of activity. What information would you wish to have before proceeding with this venture? Given that most of the employees have been with ABC Ltd for many years, how should you break the news to them if the merger goes ahead?

2 What are the dangers to a firm acquiring companies outside its area of competence?

3 What are the alternatives for growth when a company relies solely on existing products or services?

4 What is the difference between a joint venture and a merger? What advantages might there be in a demerger?

Macroeconomic and Other Environmental Factors

What is meant by fiscal policy? How does the manipulation of taxation and government spending affect the level of economic activity? Illustrate the effects this might have on the business sector.

Tackling the question

The big danger here is that you end up writing an economics answer and not a business studies one, so be careful. You will need to use and show some theory but be selective and indicate how such theory or economic models can aid business management both at the shop-floor level, which is all about sales and cash flow, and in its decision making. Similarly, government policies may affect both demand and business costs and you should show how and why. To a large extent, of course, it depends on what business the business is in. Some companies will feel the effects of economic measures more than others — say which, and why. A final thread is that the government remains the biggest employer and the biggest spender. Its actions can have tremendous knock-on effects. Why?

Answer

There are several weapons in the arsenal of economic measures that a government can take to regulate and influence the wider, macroeconomic environment.

Taxation, government spending and government borrowing are referred to as fiscal measures. By means of these measures, the government can influence the level of aggregate demand and, to a lesser extent, aggregate supply. At a time when there is unused production potential and under-utilised resources, the government may seek to stimulate demand and thus increase the level of economic activity. Conversely, when the economy is suffering from inflationary pressures and is overheating, the government may act to reduce the level of aggregate demand.

In fiscal policy, the government can seek to influence the level of demand by operating on the level of taxation or expenditure or, of course, both. However, fiscal policy is concerned not only with the overall amounts of government income and expenditure, but also with their structure and timing. The government is both a spender and a lender of money in its own

Guidance notes

Any macroeconomic question must be brought down to the operational, shop-floor level of the firm. The important point here is the effect of fiscal policy on a business. Not all economic measures affect all companies in the same way; nor, indeed, do they affect all consumers in the same way.

account. It can finance these activities in several ways: by printing money, by taxation and by borrowing and charging for its trading activities, e.g. the interest it receives for the loans it makes. The government can alter the timing of its expenditure programmes and, in general terms, it can control consumer expenditure by increasing or reducing personal disposable incomes, achieved through raising or lowering taxes and introducing changes in allowances and social security benefits.

Taxes can be divided into two broad groups: direct taxes, such as income tax and corporation tax; and indirect taxes, such as value added tax and excise duties. However, there are other compulsory deductions from earnings, such as national insurance contributions, that are not called 'taxes'. Businesses must pay the national non-domestic rate (the NNDR), and householders must pay the council tax on dwellings. In recent years there has been a much greater emphasis on, and increase in, indirect taxes. There are two basic reasons for this change of emphasis:

- Excessively high, direct tax rates cause people to exploit every possible loop-hole in the law to avoid tax. Avoiding tax payment through legitimate allowances is legal; evasion of tax payment is not.
- Lower direct tax rates, it is argued, increase the incentive to work harder. Marginal income is subject to a smaller tax deduction than before. Hence it is argued that people will work harder to earn the extra income.

Changes in corporation tax (and NNDR) will influence the levels of corporate investment, the retention of profit and the size of shareholders' dividends. In recent years there has been a marked reduction of corporation tax in an attempt to stimulate investment and research, to engender business confidence and to reinvigorate commerce and industry.

The government finances a large part of its repayments by additional borrowing. Government expenditure plans cannot be stopped overnight. Any increase in investment or government expenditure will (by the multiplier and subsequently through the accelerator) increase the level of economic activity.

Similarly, a cutback in government investment programmes will have the effect of reducing the pressure of aggregate demand by reducing the level of economic activity. If aggregate demand falls, firms may be left with spare capacity, particularly personnel, and unemployment may follow. Increasing unemployment further depresses aggregate demand, causing government expenditure to rise because it must now fund unemployment and other benefits. Further, there is a loss of indirect taxes, such as VAT, as the unemployed reduce expenditure, and a loss of income tax as the unemployed are no longer earning. In effect, a vicious circle is established. The government is the biggest spender. A small and unexpected cut in that spending may have massive repercussions throughout the business community. Many would argue, therefore, that an overriding emphasis on fiscal policy to regulate the level of economic activity is crude. It leaves many businesses bewildered as corporate planning and sales forecasting become more problematical.

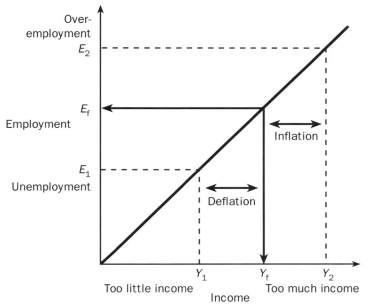

To shift Y_1 to Y_f increase government expenditure and/or decrease taxation
To shift Y_2 to Y_f decrease government expenditure and/or increase taxation

Figure 17 Fiscal measures

Fiscal policy changes are usually effected in the annual budget. Budgetary policy aims at reducing expenditure when the forecast for aggregate demand in the months ahead looks like exceeding the capacity of the economy to produce it; or, conversely, to stimulate aggregate demand when it is felt that it will be deficient. If demand is expected to grow too slowly, the government can take action to stimulate the economy by measures designed to cause an increase in the disposable incomes and spending capacity of consumers. If the growth of demand is expected to be excessive, it will be necessary to apply restraint in a variety of ways to mop up the excess. Further, if the Chancellor, through the budget, seeks to regulate aggregate demand, this will clearly affect the balance of trade and payments. Action aimed at reducing demand (and hence inflationary pressures) will involve cutting consumers' expenditure and this will probably lead to a fall in the demand for imports;

Here's the kernel of what fiscal measures are all about. Of course, it's much more complex than this, and professors of economics may shudder at this simplicity — but it tells the examiners what they need to know!

at the same time, consumers will have less disposable income as a result of higher taxes and this will release home-produced goods for the export market.

The following paragraphs explain, fairly simply, how the government implements its fiscal policies.

However, difficulties can arise during the time for which the Treasury forecast has been prepared, owing to the almost infinite number of variables in the national and international economic systems. If people have more after-tax disposable income, this will affect consumer demand, the activity of many firms — depending on their products and markets — and the level of employment. If business confidence rises, there will be a much greater inclination for companies to invest in fixed assets and capital goods, and new technology. There will be a greater stimulus to research and development. However, critics have argued that the boost to consumer spending can over-stimulate the economy, leading to inflationary pressures, excessive imports, a balance of trade deficit and consequent pressures on domestic interest rates.

In principle, taxation can be a flexible weapon in economic policy because some tax rates, such as excise duty on petrol, can be changed fairly easily. In practice, however, this is not always so. In the case of income tax, for example, changes in rates or allowances are very difficult to implement at short notice, since this means that new code numbers must be calculated for each person and, where PAYE (pay as you earn) schemes are in operation, employers must be notified of individual tax changes.

Expenditure rates can be more easily adjusted and the burden of effecting such changes falls not on the government, but on the distributors — the wholesalers and retailers — and the Customs and Excise departments responsible for collecting VAT and excise duties. Administratively, this is very much easier to achieve. However, unless there is a high degree of income and/or price elasticity of demand for a product, a marginal change of this nature may not have a very significant effect on the demand for a product.

Finally, it should be noted that the government is able to finance its activities in a variety of ways. Apart from using its revenue from taxation and direct charges for services and various trading activities, it is able to finance some of its activities by borrowing. This is known as the Public Sector Borrowing Requirement (PSBR).

Related questions

1   It is suggested that companies should set the return on investment goals higher than the current cost of capital. Discuss the implications of doing so in inflationary periods, and suggest what the limitations of this policy are.

2   It has been suggested that reducing direct taxation will stimulate the economy and bring greater prosperity than keeping interest rates artificially low. Consider this statement and discuss the implications of such a policy.

3   'Fiscal policy measures to control and regulate the economy are slow, crude and cumbersome, whereas monetary measures are quick and incisive.' Discuss.

4   What evidence do you think there might be that supply-side economics stresses the importance of a free market economy?

The manner in which businesses develop is determined by the complex interaction of a variety of forces, both internal and external to the firm. Identify some of these forces and examine the ways in which they might influence the activities of a business.

Tackling the question

Many managers spend a great deal of their time reconciling the activities of their company with the many demands that come from the broader environment in which the firm operates. There are many areas, therefore, around which this answer could be structured. Some writers talk of a 'general' environment that affects all or most businesses — such as the culture — and a 'task' environment that embraces the forces relevant to an individual business and its specific operations, such as specialist technology, regulations and customers. You could structure your answer around each of these headings. There is an enormous variety of businesses; it follows that there must be equally varied environments.

Answer

In determining its corporate objectives and associated plans, the firm's decision making is a function of both the quality and quantity of information that it receives, evaluates and subsequently analyses. No firm can operate successfully in a vacuum and it must solicit information from two primary sources: internal (i.e. organisational) data and external (i.e. environmental) data. Any business is an integral part of the society in which it operates. Its growth, development and survival are influenced by trends in society and by the effects of such trends on its products and on its personnel. The state of the market, therefore, is of prime importance in terms of the competition, the technological advances in manufacture, the product itself, the anticipated lifetime of the product and how quickly the product will become obsolete.

The market is influenced by the overall health of the economy and government measures to control and regulate that economy towards achieving desired political, as well as economic, results. The government sets the climate for entre-preneurial activity and the nature of the competition (whether domestic or foreign). How efficient and effective that competition is will depend, to a large extent, on both political and economic factors. For example, efforts to stimulate domestic consumption and restrict the flow of imports are governed not only by political treaties such as those effected within the European Union, but by many other factors including the strength of sterling and the price attractiveness of imported goods. Similarly, domestic manufacturers will be reluctant to satisfy a fickle home market if they are able to export much of their output at competitive prices. UK government, the EU and international organisations such as the United Nations circumscribe the economic and social environments in which the firm is able to operate both at home and abroad.

Society increasingly places demands on companies in a number of ways, including:

- the minimisation of atmospheric and noise pollution — it is calculated that in a typical UK chemical plant, 20% or more of the overall investments aim at protecting the environment in terms of plant safety and reducing toxic emissions;
- attempts to enforce control and improvement of the environment through the production of 'green' products, ranging from organically grown fruit and vegetables to low-energy consumption, reusable packaging and the recycling of paper and glass;
- transport controls (e.g. lead emission, speed restrictions, axle numbers, the use of tachographs);
- consumer protection against faulty or dangerous goods;
- prevention of misleading or tasteless advertising, with the Advertising Standards Authority acting as watchdog.

In addition, a plethora of legal constraints and obligations are imposed on businesses. These include:

- Inland Revenue and Customs and Excise requirements;
- statutory national insurance contributions;
- mandatory pension schemes for employees;
- local rates and planning controls by local authorities;
- the Health and Safety at Work Act and other factory premises Acts.

The business person's problems are complicated further by the extent and complexity of industrial law, designed in most cases to protect individual employees from unfair treatment and

It's only fair to comment, however, that the largest multinationals — particularly in developing countries — can often influence governments that are reliant on the income generated by the multinational. So it's not just the case that businesses are affected by forces; sometimes, businesses are the very forces that cause change.

unfair dismissal, such as the Equal Pay Act, a number of Employment Acts, the Redundancy Payment Act, and many others. Much of what a firm can or cannot do, therefore, is prescribed and frequently proscribed. However, there are other obligations to which businesses are expected to subscribe. In a private sector firm, management has an obligation to add value, achieve a profit and distribute part of that profit to the firm's shareholders; it may also be considered to have an obligation to its employees. But employees and shareholders are not homogeneous. They may well have diverging objectives. The perceived level of the firm's accountability will differ from group to group, and will be largely a function of each group's objectives. These may clash with those of the firm and lead ultimately to disaffection and conflict.

An important external and internal force is that of the trade unions. The nature and style of the industrial relations inherent within a firm are a significant influence on a company's decision making. The history of such relations, the work patterns that have emerged and the styles of management will all contribute to the effectiveness of implemented plans. Increasingly, firms are adopting a participative/consultative style of management and there is much empirical evidence to suggest that such a style of management is, in the long run, beneficial to both firm and employees.

We can well understand, perhaps, why some business people and managers, faced with so many pressures, get impatient and irritated. There are so many external (and internal) factors which need to be taken into account. In particular, the media require very careful handling, which is why many organisations, especially the larger ones, employ public relations specialists. But companies do have a moral, social and ethical responsibility for the environment, just as much as you and I do. Some take such duties more seriously than others, not least because of the cost implications.

There are other pressure groups concerned to protect the environment, such as Greenpeace and Friends of the Earth, which may lobby Members of Parliament and the media in an attempt to dissuade a firm from a particular course of action. Protecting the environment and making a satisfactory profit at the same time may cause a dilemma for the company. There are, however, many activities that serve both purposes, such as saving energy, conserving water, finding cheaper alternatives to scarce raw materials such as mahogany, and using an efficient transport fleet.

Environmental scanning is a relatively new concept that enables the firm to deal with environmental change and take advantage of early opportunities. In addition, such scanning sensitises the firm to the changing needs of customers and the changing priorities of society, and provides a base of information for strategic planning and direction. The environment of a firm has been described as consisting of those factors that are outside the firm's control, but which determine, in part, how the firm performs.

The media exert some of the most significant influences on society's tastes and fashions and on its attitudes and opinions. In addition, many other factors influence and stimulate consumption of a particular product, such as seasonal factors, attempts to 'keep up with the 'Joneses', the age and socio-economic group of the potential buyer, the speed of supply, the perceived quality of the product, the reputation of the firm and, not least, the perceived satisfaction which the potential customers think they will get from that product.

The major areas of environmental influence are as follows:

- *Sociological*: class structure and mobility; cultural factors including values, beliefs and ideology; educational factors including levels of knowledge and abilities; changing patterns of population.
- *Legislative*: specific laws affecting businesses, the nature of the legal system, and the jurisdiction of the many government agencies.
- *Economic*: the general economic framework in which the firm operates both at home and overseas, fiscal and monetary policies, and the capital and finance markets.
- *Political*: the political climate of the country, the shifting sands of power and influence, the nature of political organisations and pressure groups.
- *Technological*: the technology of manufacturing and the commitment to research and development.

The response to these forces will be unique to the firm because the circumstances are different for each enterprise. However, there will be areas of commonality and concern among companies, such as:

- the availability of finance for research and development of new products;
- the development of new environmentally friendly products;
- the expansion of markets and the development of new markets;
- investment in new, fixed assets to accommodate customers' changing demands and expectations.

Patterns of trading, particularly in retailing, continue to change dramatically. Technology, for example, continues to revolutionise business operations. Tele-shopping, now in its infancy, and the growth of the Internet have the potential to alter markedly the way that the distribution and retailing industries operate, with enormous implications for employment patterns and capital investment.

Related questions

1 'There really is too much government interference as well as intervention. Business interests would be better served if the government just let us get on with it,' said the managing director of one company. Consider this statement from the point of view of (a) an employee, and (b) a customer.

2 Discuss the ways that government policies might affect and influence corporate decision making.

3 'Running and organising a commercial enterprise is far too important to be left to the politicians. We should each stick to what we know best.' Do you agree with this statement? Consider the implications for consumers if it is accepted or rejected.

4 Consider how national and Economic Union legislation has affected UK industries in the past. Is UK industry too heavily policed and regulated?

Question 35

'Theory and practice are quite different: the best education comes from experience.' Are economic models or theories of psychology of any use to a practising business person or manager?

Tackling the question

This is quite a challenging question. In a sense, it requires you to justify why you should study something as vague or, if you like, as comprehensive as business management. Clearly, therefore, your justification must include something about optimising decision making and that cannot be done without gathering data, turning such data into information and then interpreting it. But how is this to be done? Discuss the use and limitations of models — just as a physical scientist might use hypotheses and models in the laboratory. Show also how experience and theory can work in partnership; how they complement each other, and how one can build on the other. It would be useful to select relevant theories and show how, over a period of time, they have laid the foundation stone for both experience and practice.

Answer

The question is a valid and pragmatic one. Business management involves many of the social sciences, such as economics, psychology, marketing and politics. All seek to analyse, predict and understand human behaviour, particularly as it relates to the allocation of scarce resources, the distribution of power and influence, and consumer behaviour. In attempting this analysis, a number of approaches are valid. Economists, for example, try to explain the workings of an economic system and the observed behaviour of those within that system. The possible explanations of that behaviour, however, are many and varied, so they must try to determine the reasons for and estimate the strengths of the influences acting upon and shaping that behaviour.

The universe that economists and other social scientists study is very volatile and never stationary; it is highly dynamic. There is, therefore, only a limited stock of accepted principles or explanations. So social scientists must theorise; they must build models; they must advance hypotheses. Well-tested theories are few and often highly qualified. Much of modern

Guidance notes

It's a valid question because there are many people in business who trumpet the importance of experience relative to learned theory. But you wouldn't expect brain surgeons to start performing without a certain amount of study and theory behind them. Experience, in most jobs, takes a long time to obtain: theory and study can shorten that time period.

economic theory, for example, lies within the area of speculation and controversy. Consequently, there is often significant disagreement between professionals in expounding many elements of the subject.

Economists advance hypotheses, or sets of propositions, which may be capable of explaining the facts. Like other people, they attempt to understand the world as it really is (i.e. appearance versus reality) and, in doing so, they begin with certain assumptions, e.g. about human behaviour. They then go on to derive a logical conclusion. The conclusion is therefore implied by the assumptions. A model may be absolutely perfect and sound; it may be irrefutable, in that its logic cannot be challenged; but if the assumptions on which that model is based are inadequate or unrealistic, then the model will be of little practical use.

The appearance of an economic system may be logical but irrational, where rationality is based on reasonableness and reason, in turn, is the product of attitudes, beliefs and values. Little if any human behaviour is logical, for 'logic' implies mathematical precision and predictability. Truth about an economic system cannot be determined without reference to observation. So, to some extent, economic theories, or any theories in the social sciences, attempt to restore order to the study of economic systems and economic phenomena.

Economists help societies and companies to determine the most efficient use of resources and the probable consequences of various projected uses of them. They cannot tell what will happen. However, they can indicate the various possibilities, with their associated risks and implications. It is then up to the manager, or business person, to make the rational choice of ends. In other words, the economist's job ends where choice begins. The job of an economist, or any social scientist, is to analyse not to prescribe, for choosing a particular course of action may be deemed inappropriate and inadvisable in economic terms, but highly desirable politically or socially. However, few social problems are of a purely economic nature; many contain legal, ethical and moral aspects, and it is not within the economists' expertise to advise on these aspects, although, like others, they will no doubt have opinions.

One reason that disagreements tend to persist among social scientists is the difficulty of conducting controlled experiments using people as guinea pigs. So, predictions deduced from economic theories are subject to the 'all other things equal' clause — *ceteris paribus*. But economists and social scientists cannot exclude other kinds of interference, such as technological change, unexpected international events or political turbulence.

This, of course, is the key point. Most economists, or social scientists, would refrain in public from prescribing a cure even if they had private opinions: well, they would if they wished to retain their credibility. In the social sciences, which, by definition, deal with societies — people, consumers, husbands, wives, mothers, bank managers and nurses — few of us can be certain what anyone will do in a given situation or what a society will do. Politicians appear on television to reassure us that inflation is under control: it might be, or it might not be. But if we think they're hiding something, we are likely to go out and start buying before prices really do start rising. The net result? Inflationary pressures. A national fear of inflation may become, in the end, a self-fulfilling prophecy.

Besides theories, one of the dominant characteristics of the scientific approach to social studies is the construction and uses of mathematical representations, in the same way that a manager might use operational research techniques to narrow down the range of choices. The use of economic models to analyse and study problems is an adaptation of the scientific methods used by the physical sciences, such as chemistry. The primary requirement of such model building is the identification of the real problem, otherwise any theory that might emerge, and any prediction that might be made, will be invalid.

Economic problems, whether at corporate or national level, usually come to light because signs and symptoms manifest themselves. No single model can hope to reflect a mirror image of reality, for a model is simply a static representation of a dynamic situation. With this caveat in mind, social science theories do, nonetheless, assist in explaining and predicting social and economic behaviour, particularly where such theories are positive (i.e. a statement of what is or will be) and testable (i.e. based on empirical evidence). A theory is, in essence, an abstraction from reality. A theory that is testable, positive and repeatable, *ad infinitum*, becomes a law of that particular science, e.g. the law of diminishing marginal utility.

Both laws and theories are not only relevant but essential to the study and understanding of the complex web spun by the business community. However, the more a theory is investigated, the more it gets tested and expanded. In essence, therefore, the test of validity for an economic theory is not whether it realistically describes the situation, but whether it advances the understanding and interpretation of social phenomena that appear to have economic origins. Essentially a social science theory goes through the process of observation, hypothesis, testing, synthesis and, finally, prediction.

The study of business requires a multidisciplinary, integrated approach, ranging from accountancy to psychology and from sociology to operational research. To over-emphasise any one of these disciplines, including economics, at the expense of the others may result in a narrow-minded technical approach, lacking in flexibility. It is this that distinguishes the successful firm from the unsuccessful. The theories offer tools for management analysis and judgement. They do not provide prescriptive ingredients for action. The whole point of social science theory is to increase understanding and subsequently improve practice. No one theory or technique is applicable in all circumstances.

In essence, then, a theory both in the physical and in the social sciences should be regarded as a systematic method for increasing our understanding, rather than as a given solution

In the case of business studies, it's our understanding of human behaviour that we're trying to increase. The problem is that human beings are often unpredictable. They're a funny lot and often behave in unexpected ways. Thank goodness!

to all problems that may arise. The awareness of theories and models will sensitise managers and business people to the multitude of important factors that need to be considered in their efforts to understand the problems associated with the management, development and survival of any business enterprise.

Related questions

1   The application of the theories of social science may be very different from the application of the laws of physical sciences. Explain why that might be so and suggest the limitations of models in business management.

2   Discuss the role and importance of social scientists, such as economists, in advising business or the government.

3   How far should training and development of managers require the formal study of social science theories? Consider what use managers might make of such theories.

Question 36

Tackling the question

In recent years less, perhaps, has been written and said of trade unions than in the past, but they remain a substantial and potent pressure group. Their bargaining influence and activities impinge on many organisations. In any discussion of trade unions it might be appropriate to mention also the role and function of staff associations. Another approach might be to consider independent trade unions and those that are members of the TUC. Industrial legislation is wide and complex and one of the primary sources of help and advice may well be the employee's trade union, especially in cases of redundancy or allegations of unfair dismissal.

Answer

Guidance notes

The classical definition of a trade union is a continuous association of wage earners for the purpose of maintaining or improving the conditions of their working lives. In substance, this definition remains largely correct, albeit that increasing numbers of trade unionists earn salaries rather than wages, particularly since the appearance and growth of the 'white-collar' unions. It is a common complaint that there are still too many trade unions in the UK — unlike, say, Germany — and that many of our industrial relations problems are exacerbated by multi-unionism in factories and other organisations. It is further alleged that the trade union movement is far from united and that inter-union demarcation disputes still frequently arise. While there is probably an element of truth in these charges, the fact is that there is a very high proportion of union membership concentrated in a comparatively small number of trade unions. The main reason for the reduction in the number of independent unions is the amalgamation of unions.

In a sense, it's difficult to consider the role and relevance of the trade unions today if we don't have some appreciation of their origins. So a short historical perspective seems perfectly reasonable to me, if it helps to answer the question and put things into context.

Trade unions arose primarily in the nineteenth century as a response to the poor conditions of the working class. The chief aims of the early trade unions were to improve the wages and working conditions of their members, who, without doubt, had just cause for complaint. The trade union movement had some notable successes and setbacks, such as the repeal of the Combination Acts in 1824 and the first Trades Union Congress in 1868; the unfavourable decision of the Taff Vale dispute and the subsequent Trade Disputes Act of 1906.

As unions were formed, they adopted democratic constitutions that gave their members ultimate control over the union's policy decisions and organisation. The nature of this democracy has led some observers to conclude that the retention of individual freedoms and of collective rights within a pluralist democracy, such as prevail in the UK, are bound up with the problem of trade union internal democracy. The constitution of most unions emphasises the right of their members to debate motions and advance resolutions at local level, which can then be processed to the executive policy-makers, most of whom enjoy security of tenure, unlike the union officials at lower levels who must stand periodically for re-election. Unfortunately, the attendance at union meetings of members at grass-roots level is generally poor, and democracy can hardly occur if a cohesive and determined minority successfully imposes its views on an apathetic majority. Nonetheless, evidence suggests that there is little enthusiasm among ordinary members to become involved in a union's policy making unless there is a nationally contentious issue that may then give rise to opposing factions within a union.

This might be something of a dangerous statement without naming names or giving evidence!

To most union members, the union is represented by the elected member of the workforce, the shop steward. In large organisations, the shop steward can be a very influential figure. Some union practices, such as the establishment of closed shops, have certainly caused conflict. Yet the unions argue, with some justification, that workers must be united at a workplace and, further, that negotiated improvements are afforded to all, not just the union members. It is the objective of the trade unions to look after the interests of their members, chiefly in the areas of wages, working conditions (including health and safety), job security and redundancy negotiations. The unions attempt to do this through the mechanism of collective bargaining with the employer's representatives. Trade unionists generally regard this collective bargaining as of paramount importance and view suspiciously any attempts to dispense or interfere with its process.

Most observers would agree that employers, with the help of central government, have in the last 20 years reversed the influence that shop stewards and unions once had over their decision making. Discipline and the 'right of the manager to manage' have significantly increased in many factories and organisations, while trade unionists have looked on, relatively impotent. Whether this industrial castration of the trade unions is in the interest of the third of the working population who belong to the trade union movement remains to be seen. What cannot be denied, however, is that there has been a period of comparative industrial peace unprecedented in industrial relations history.

There are several reasons for the waning influence of the trade union movement in the last two decades:

- specific legislation aimed at curbing the power of the unions;
- high unemployment during the 1980s, which weakened the bargaining power of the unions;
- an increased emphasis on monetarist economic policies which, initially, required historically high interest rates and resulted in company closures, redundancies and increasing unemployment;
- the changing nature of jobs in the UK and in many other parts of the world, including faster communications, improved and increasing technology, and the development of 'the global village';
- the political will and intentions of the elected government.

If the influence of the trade unions has waned — and it has — it seems sensible to suggest why that should be so, but we don't need to go into great detail.

There has been a plethora of industrial legislation since 1980, including two consolidation Acts. Most of this legislation has been aimed at improving the protection of workers — the Equal Pay Act, the Race Relations Act, the Redundancy Payments Act, the Health and Safety at Work Act, etc. However, some of the statutes have also attempted to curb the influence — some would say 'power' — of the trade unions. The Employment Act of 1980 removed the immunity of trade unions for secondary action and secondary picketing, and enabled the government to approve public money for independent trade unions to conduct certain secret ballots. The Employment Act of 1982 further curtailed the operations of the closed shop and required secret ballots to be held regarding proposed closed-shop agreements. In addition, it introduced a prohibition of union membership requirements in commercial contracts.

This summary of the legislation is quite sufficient. We don't need a line-by-line account of what the laws actually say. It's sufficient to know what effect they have.

This is a significant point because many of the 'old', often labour-intensive industries, which relied heavily on craft workers — from boiler makers to shipwrights — have largely disappeared and, with them, the loyalty and membership of the shop-floor trade unionists. The economic base of the country has changed and so, too, has the distribution of wealth. Some of the old trade unionists would turn in their graves if they knew that many of today's trade unionists are part of the 'share-owning democracy'. However, none of that reduces the need for trade unions: in fact, many managers prefer to deal with them.

'Sunset' industries, such as coal mining and shipbuilding, which were traditionally heavily unionised, have declined. 'Sunrise' industries, particularly in micro-processing, chemicals and electronics, have emerged. New technology, computer-controlled machinery and robotics in the workplace have reduced a company's dependency on personnel. Interestingly, studies in the late 1980s found overwhelmingly that managers had more difficulty in getting to grips with new technology than the shop-floor operatives. On the whole, trade unions have not resisted new technology; many managers have.

Some unions, such as the Electrical, Electronic, Telecommunication and Plumbing Union (the EETPU), have largely abandoned their original socialist tendencies in favour of a more pragmatic approach to industrial relations. Their original objectives of protecting workers and improving their lot substantially remain, but their approach is less confrontational. It is ironic that many trade unionists have moved so far away from their origins that over 4 million of them are now part of the share-owning capitalist society that they once despised. Many organisations have developed channels (such as employee surveys) for monitoring employee concerns and providing employees with channels of communication (through, say, work committees), so that their views on the quality of their working life can be made known without fear of reprisal.

The evidence is both impressive and overwhelming that the high-performance workplace is characterised by high employee involvement and performance-related pay. Unfortunately, because of the initial costs of establishing such high-performance systems, many companies and organisations have not adopted or implemented a more enlightened approach to human resource management. Until most or all companies do so, which is unlikely without significant stimuli of some kind, there will continue to be an important role for the trade unions, the trade union movement, and employees' representatives in one form or another.

Related questions

1   Why might an employee claim unfair dismissal even though he is being made redundant? What are the reasons that enable him to do this?

2   Explain how the disclosure of information, under the Employment Protection Act of 1975, can help industrial relations. Describe the extent and limitations of this requirement.

3 What do you think might be the advantages of a fixed-term wage agreement? How might the employees be compensated subsequently?

4 Why might employees be reluctant to use industrial action, and what factors might influence the success of such action?

Describe and discuss the problems experienced by a company manufacturing consumer durables as a result of a high level of unemployment in the economy.

The temptation to answer this as an economics question must be resisted. Of course, unemployment should be discussed, but the analysis must focus on the consequences for the firm. Tactical and operational considerations are the primary areas of concern. The optimisation of plant capacity, the possible 'downtime' of expensive resources, falling revenues, squeezed cash flows, increased bad debts and falling contribution are all issues at the shop-floor level. How can the firm retrench, put up the barricades and take defensive measures to protect itself from the storms of unemployment, falling incomes, reducing profits and increasing competition?

Answer

Before considering issues for the firm at shop-floor level, we need a brief explanation of how unemployment is caused and what the government might be doing to address it.

There are a number of different types of unemployment (structural, frictional, seasonal), but whatever the cause, the primary effect of such unemployment is to reduce both individual and aggregate discretionary spending power. Some consumer goods will have relatively low importance in some households, so demand for a particular product will depend on the nature of that product, the price and income elasticity of demand, the availability of substitute products and the relevance of complementary products. However, the national economy is far from homogeneous, and regional variations in local and aggregate demand will occur, which may affect total demand only indirectly. The impact of unemployment, therefore, will depend on the location of the firm, the political objectives of local government leaders, and other social and infrastructure problems and initiatives. Chronic structural unemployment, such as occurs in north-east England or Northern Ireland, will result in a persistently economically depressed area. Government measures to afford special consideration and development status to these areas may be no more than meaningless cosmetic measures. Entrepreneurs and overseas investors may be unwilling, even with government aid, to invest in new plant and new ventures because of the lack of reward for the perceived high risk and the low marginal efficiency of capital.

As incomes fall, so too will demand. The high level of unemployment will cause a fall in overall aggregate demand. In effect, there will be a shift in the position of the demand curve from D_1 to D_2 in the diagram. As supply is now greater than demand, price disequilibrium follows. To move excess stock and to utilise excess capacity, manufacturers will be forced to reduce prices to P_2. Although the demand curves are parallel to each other, many changes in demand will involve only sections of the curves and may also involve changes in the slope or elasticity at the same time. One of the most obvious causes of a change in demand is variation in consumer tastes. However, while tastes may remain the same during high unemployment, there may be a search for substitute products in an attempt to reduce individual expenditure. The demand for complementary products will also be affected. The major variable, however, will be aggregate consumer purchasing power causing changes in demand. A change in the size and distribution of national income and wealth will take place.

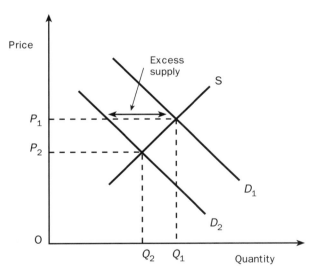

The use of diagrams will make your discussion clearer.

Figure 18 Effect of a fall in aggregate demand on price

If the unemployment is accompanied or precipitated by central government measures to control and regulate the macro economy, the overall problems may deteriorate further. Accompanying measures might include a tight monetary policy, resulting in higher interest rates, as a result of which consumers may be unwilling to buy goods on credit. Attempts to control the Public Sector Borrowing Requirement may reduce the level of the rate support grant and local authorities may be forced

Now we can start to get into the micro details of what is likely to happen in the firm itself. Remember that the question asks about consumer durables — products that are going to last; 'white goods' such as washing machines, dishwashers, hi-fi equipment, tools and cars. Generally, these are the goods that consumers can do without — at least in the short term. In economic terms, there's a relatively high income elasticity of demand for such products.

If the firm takes one particular course of action, it will almost certainly cause another action or reaction within the company; so we need to consider the 'knock-on' effects.

into raising local rates (the 'Council Tax') to maintain the level of service and employment of local government services. These measures will increase the cash flow problems of many firms which, in an attempt to improve their liquidity, will tighten credit control procedures while at the same time attempting to delay payment of their own creditors.

As revenue and profits fall, cost consciousness will prevail and the firm's peripheral activities and philanthropic acts will be severely curtailed. Stocks of finished goods will rise and so will the associated costs of stockholding. The firm will attempt to de-stock by offering favourable discounts and promotional offers. As demand falls, excess plant capacity will occur and the firm may attempt to reduce this capacity, by shedding some fixed assets and realising their liquidity and/or by reducing labour hours. If it does the latter, however, it may then be faced with recruitment and selection costs if trade should subsequently improve and additional labour is then required.

Part-time workers (such as twilight shift-workers) may be laid off; full-time operatives may be put on short time or a reduced working week or a shared working week. Eventually, redundancies may be contemplated. However, redundancy proposals will incur the vexation of the trade unions, which are committed to protecting the livelihood of their members, and protracted and occasionally bitter negotiations may ensue as unions attempt to obtain the best deal for their members. There may be protective strikes and a general lowering of industrial morale. Redundancy payments will weaken further the liquidity position of the firm, and the shedding of labour will further depress the aggregate buying power of the local community; other local traders and retailers will begin to feel the effects as debts mount and demand falls even further.

The business decisions will impinge on the local community, and the future development and prospects of the region may be put at risk. As demand falls, the firm's fixed costs will be spread over fewer goods and the profitability of those goods that are sold will fall even further. In an attempt to recover markets and stimulate demand, the firm may be faced with the prospect of spending greater amounts of cash on efforts to stimulate demand using aggressive marketing techniques and promotional measures. However, it may also investigate diversification possibilities, as well as exploring the potential for new and different markets, both at home and overseas, and the opportunities for amalgamation with other similarly placed companies to ensure their ultimate survival.

Many of the firm's actions will depend on the nature and structure of the firm, the type of equipment it possesses, and the quality and expertise of its management. The problems experienced may ultimately lead to the substitution of labour by capital and more efficient, technologically advanced production methods. However, to overcome the short-term problems associated with sales, revenue and profitability, the firm may be forced to resort to borrowing. If high interest rates prevail, the costs of such borrowing may be the last straw for a firm already financially weakened by the fall in consumer demand and sales turnover. High-growth, entrepreneurial companies with significant capital investment and, possibly, high gearing may be the hardest hit by rising interest rates.

As the company's fixed costs per unit increase, in the face of falling demand, investment will be curtailed, projects will be shelved and there may be a fall in productivity relative to other countries that will further diminish the firm's international competitiveness. Ironically, the government may be encouraging companies to invest in an attempt to reduce unemployment, but a firm will invest only if there is business confidence and a reasonable prospect of a satisfactory return on investment.

This is important because unemployment will affect different companies in different ways. It's not just the obvious reduction in disposable incomes and falling demand; what of the skills market, the availability of labour, the effects on wages in a region, the effects on families, shopkeepers, etc? Perhaps a company can take the opportunity to reduce its personnel and run a tighter, leaner ship. Which wag said: 'There is no such thing as a problem; only an opportunity'?

Related questions

1 As a manufacturer of gardening equipment, would you prefer the government to rely more on monetary policy than fiscal policy to regulate the economy?

2 In what ways might a government stimulate economic activity and reduce unemployment? What effects might such action have on the rate of inflation?

3 How far should the government intervene in its attempts to reduce unemployment?

4 'It could be argued that unemployment is a natural and inevitable consequence of an overheated economy. It acts, in effect, as a safety valve.' How far do you agree with this view?

What are the principal factors that cause a change in the international value of sterling and how can a balance of payments deficit be arrested? What measures can a company take to protect itself from fluctuations in the exchange rate?

Tackling the question

Here another temptation to burst into a frenzy of economic modelling and concepts presents itself. Resist it. However, it would be quite legitimate to consider in greater detail the role and importance of both domestic and international interest rates and, particularly, their effect on a company's cost of capital as well as its revenues. A government can, of course, take fairly stringent measures to limit movements in exchange rates — protectionist measures, supply-side policies, deflationary measures, etc. — but the key point is what effects these measures might have on a company in the UK. Some companies will be international or even multinational, and various changes will affect them in different ways.

Answer

Changes in the value of sterling are caused by three main factors:

- *speculation.* People buy and sell currencies in the short term, in the expectation that the currency will rise and fall. If speculators feel that the value of the pound is going to fall, they will not buy pounds — and the pound's value will fall!
- *changes in UK domestic interest rates.* A rise in interest rates encourages other countries to invest in the UK, in preference to another country. However, they must first convert their currency to pounds sterling, which will lead to an increase in its demand, a reduction in its supply and a rise in its price. The same effects will be felt if there is a demand for UK exports.
- *inflation.* This tends to cause imports to rise faster than exports. Because the pound is effectively depreciating, exports become more expensive and imports cheaper. As the exports are now more expensive to overseas customers,

fewer exports are demanded; in turn, fewer pounds are demanded, so the value of the pound falls even further.

In the early 1970s, the fixed exchange rate system was replaced by floating exchange rates, so that currencies could appreciate and depreciate according to international supply and demand. Such rates do not freely go up and down of their own accord, however, for government agencies will intervene by buying or selling currencies and by altering UK interest rates.

International trade is important to the UK. Although small and with less than 2% of the world's population, the UK is still one of the major trading nations along with the USA, Germany and Japan. The evidence shows that, for the past few years, the people of the UK have consistently lived beyond their means, and are continuing to do so. The value of the UK's imports exceeds the value of its exports, producing a balance of payments deficit. Some of this deficit, however, was due to the import of capital goods, which, in the long run, will benefit the UK economy by helping to modernise industry, increase productivity and reduce average unit costs, so improving the competitiveness of UK goods.

The exchange rate is defined as the price of one country's currency denominated in terms of another country's currency. Capital flows, arising from trade in goods and services, international investment and loans, create enormous demands for foreign currencies. In 1990 it was estimated that the global turnover in foreign exchange currency dealings approached $640 billion each day.

There are three types of participant in the foreign exchange market:

- the customers, such as multinational companies that require foreign currency for cross-border trade and investments;
- the banks, which act as market-makers, buying and selling foreign currencies and making a profit on the difference;
- the brokers, which are specialist companies acting as intermediaries between banks throughout the world, and which charge a commission for their services.

Each currency comes to have a value not only within its country of origin, but also in terms of the other currencies that can be bought and sold for it. Changes in sterling exchange rates may have a marked effect on the volume of exports and imports. Any firm that relies heavily on overseas markets is very vulnerable to changes in the exchange rates and specifically to a rise

Because of the importance of exporting to many UK firms, the value of sterling and fluctuations in that value can leave many firms seriously exposed. Explain how this leads to a balance of trade deficit.

in the value of sterling, which will cause UK exports to increase in price. The British government's attempts to control inflation through, say, the imposition of higher interest rates may seriously affect the volume of overseas exports (and, of course, imports). The ability to compete in world markets is essential for the success of UK firms.

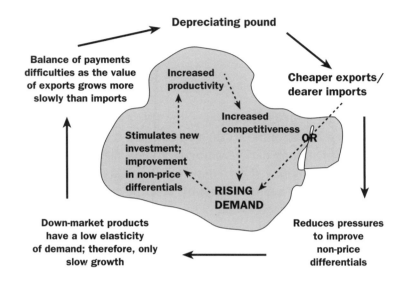

Figure 19 Virtuous and vicious circles

Exchange rates vary considerably with changes in the demand for currency relative to supply. The major influences affecting the demand for currency and its supply are:

- *capital movements.* Investment in foreign countries for speculative purposes gives rise to large movements of capital. To a great extent this movement of capital is 'hot money', i.e. money that goes from country to country seeking the best return; it is thus liable to sudden withdrawal. Capital always seeks the most profitable market where it can be safely invested. In addition, there are currency speculators who attempt to make profits out of the movements in exchange rates, e.g. buying dollars when they are low and selling them when the dollar exchange rate rises. Currency speculators can precipitate a change in exchange rates.
- *trading operations.* A rise in the volume of goods imported by a country without a corresponding change in the volume of exports will cause a reduction in the demand for sterling (and a corresponding increase in the demand for foreign currencies with which to purchase those imports). The pound will fall in international value.
- *monetary policy.* Deliberate action by the monetary authorities, namely the central bank or government, to control inflation will affect the value of the currency.

There are three important areas for an exporting firm to consider. First, what is the company's foreign exchange exposure; just how vulnerable is the company to fluctuations in currency exchange rates? Second, what decisions need to be made about hedging techniques? Third, what is the possibility and advantage of using external money and foreign capital markets? Companies can take various measures to mitigate the effects of fluctuating exchange rates, but none is easy and few are short term. The company might consider any or most of the following:

- It can reduce the price elasticity of demand for its products by going for improvements in quality and improving the non-price differentials.

Now we can get down to the actual measures that a company might consider. Not all will be appropriate, but there's a range of options. Some of these are quite specialist, and if the firm cannot undertake them itself, it might be able to employ a specialist in the field to do the job.

- It can buy and sell forward on the foreign exchange markets. This may have implications for the company's cash flow and liquidity. However, a policy of 100% cover against unfavourable exchange rates, by using the forward market, does at least lock into a known rate of exchange, if not necessarily an advantageous one. In the end, using the forward markets is just as speculative as waiting for payment to be made in several weeks' time.
- It can alter debtor and creditor periods according to its expectations of exchange rate movements. This is called 'leading and lagging' — speeding up some payments but delaying others.
- It can turn to alternative and additional markets, and/or restructure its marketing department towards domestic markets.
- It can attempt to reduce costs, particularly labour costs, and improve productivity (but there may be implications for working capital).
- It can consider stockholding 'insurance' against appreciating imports.
- It can consider hedging the potential foreign exchange problems by operational means rather than purely financial ones. For example, a firm that has a reasonable export market in, say, France could consider importing its own raw materials and supplies from France.
- It may be possible to use foreign banks more advantageously than domestic ones, and to use external money and capital markets. Corporate management may be surprised that banks operating in the 'Euro' market can often pay a slightly higher interest rate on deposited funds than the domestic banks, but at the same time can charge a slightly lower rate on the loans they make.

Related questions

1   How might a significant rise in the value of sterling, relative to other currencies, affect the fortunes of a company that exports 60% of its output to European Union countries?

2   'Given that the pound is now floating, the government need not be too concerned about the balance of payments.' How far do you think this is true?

3   'It is only a matter of time before the UK joins a single currency, and there will be significant benefits for the business community.' What might be the benefits of joining the single currency arrangements?

4   Explain what measures the government might take to protect the value of sterling. Why is it considered important to do so?

Marketing
Management

'There is probably no other part of the business to which we allocate resources that provides so little justification for their use.' 'I am aware that half of the advertising budget is wasted. Will somebody please tell me which half?' Bearing in mind these statements, and with examples, consider and discuss the function and effectiveness of advertising.

Tackling the question

This is open season for those who have studied advertising in some depth. It offers plenty of opportunities to discuss the various approaches and the advertising aims of companies. You might consider introducing the major forms of advertising, such as direct mailing, which is becoming increasingly important, and the many media outlets, along with some examples of dealer promotions that encourage dealers to participate in a promotional drive. Promotion, in all its many guises, is an enormous subject, but this question deals specifically with advertising, which is only one part — albeit an important part — of promotion. Similarly, the importance of merchandising — assisting the retailer with publicity at the point of display — should not be overlooked, although strictly speaking it is promotion rather than advertising.

Answer

Guidance notes

Advertising is probably the most reviled, the most controlled and yet the most pervasive and persuasive form of mass communication. It consists of any paid form of non-personal presentation and promotion of ideas, goods or services by an identified sponsor. The simplest form of advertisement, with a memorable strapline (e.g. 'Beanz Meanz Heinz'), sells the product itself, but more complex and subtle forms of advertising sell ideas and attitudes and leave the consumer to turn them into reality. It is an essential feature of good advertising that the receiver should identify with the message and not merely receive it.

An essay on advertising lends itself to the use of examples. But choose them carefully, and don't trivialise your answer with silly or irrelevant ones.

These are the main reasons why advertising (and promotion) might be used. You may be able to think of a few more — but would they add to your answer? You have to draw the line somewhere.

The objectives of an advertising strategy are many and varied but will include:

- supporting an existing brand by stressing the advantages of a product — the unique selling proposition (USP) — that consumers are believed to have identified;
- attacking the competitors and increasing the firm's market share within the same total market. This is directly competitive and may include veiled statements about other, less successful products. However, a direct comparison to the detriment of competitor products is not permitted in the UK.
- increasing total sales by retaining the same market share within a larger market. This is normally achieved by co-operative advertising with other firms.
- co-operating with producers of jointly used products to suggest mutual approval. Examples of this are 'Hoover recommend Daz' and 'Leading manufacturers recommend Bold for front loaders'.
- appealing to a new market segment — very often a niche market that may have potential for growth. Here the consumer will need to be informed in the first instance, and it is only the later advertisements that will switch to persuasion and attitude development. This kind of approach is also relevant to the marketing of a new and innovative product.
- conveying an image of the firm rather than a specific product. This is often the way in which service industries, social services and welfare organisations advertise.
- supporting a particular marketing policy. This is particularly necessary when it is proposed to do something that the consumer will not readily accept, such as charging too much or too little: for example, 'Deservedly the most expensive pen on the market'.
- supporting a decision to buy after it has been made. Many who make an important decision to buy have second thoughts about it once the decision has been made. This is particularly important for expensive and up-market goods.

There are two basic types of advertisement. The first relies on rational argument and is most common in industrial advertising. The second kind of appeal is to the emotions. Here the advertisement claims to convey benefits such as status, safety, personal achievement and sexual prowess. Examples of products that depend upon this sort of approach are toothpaste, cosmetics, toiletries and air transport.

Successful advertising relies on a variety of methods and appeals, depending on many factors, including the target group at which the product is aimed. Advertisers might have a number of market segments — through pin-point targeting — that they wish to enter. They will also have a number of objectives for their advertisements in each market segment and for each product. They will need to determine what kind of consumer they are aiming at, and to what forms of approach that group is most likely to respond. Whatever else they decide, a strong initial impact is important.

Increasingly, advertisements and, indeed, promotion concentrate on the lifestyle and attitudes of the prospective customer. This is known as psychographic segmentation. The Legal and General umbrella advertising campaign, for example, is aimed at the mainstreamer group, which prefers the security associated with well-known branded products. Customers in this group, which is the largest group and comprises some 40% of the population, do not take risks; they tend to shop at high street shops and are willing to pay that little extra in return for the reassurance that they are undoubtedly getting value for money.

However, simply advertising the product or service may not translate into sales; there may need to be additional supportive promotion, including sales promotion and merchandising at the point of sale. At this stage, the marketing process involves another and separate form of communication to persuade the retailer to stock the product and ensure that it is on the shelves when the consumer wishes to buy it. When the advertising campaign has reached this stage, the promotional campaign may change its thrust, now beginning to associate the consumer with the product in a purchasing or use situation.

Much advertising does little more than maintain an existing position, but experiments have shown that this is an essential feature of marketing, as 'brand loyalty' may be very fickle. The most effective advertising is that associated with a new product, particularly because there is information on which the consumer can focus and because it is easier to create new attitudes than to change existing ones.

Research suggests that consistency of advertising is a better guarantee of success than brilliant artwork or heavy spending, and that success is measured by the percentage of people surveyed who remember seeing a brand being advertised from a prompt list they are shown. Success in money terms is measured by the cost per percentage point of those who could remember the advertisement. However, there are difficulties in assessing the impact of promotional expenditure because of the delayed nature of the possible results.

While many consumers may view advertising with a jaundiced eye, the growth of consumerism and intensely competitive

You need to understand the nature, purpose and usefulness of market segmentation and, increasingly, the use of 'lifestyle' segments as well as traditional ones, such as demographic and geographic. Lifestyle segments have to do with the way that people run their lives, how they conduct themselves, what they believe in — in other words, what makes them 'tick'.

It is important to stress that while advertising is very important and billions of pounds are spent on it each year, it is only one ingredient in the total promotion package. In terms of communicating with the consumer, we must not forget the tremendous impact of packaging — especially of fast-moving consumer goods (FMCGs), which leap off the supermarket shelf.

markets have ensured that advertising is as much a science as it is an art. Few firms, if any, could dispense with advertising. However, advertising must not be seen in isolation from the other promotional factors. Similarly, the synergistic possibilities of the communications mix — promotion and packaging — must not be overlooked. The importance of advertising and, indeed, promotion lies in its recognition as a major ingredient of the marketing mix; altering or emphasising one variable within that mix will almost certainly have effects on the remaining variables.

Related questions

1 How does the government attempt to prevent misleading advertisements? Consider the role of the Advertising Standards Authority and whether this organisation is effective.

2 'Advertising and promotional expenditures invariably raise the final price of the product.' Consider this statement and examine whether it is true or not. What benefit, if any, does 'above the line' advertising bring?

3 Develop a set of advertising objectives for an actual or a hypothetical brand that reflects (a) message; (b) media; (c) utility.

4 Consider the principles of effective advertising and draw up a timetable for an advertising campaign.

Question 40

Suggest how the organisational structure of a firm might affect managerial pricing decisions, and consider how much discretion to set prices a manager should have.

Tackling the question

This is quite a tricky question because it's asking you to bring together several concepts: the organisation of the company, who sets the prices, and how much empowerment, discretion and delegation a manager should have. And you will have to weave these concepts throughout the answer. In doing so, you must mention organisational objectives, departmental or divisional goals and, equally important, the fact that an action or decision in one part of the company may have effects in others parts of the firm. In other words, a systems approach is required. It would be a good opportunity to discuss the importance of profit centres and cost centres, and the need for a commercial organisation to be flexible and responsive in a dynamic market place. The problem may be knowing what to leave out rather than what to include.

Answer

The setting of prices is not an end in itself. It is part of the process of achieving the objective of the company, and the appropriate pricing policy is therefore important to that objective. In a functionally structured organisation, the objective of the chief executive can be expressed in terms of making a profit by exercising discretion within prescribed limits set, perhaps, by the board of directors. This cannot be said of any of the subordinates, since none of them has authority over both production and sales. The inability to push accountability for profit to levels below chief executive may be seen as a weakness of the functionally structured organisation, since profitability is seen as a measure of efficiency and, therefore, as a means of control. It is to obtain this control that the organisation becomes more product or federally structured.

In such a structure, product, divisional or regional managers may have their own business development manager or, alternatively, this function may be centralised under the chief executive. Product managers would be accountable for profit in a

Guidance notes

Setting prices is no easy matter — well, I suppose it can be an easy matter if a firm simply adds 20% or 50% to its costs (however it decides what they are), but that's not very sensible or very precise, not least because different firms have different cost structures. So a key issue must be how much discretion a manager might have to set prices, given local conditions and local competition. Does it make sense to make a manager responsible for profit when he or she has little or no control over prices — or costs, for that matter?

more limited way in the latter case than in the former because the discretion to decide what products to make and sell is largely removed. However, so long as this is borne in mind, it is still reasonable to hold them accountable for profit because they have authority at least over production, over many costs and over sales.

A manager accountable for the success of a profit centre may be called a profit manager. This term covers the chief executive of a functionally structured organisation as well as a product or brand or regional manager in a federally structured organisation. Pricing policy is an instrument essential to a profit manager. The product price is an important determinant of sales volume and hence of revenue. At the same time it determines, through volume, the level of plant capacity utilisation. Unless profit managers have authority for the local pricing policy, and are able to exercise it, they cannot rationally be held accountable for profit.

Where there are too many individual pricing decisions for profit managers to make them personally, they must delegate a policy for their subordinates to implement. This situation is typical of a firm making a large variety of non-standard products in batches for commercial customers to the customers' specifications and against the customers' orders. As the products are to customers' specifications, the potential range is virtually infinite. Pricing cannot be by means of a pre-set price list and discount structure, as in the case of producers of standardised products. Instead, pricing must be done on an individual basis on the receipt of enquiries from customers. In this case, many factors — including associated costs, demand and competition — must be remembered.

Managers need to be able to ensure that their subordinates are, indeed, implementing the company pricing policy within prescribed limits. The prices must be oriented towards the market level, but they must, nonetheless, allow their subordinates a significant degree of autonomy. If there are few limits to the discretion that a subordinate can exercise in the performance of price setting, then the manager cannot be sure that the price set will contribute to the firm's objectives, or indeed that it will not be prejudicial to them. In delegating pricing policy, managers are very much interested in the way the subordinates use their discretion, and they must be able to communicate to the subordinates the sort of results that will be acceptable to them.

There are, broadly, two groups of product: those that might be deemed standard and those that are non-standard. One of

You should know about profit centres (and cost centres) and with them, perhaps, something loosely called 'management by objectives'. If head office is going to set how much profit my division must make, I would like some say in what's realistic and what isn't. Profit centre performance might be connected, of course, to performance-related pay.

In a sense, it's about how much autonomy — self-government — a company is willing to delegate. And delegation is about trust: I trust you to do the job, therefore I am delegating it to you.

the principal differences between pricing standard products for the consumer and pricing non-standard products for the commercial customer is that, generally, standard products are specified by the producing firm and sold to a lay customer. Non-standard products, however, are specified and bought by an expert buyer. The effect of this distinction on pricing strategy is profound. In the former case, customers often have no way of assessing quality other than by experience of the brand and comparison with competitors' products. They may be tempted to use price as an indicator of quality in the rather naive hope that the more expensive it is, the better the quality.

Expert buyers of non-standard products are in a very different position. When they invite tenders, they need only check the specifications of the quotations to see that they meet their own specifications and, in the knowledge that quality is adequate, they can then base their selection on the lowest price. In practice, a number of other factors will affect the decision — whether the delivery date is satisfactory, whether the price is so far below competitors' prices that the ability to maintain supply becomes suspect, and so on. Nevertheless, and broadly speaking, the expert buyer is much more able to discriminate on price than the lay counterpart, and the seller of non-standard goods must match the quoted or tendered prices of the competitors, both local and national, to sell. This means the profit manager requires access to a comprehensive marketing information system.

Whatever pricing system is used for individual jobs, it is vital to determine what the customer is likely to pay for that one-off contract. Pricing managers must consider whether, at the price proposed, the firm is better off taking the job or refusing it. To resolve the problem, it is necessary to consider the alternatives. They could utilise the firm's capacity by accepting the order; they could use it to take on another task; or they could even leave the capacity idle. The real cost of taking on the first job is what the firm is sacrificing by not exercising either of the alternative choices available; economists describe this concept as the opportunity cost.

In the short run, it may be sensible to accept a non-profit-making order as long as the revenue from the order is ultimately making a contribution to the fixed costs that will have to be paid regardless of the order. A functionally organised firm may not possess the flexibility and responsiveness necessary to meet these conditions, or to react to a dynamic market place.

In practice, such a firm would almost certainly have a centralised purchasing policy for, say, raw materials; it may also have a corporate agreement with trade unions on its wage

It's an interesting problem. A firm may want to delegate — give greater autonomy — but Marks and Spencer can't really allow a store in Inverness to charge more for a jumper than a store in, say, Truro. So how does a firm justify making individual managers responsible — giving them targets — and then telling them what prices to set? Perhaps the good people of Inverness buy more jumpers and are willing to pay a higher price. Is that dilemma really a dilemma?

policies, although there may be some discretion for local plant bargaining. Very few profit managers will have total control over costs and/or prices. However, where there are too many individual pricing decisions for profit managers, they, in turn, must delegate some pricing responsibility to their subordinates, such as salespeople in the field.

Related questions

1 What factors do you think should be taken into account when deciding how far a company should be decentralised?

2 Why might the communication process between management and the workforce become increasingly ineffective as the company grows?

3 'Managerial autonomy and pricing decisions go hand in glove. It does not make good marketing sense to interfere with a manager's pricing discretion.' Explain the apparent reasoning behind this statement.

4 Explain how pricing decisions are likely to be made in a company manufacturing consumer durables for export to the European mainland.

What are channels of distribution? Consider the factors that might influence their use.

Tackling the question

Distribution is about providing the link between producer and consumer, where any distribution gap exists because of, say, geographical separation, ownership, time or sorting goods into more convenient packages. Several factors are involved in this process and an examination of any or all of these would be a reasonable way of answering this question. The factors include transportation, storage, merchandising, selling and packaging. Distribution to overseas customers may present particular problems and the use of expert agent intermediaries may have to be considered.

Answer

A modern trading economy deals in millions of products that need to be distributed quickly and economically. A fast and efficient distribution system is a key marketing tool that may provide a competitive edge for companies eager to develop an image for reliability and service. The introduction and wide acceptance of just-in-time management have made an effective distribution system even more imperative. In a sense, a distribution system is a key external resource that may take years to evolve and is not easily changed. Nonetheless, it must be flexible enough to change in response to changing demand patterns and shopping habits.

The distribution function in marketing is concerned with the flow of products and services from the producer to the ultimate consumer. While a concern for the efficiency of distribution (in terms of cost) is important, the real issue in distribution must be its effectiveness and the improvement to customer service that can follow. Improving customer service adds value to the product, which is just as important, if not more so, than cutting costs. The objective of a distribution network is to make the products available to consumers at the right place and at the right time, in the right quantity and at a price acceptable to the

Guidance notes

Getting products to the point of sale is something of a logistical exercise. In fact, a new 'science' has sprung up called physical distribution management, which considers the raw materials and component parts going in at one end of the firm, the transfer of work in progress through the organisation, and the distribution of the outputs to the final consumer — or, at least, to the retailer or wholesaler.

Although many firms still use these traditional distribution channels, many factors are contributing to their decline. (See Question 42 on direct selling.)

target consumer. The current methods of distributing products follow basic channel patterns, which are as follows:

- M — A — W — R — C
- M — W — R — C
- M — A — R — C
- M — R — C
- M — A — C
- M — C
- M — direct selling organisation — C

where M = manufacturer; A = agent; W = wholesaler; R = retailer; C = consumer.

Products may be channelled directly from the producer/manufacturer to the final consumer. On the other hand, a longer channel may be adopted, involving the use of merchant or agent intermediaries. Agent intermediaries negotiate the transfer of the title but never own the goods, e.g. stockbrokers and mail-order agents. Merchant intermediaries, such as retailers and wholesalers, take ownership title to the goods.

Many factors govern the choice of appropriate distribution channels, including:

- the type of products to be distributed, including their fragility and perishability;
- the experience of the manufacturing company and its network of distribution agencies;
- the marketing facilities and marketing organisation available within the company;
- the availability and experience of the intermediaries;
- the financial resources available and the associated costs of distribution;
- the proximity of the markets and of the final consumer;
- the cost, flexibility and convenience of transport facilities.

The key point is that different types of good will require different channels of distribution. It sound a little trite, but it's reasonable to ask what the objective is — yes, to get the goods from A to B, but how quickly and at what cost?

Broadly, three categories of product may be differentiated: consumer goods, industrial goods and capital goods. More often than not, it is the type of product and its ultimate market that dictates the channel of distribution employed.

Consumer goods
These, in turn, can be classified into three groups:

- convenience goods (e.g. detergents, soap, soft drinks and many other household items, known as fast-moving consumer goods, or FMCGs). These are used more or less regularly by large numbers of consumers. Manufacturers usually adopt an intensive and extensive distribution strategy. These companies generally have their own marketing team and facilities to distribute to wholesalers and retailers, without requiring the services of a national agent. It should be noted that the patterns of distribution are flexible, depending on the nature and requirements of the trade and the market. For instance, many manufacturers distribute their products not only to wholesalers, but also to retailers on a selective basis.

Clearly, in any essay about distribution the role of the wholesaler and the retailer must be considered. The problem, however, is knowing when to stop!

- shopping goods (e.g. cosmetics, shoes, watches, jewellery, electrical goods, 'white' goods). These products are not purchased as regularly as convenience goods; therefore, fewer retail outlets are necessary. The manufacturer usually adopts a selective distribution strategy — that is, selects only a limited number of retail outlets in each area.
- speciality goods (e.g. motor cars). These items are purchased very infrequently. The manufacturer may appoint (or franchise) and support an exclusive agent in each territory, town or region.

Industrial goods

These products are not for household use but for industrial consumption. There are three main groups:

- raw materials (e.g. agricultural produce, chemicals, plastics, timber, fish, oil);
- semi-manufactured goods (e.g. canvas, leather, cement, steel);
- accessory materials required in production (e.g. bottles, cans, other packaging materials, component parts).

Generally, most local manufacturers of these categories of product sell directly to the industrial consumer. Orders are likely to be substantial and may entail long-term commitments.

Capital goods

Examples of capital goods include buildings, machinery (e.g. generators and lift trucks) and equipment (e.g. computers, desks and benches, shop fittings). Usually, close contact between the manufacturer and final consumer is necessary. There is often little need to have an intermediary, except perhaps a manufacturer's agent or franchisee.

Channels of distribution have, however, become increasingly complex, markets more dispersed, consumers better informed

Channels of distribution have changed and are changing. What do you think is next on the horizon, given the growth in computer technology and the Internet? Some even forecast the eventual demise of the traditional retailer, but there will still be a need to get the product — whatever it is — from A to B and possibly to C.

and their buying behaviour more cosmopolitan. The introduction of sophisticated technology heralds another revolution in retailing. In consequence, many manufacturers have tended to lose much of the personal relationship with customers and the intermediaries have become very important — despite the growth of supermarkets and hypermarkets where retailers, such as Asda, buy directly from the manufacturers. Often intermediaries own the goods (i.e. they take title to the goods), or they may negotiate transfer of the title (e.g. an estate agent). However, an intermediary may not be necessary when:

- the manufacturer appoints sole agents, such as a franchisee;
- the manufacturer can supply retailers directly, such as the large supermarket chains that either have strategically placed depot warehouses or are sufficiently large to carry considerable stocks themselves;
- there are many smaller retailers that are geographically concentrated. It may be cheaper and easier for the manufacturer to supply these retailers directly, particularly when handling the products must be minimised (e.g. frozen food, crockery).
- manufacturers own their own retail outlets (e.g. farm shops, wool mill shops);
- the products are very large or very expensive;
- the product is either custom-made or requires complex installation;
- the manufacturer wants closer contact with the markets.

This must be a very relevant point to make. It emphasises the partnership that exists — or, more precisely perhaps, that should exist — between central and local governments and the business community. It's local government that sets the highways priorities in each area, while the government provides about 50% of the funding. But the government, through the Highways Agency, determines the priorities for trunk roads and motorways.

However, any distribution system is only as good as the infrastructure that serves it. Demand for all types of transport rose sharply during the 1980s. Freight carriage rose by 25%, but by 1991 the railways' share of the total freight transported was a mere 7%. The spread of just-in-time manufacturing strategies, the increasing emphasis on fresh and perishable food in retail markets, and the tighter control of stock made possible by recent advances in information technology have combined to make suppliers very sensitive to being able to meet their delivery promises. It would appear, therefore, that if mounting traffic congestion is to be avoided, there is no alternative to increased investment in the UK road network. The impact on businesses of road congestion is a matter not only of increased commercial costs, but also of missed opportunities to improve service and distribution times. For example, a fast and effective road system allows manufacturers to have fewer strategically placed depots and warehouses. It is estimated that road congestion in the UK is costing the economy £18 billion per year, and adds over £60 per month to the average shopping bill.

Related questions

1 What advantages might the community obtain if there were government incentives to switch freight traffic from road haulage to rail? As a road haulier, oppose this proposal.

2 Does it follow that a company offering high customer service bears high physical distribution costs in relation to sales?

3 A colleague suggests that the distribution function of a company has got nothing to do with the marketing department. How would you reply to this assertion?

4 Explain how distribution logistics and marketing can combine together to provide a powerful means of achieving a competitive advantage.

Consider the growth and advantages of direct selling in the distribution network. Comment also on the functions and role of the wholesaler as a merchant intermediary.

Tackling the question

This is a very topical question because the increasing trend is to sell without retail outlets, wholesalers or any type of intermediary. Quite sophisticated direct selling has been successfully undertaken by some companies for many years, e.g. Avon and Tupperware. Any selling process can be identified as having seven key elements: the opening, the need identification and stimulation, the presentation, dealing with objections, negotiation, closing the sale and the follow-up. It would be both interesting and useful to consider how these seven stages might be used in direct selling. It would also be relevant to consider the relationship between direct selling and direct response advertising.

Answer

One of the significant developments in product distribution in recent years is the growth of the direct selling industry. Many of the companies involved in direct selling confine their activities to certain localities, while a few have grown and expanded their business nationwide and internationally. The direct selling companies sell products ranging from shopping and speciality goods to fast-moving and regularly consumed convenience items. Some well-established firms make use of contract manufacturers to produce various items under their own brand names.

There is no doubt that the traditional retailer, not just the corner shop outlet, is facing some difficulties. Many changes have affected and are affecting the retailer, and the wholesaler, and they are having to think of even more sophisticated ways of enticing us to spend.

While trade selling usually involves distributing products through traditional retail outlets, direct selling means that the products are sold to consumers by means of a personal approach or by personal selling and telesales. A well-established direct selling organisation typically has a large network of thousands of distributors (some companies call them agents, dealers, etc.), supplied from distribution depots, who reach out to the ultimate consumers. These distributors are private individuals who operate the business independently, either on a part-time or full-time basis. They are people from all walks of life and, strictly speaking, they are not employees of the parent company. Many hold 'parties' regularly to demonstrate, merchandise and promote the products. Many even go door-to-door, although some direct selling companies do not encourage their distributors to do so for image reasons. This is in contrast to companies that have established a well-known, international and reputable image for doing just that, such as Avon.

There are several advantages in distributing consumer goods through direct selling channels instead of selling through the trade or though traditional retailing outlets. In particular, there is a saving of advertising and promotional costs. Selling through the trade and traditional outlets requires intensive advertising by mass media to 'pull' customers to the retail outlets. Direct selling, on the other hand, involves personal efforts to create the 'push' effect of promotion. The advertising cost that is saved can benefit the consumers in the form of lower prices and makes the products more price competitive. In addition, there will be a marked reduction in the related distribution costs. Trade selling usually involves a series of mark-ups through several intermediaries. By direct selling these costs can be minimised and the company can afford to give attractive incentives to its distributors as well as price concessions and special offers to customers.

Other advantages of direct selling include:

- immediate or near-immediate finance and liquidity. Many types of trade selling are traditionally linked with long-term credit terms. This means that considerable capital may be necessary to finance the trade outlet. Direct selling is usually based on cash terms or credit card terms.
- personalised service. By direct selling, consumers can receive a more personalised type of service from distributors. They can even enjoy the convenience of 'shopping in their own home'. The arrival of the Internet and telesales has brought this concept even closer to the final consumer.
- consumer education. Because of the nature of direct selling, which is based upon the personal approach, consumers have a chance to know more about the features and benefits of the products that they pay for.
- shelf space. With increasing competition for limited shelf space in shops, and pressure and incentives to display a host of competitive products, a brand may become submerged among many others. This problem does not arise in direct selling.

Key among these changes is, of course, the rapid advances in computer technology. That's not all bad for the retailer. The service has improved enormously — in some ways — but it does mean that increasing use of direct mailing, direct selling and the Internet are gnawing their way into traditional retail practices. Armchair shopping is with us.

It begs the question as to what the final consumer is looking for. Is it mainly value for money and cheapness? Or quality, convenience or after-sales service? What is the USP — the unique selling proposition — and why should I shop with you rather than with someone else?

With this list you can begin to see how attractive direct selling becomes.

According to conventional marketing philosophy, consumer goods — especially those convenience items that are widely and frequently consumed (e.g. FMCGs) — should be sold through retail outlets. In direct selling, however, these items are sold by means of a person-to-person approach. This is made possible because of a feature in direct selling known as 'sponsoring'. A distributor can recruit others to become distributors, and earn an attractive commission on their sales as well. An individual can, therefore, build up a large network of distributors under him or her, and the outcome of this sponsoring feature is the creation of numerous networks of distributors.

Although the manufacturing or producing company is concerned with the final consumer's reaction to its product and its price, the immediate buyers are very often wholesalers and, in some cases, retailers — especially the large supermarket chains and multiples. The role of both agent and merchant inter-mediaries remains important and may, depending on the type of product sold, be indispensable. One such type of merchant intermediary is the wholesaler. Some manufacturers have taken on the wholesale function themselves by establishing outlets that carry stocks of finished goods for resale. Often these outlets are located in high-volume market areas. Large retailers can also assume the role of wholesaler by backwards integration and, in doing so, gain several advantages including lower costs, more variety, better quality, improved stock control and quicker delivery.

The wholesaler remains, therefore, an important link in the commercial network, even though there is an increasing tendency for manufacturers to supply the final retailer or consumer directly, in which case the manufacturer must assume the role and functions of the wholesaler (i.e. develop a vertically integrated marketing system). A wholesaler attempts to reconcile supply and demand on a regional or local basis and, in doing so, helps to relieve the manufacturer of this task.

This is what the question asked for and this is what the wholesaler does. But go further. Like retailing, the wholesaler's role is being squeezed. Wholesalers are having to find new ways of making themselves attractive. After all, who wants to pay yet another inter-mediary's margins when they can cut them out altogether?

The main benefits that the traditional wholesaler offers are as follows:

- It helps to create and expand markets in co-operation with the manufacturer, which may offer discounts and promo-tional activities.
- It is able to make the manufacturer aware of changing consumer preferences, and the nature of demand for other goods and associated market trends.
- It is able to stabilise prices by varying supplies and by stock-holding.

- It relieves the manufacturer of some risk by taking title to the goods (if a merchant wholesaler).
- It may grade, pre-pack and price the products, so that they are ready for immediate retail sale.
- It may offer point-of-sale promotion and assist with merchandising of the products.
- It is able to keep abreast of competitive product innovation and to advise the retailer accordingly.
- It is an important link between manufacturer and retailer.
- It is often situated locally, which allows for easier communication and delivery services.
- It breaks down bulk products into smaller units and so provides convenience for the retailer.

Against the competition of company-owned wholesalers and the large supermarket chains, many independent wholesalers have significantly improved their services. Changing to 'superior' products only, or introducing appropriate technology for distribution planning and stock control, has increased turnover, reduced costs and improved margins. Inevitably, the latter improvements have required major capital investment that may not be available to the smaller, traditional wholesaler.

Related questions

1 Given the increasing use of information technology and changes in distribution, consider whether or not the traditional role of the wholesaler is becoming increasingly redundant.

2 Direct selling is deemed by many to be both invasive and intrusive. Should it be regulated and, if so, how?

3 What is the difference between an agent and a broker? Explain why manufacturers use wholesalers.

4 Discuss the role of the intermediaries who act as a link between manufacturers and retailers. Why do manufacturers not bypass these intermediaries?

5 Suggest what the reasons might be for wholesalers failing to invest much in promotional activities. Would increasing this investment stimulate their sales?

Retailing has changed markedly during the past two or three decades and new technology promises even more fundamental changes. Consider the different types of retail outlet and discuss the evolution of retailing and the influences that have stimulated the changes.

Tackling the question

There are several ways of tackling this question, including offering a detailed analysis of how the functions of the retailer are changing. These functions tend to include the movement of goods, the transfer of title, the standardisation of goods, the immediate availability of goods and the financing of stock. The concept of the retail audit makes a systematic evaluation of the retailer's strategies and marketing activities. There have been broad structural changes in retailing and these changes are continuing. Some writers talk about the low-cost, low-margin operations attracting price-conscious customers. This is another interesting angle.

Answer

Retailing and patterns of retailing have changed and are changing dramatically. There aren't many of the traditional shops left, except in the more remote areas, for they have been squeezed out by supermarkets and hypermarkets. But now even they are having to look to their laurels. And that's good for the consumers — they benefit from lower prices, more variety and more pleasant shops with all sorts of amenities and conveniences. But technology and telephones are revolutionising the retail industry. Read on...

Retailing includes all activities related directly to the sale of goods or services to the final consumer. As retailing has evolved from the personal service once offered by small and individual shops to the increasing trend towards self-service and mail order, manufacturers have modified their promotional and communication strategies by developing sophisticated branding and loyalty campaigns to create consumer insistence for a product or service. Merchandising consists of the use of display and promotional devices specifically at the point of sale, including free samples, cut-price offers, interior displays, loss-leaders and the judicious use of gondolas. Competition for shelf space is very fierce, and many manufacturers are willing to grant some kind of discount (called dealer loaders) to retailers if they site their products on certain shelves in specific parts of the store. The effectiveness and the efficiency of a retail outlet are usually measured in contribution (or profit) per square metre of floor space. This is a good basis for comparison with other shops, or between departments in the same shop.

Traditional retail outlets include the following:

- Independent traders. They own their own shops and usually supervise personally. However, they are likely to have limited financial resources and will restrict their expenditure on elaborate shop-fittings. They may also have some difficulty in matching the keen prices of the larger shops. Nonetheless, they survive because of the goodwill they build up, their convenient opening hours and their convenient location.

- Multiples or chain stores. These organisations have a number of branches located over an area of the country or throughout the country. Invariably, the outlets have identical shop fronts. Chain stores are immensely powerful buying organisations and are often able to obtain significant discounts from their suppliers. In essence, they rely on a high turnover and comparatively low profit margins.

- Department stores. Enormous improvements in transport and communications have made it profitable to establish large-scale retail outlets in densely populated areas — often in city centres that attract shoppers from a wide catchment area. In addition, there has been a succession of department store acquisitions, mergers and takeovers; increased capital has been available, and rationalisation and modernisation have followed. Customers are often attracted by the palatial surroundings, the comfort and convenience of one-stop shopping, and the enormous variety of products on sale. Each department is run as a separate business and is under the control of a manager or buyer.

- Supermarkets and hypermarkets. The concept of a supermarket developed in the 1920s in the USA, but it did not catch on until the depression years of the 1930s when wages and incomes were low, and the buying public became very price conscious. The first self-service store in the UK was opened in 1942. A supermarket is a self-service store with a floor area of more than 2,000 square feet and more than three check-outs. There is emphasis on food and household goods — FMCGs — at very competitive prices (bulk buying enabling economies of scale), fewer employees (meaning lower labour costs) and fast turnover of goods.

The question does actually ask you to consider the different types of retail outlet, so here they are. Well, most of them.

Although most products continue to be sold through shops and traditional retail outlets, non-store retailing has been growing much faster than has store retailing.

In terms of an appreciation of the retail industry and, indeed, changes to marketing practices, technology is clearly the force of the future. Soon, you won't have to move from your armchair to order anything you want, and for immediate delivery. It will certainly take the fun — and the frustration — out of shopping, which is as much a social activity for some as it is a purposeful one to replenish the deep freeze or pantry.

- Mail-order businesses. A mail-order house operates its business through extensive advertising and through the production of a detailed and illustrated catalogue. Although designed originally to reach the rural markets, this method of retailing is appealing more and more to urban buyers, who are able to 'shop' from the comfort of their own home, selecting from the retailer's glossy and descriptive catalogue. Although mail-order retailing is not without its disadvantages — lack of personal contact, limited stock range, the problems of after-sales servicing — it is one of the fastest-growing areas of retailing.
- Direct mailing. This is a development from mail-order business, but appeals to specific market segments by mailing potential customers for a specific type of product. It uses various media to interact directly with carefully targeted consumers and to disseminate promotional material.
- Telemarketing, direct radio and on-line computer shopping. These are further extensions of armchair shopping. Customers are able to view the goods on their televisions or computers and to place an order for the product through the interactive facilities that companies such as British Telecom have developed.

Changing social and environmental factors, such as more women going to work, congested town centres, free telephone facilities, environmental pollution and stress have all contributed to the phenomenal growth in direct marketing. In addition, companies can target specific consumers, who have specific interests and needs, even more precisely. Such vendors can build up an enormous database of potential customers and, with it, an improved customer relationship.

The retail market has been, and is being, affected enormously by the introduction of new technology and, particularly, computer technology and information processing. The widespread use of 'plastic' money, including direct debit cards that allow for electronic funds transfer, has not only reduced the problems associated with cash security; many would argue that such cards have stimulated sales dramatically. Developed nations are fast becoming cashless societies.

In addition, the cumulative data amassed by credit card agencies can be analysed to show changes in tastes, fashions and buying behaviour. The development of electronic point-of-sale (EPOS) systems has had a major impact on the quantity and the quality of information available to retailing organisations and, in addition, has improved enormously their stock control and stock-ordering procedures. Bar coding was introduced into the

UK in 1977. A typical, large supermarket or hypermarket will carry over 16,000 bar-coded items. The printed lines on the packaging consist of magnetic symbols that are interpreted by an optical scanning device. A computer screen displays the price and the customer is given an itemised till receipt. At the same time, the computer automatically adjusts the store's stock figure for each item, and subsequently and electronically will initiate reordering of stock from a central warehouse. There are many advantages to such a system, including:

- better data collection and analysis on the movement of goods, sales patterns, new product preferences, promotional campaigns, product life cycles and price elasticities of demand;
- automatic reordering at pre-set stock levels;
- no need to price each item;
- at the check-out, a reduced number of operator mistakes, increased throughput of goods, increased productivity of operators and better cash reconciliation;
- for the customer, an itemised receipt, greater confidence, a quicker service and reduced waiting time.

Retailers are investing a great deal of money in innovative technologies, designed both to influence consumer behaviour and to provide better information about demand. Other innovations include 'the people meter', which assesses the flow of shoppers into and within a retail outlet by criss-crossing the store with infrared beams. From the immediate information received by the store's central computers, the number of sales staff required at any one location can be quickly determined. The level of activity within the store, or on parts of the floor, can be monitored. Even the effects of the weather and the seasons on demand, shopper activity and buying behaviour can be analysed. Any retailing organisation ignores these technological advances at its peril.

A key point here is: what can retailers do to make shopping more attractive? They need the unique selling proposition. Yes, they will compete on price, but what else? What about merchandising, point-of-sale attractions, shoppers' buses, credit cards, banking and petrol? Retailers, of any kind, are having to be more and more innovative. That's good for the shopper, of course!

Related questions

1 Explain how a voluntary chain agreement between a group of retailers and a wholesaler might help the smaller retailers to compete with supermarkets.

2 Consider why and how patterns of retailing are changing so dramatically. What effect is this likely to have on the traditional distribution networks?

3 There are many different types of retailer. Explain the differing roles of each and suggest what features ensure their survival.

4 Computer-based approaches are being used more widely by banks and insurance companies to sell a wide range of related services to identified market segments. Explain what advantages this might bring to both the retailer and the consumer.

> 'Effective pricing is a necessary ingredient in achieving both corporate profitability and continued survival.' Consider this statement and discuss product pricing policies and the various pricing strategies.

Tackling the question

A key element when studying the marketing mix is pricing, and massive volumes are devoted to pricing alone. I doubt if Jack Cohen, the founder of Tesco, ever read one of these books! For many business people, pricing remains a gut reaction — whatever they think the market will bear. Nonetheless, many would argue that it's more a science than an art. It's a little more complex than gut reaction — well, it is for the exam anyhow. Until quite recently only two broad strategic approaches to pricing have been recognised: skimming, which relies on the premise that some consumers are relatively insensitive to price; and penetration pricing, which seeks to undercut the competition and increase market share. However, these approaches are fairly crude, albeit perfectly rational and legitimate in business terms. Greater sophistication in pricing now considers the potential customer's perceived value to be more appropriate. Perhaps this approach is not that dissimilar to the familiar strategy of pricing a product according to what the market will bear.

Answer

Price is one of the major variables in the marketing mix: the other elements, in marketing terminology, are the product, the place or point of sale, and promotion (with packaging). The mix is not complete until the right price has been determined, but the 'right' price depends on many variables, not least the immediate and long-term objectives of the company.

Economists state that three main factors will affect effective demand, which is defined as the willingness of consumers to pay a particular price for a particular product at a particular time. Those three factors are: the level of individual consumers' income; the price of close substitutes to the product and the price of accompanying, complementary goods; and individual consumer preferences for the different characteristics of that product.

Question 44

There's a key word in the title — 'effective' — which we might interpret as 'that which produces results'. We should remember that.

Before a company determines its pricing policies, it must first define its pricing objectives. Pricing objectives provide the direction for, and define the outcome of, the pricing process, and serve as a guide to the formulation of pricing policies. Pricing policies are merely principles or 'ground rules' to be applied to repetitive situations. Unfortunately, pricing objectives are often confused with pricing policies.

Pricing objectives may be broadly classified into non-economic and economic. Non-economic pricing objectives do not imply non-profit-making, although because of such objectives a company could end up making lower profits than it would otherwise be able to achieve. Non-economic objectives could focus on:

- expanding market share. This could be with a view towards putting the company in a better position to implement an economic pricing objective in the longer term. Japanese companies are known to favour this approach, especially in new markets.
- orderly marketing. This is to promote stable prices and ensure business stability. Traditional mark-ups are used and competitors do not feel upset.
- humanitarian motives, such as maintenance of employment opportunities.

So first, let's give an economic appraisal of what we mean by price — but not in too much depth — and then we can go on to look at the commercial or business aspects.

Economic pricing objectives emphasise optimising (some would say 'maximising') profits, or achieving a target return. This could be based on sales or on investment, or it could be a stated and fixed amount of profit.

I think it's important to mention price and price elasticity of demand together. You can't change the price without bearing in mind what will happen to demand. The whole point of calculating the price elasticity of demand is to calculate the effect on total revenue if price should change. We might sell more (or less), but what will happen to the total revenue and, hence, the profit? Elasticity of demand is often a favourite topic in case study analysis. You must be able to calculate it.

With the profit maximisation objective, a company fixes its price at a level that will allow it to earn the highest possible profits — and that price could be high or low depending on the price elasticity of demand. With a target return objective, a company would pre-determine a percentage figure (perhaps based on anticipated sales) as the target return. The price would then be built up from cost figures to provide for that target return. This is essentially a cost-plus approach to pricing. In establishing the percentage figure, the company may take into consideration the risks that are faced in the industry, the previous years' performances and the prevailing market conditions. From the target return, a target profit figure could be determined, after taking into consideration costs and forecast sales volume. The target profit will not be achieved if, on the basis of the pre-determined target return, it prices the product out of the market.

It is not unusual for a company to have more than one pricing objective. If there are several objectives, one must be dominant and the others must be subordinate to, but compatible with, that dominant objective.

Pricing policies are generally developed from pricing objectives and are intended to take care of repetitive situations, such as when costs of raw materials rise and existing prices have to be changed. A policy could be to sell always at 5% below the price of the market leader, or it could be always to be the market leader. A company could also decide as a matter of policy that its staff price will be its best wholesalers' price.

It's important to stress the objectives of any pricing strategy and its associated policies. What, exactly, does the firm hope to achieve by setting prices at this level? What is it trying to do?

Efficient and effective pricing policies save time and minimise the possibility of incurring customer ill-will. With policies providing the guidelines, those involved with setting the pricing of a company can act more positively. There is also less scope for inconsistency.

Pricing policies and practices vary from company to company. Some examples are:

- a one-price policy that applies to all customers, provided that they buy the same quantity and under the same conditions;
- a flexible pricing policy that means that different customers enjoy different prices, depending on their connections and bargaining ability;
- a policy to undercut competition and sell at below market price. This could invite retaliation and lead to a price-war.
- a policy to set price at the market level and meet the competition head on;
- a psychological pricing policy. Two variations of this are prestige pricing and 'odd' price quoting. Prestige pricing takes advantage of situations whereby consumers associate price with quality and draw irrational conclusions. In such cases, the prices set bear no relationship to costs. Psychological or 'odd' price quoting is a retailing practice whereby prices such as £2.99 or £9.99 are quoted instead of £3.00 or £10.00.
- a geographic pricing policy, such as uniform delivered price throughout a territory or a uniform zone price that applies to all outlets within each zone in a given territory.

Some pricing strategies relate to special circumstances, such as the introduction of new products. Examples of strategies are:

- skimming pricing. A high price is charged in the initial

Clearly, much of this answer reflects the fact that the final price charged depends on what the firm is hoping to achieve, what it's marketing (rather than simply 'selling'), where it's marketing, which target segment it's aiming at, and so on. Many factors will influence the final price and, even then, the final price may change fairly quickly.

stages to take the cream off the market, after which the price is gradually reduced. This was the case with electronic calculators, ball-point pens and colour televisions.

- penetration pricing. This is aimed at tapping the mass market quickly with a low price, thereby discouraging potential competitors from entering the field. The method is often employed by Japanese motor manufacturers when introducing a new model.

- initial launch pricing. This allows a special price for the first order to induce distributors to stock the product or to encourage consumers to try the product.

- product line pricing. In circumstances where a firm produces a wide range of products, it may accept a low price on one product but simultaneously stimulate sales of another, more expensive product. Essentially, this relies on consumer impulse purchasing.

- bid pricing (or tender pricing). Bids or tenders are offered for major work programmes or installations of central and local government, large organisations and utilities, agency work and plant construction. It may be difficult to change the price once the tender is accepted, except to allow for some type of index-linked pricing. Usually, the organisation seeking the tenders, subject to a detailed specification, is looking for the lowest price from a number of competitive bidders.

Here it's important to emphasise again that the price is just one of the marketing mix elements: change one of them, say promotion, and the price may have to change. The marketing mix elements are interdependent variables. They don't live in isolation from each other.

Pricing strategies tend to change as a product passes through its life cycle and as the firm employs product extension strategies, during which it will revamp and reconsider the elements of the marketing mix, of which price is but one variable. In a free enterprise society, pricing is a dynamic process; competition tends to regulate economic activity and prices, and there is need for only the very minimum of government controls. In the absence of price restrictions or regulations, and in times of high demand and low supply, the higher profits earned by suppliers through a price increase will attract new suppliers to enter the market and expand those supplies. The high prices will also serve ultimately to curb demand. In the longer run, the additional quantities made available to the market by the new suppliers will help to reduce prices.

With government-imposed price control during periods of shortages, opportunities arise for the markets to be manipulated, leading to more severe supply inadequacies and higher black-market prices. Although there is some modest price control of the utilities, price control mechanisms are rarely imposed in the UK.

Related questions

1 Under what circumstances would a manufacturer initiate price cuts?

2 Suggest and describe how a company can increase its profits without raising its prices or lowering its costs.

3 A manufacturing company has developed a totally new and innovative product for the hi-fi market. Consider how the company should set its pricing strategy.

4 The final price of a product is the result of many factors. Suggest what those factors are and how far the company should take account of them.

Question 45

As a result of technological development, a product of a manufacturing company is expected to become unfashionable. Examine the measures that might be taken to minimise the effects of such obsolescence on the company.

Tackling the question

This question tackles another major element of the marketing mix — the actual product itself. Obsolescence of a product is a major factor that affects most companies. It allows you to bring in all sorts of relevant terms and phrases, such as product screening, product survival, product planning, product policy and product life cycle (in fact, almost anything with the word 'product' stuck in front of it!). Of course, all these terms do presuppose that you actually know what you are talking about, and that you can use them in the right context. So in this essay, I try to introduce quite a few of them. They are relevant. If you know these concepts and others, such as the Boston matrix, product portfolio analysis and SWOT analysis, the essay almost writes itself.

Answer

When assessing the position of any product, three fundamental factors must be taken into account. They are considerations of demand, competition and the resources that the firm possesses, or which it can obtain within the constraints of finance and opportunity costs. Product portfolio analysis, using concepts such as the Boston matrix, may be particularly useful in monitoring the success of a product, the contribution that product appears to be making to the firm's fixed costs and profits, and the market share enjoyed by that product. Any product in a portfolio of products that fails to make an adequate contribution is deemed to be weak.

Unless there are strong reasons for retention, carrying a weak product may prove to be very costly. Falling sales and a falling share of the market will cause plant capacity to be under-utilised, and that capacity will be incurring fixed costs. Retention of weak or obsolescent products may delay the search for better and alternative products. It may be appropriate, in both the medium and long term, to sever all connections with the obsolete product and withdraw from that particular market. It can be argued, however, that if several companies are producing similar products, all of which are becoming technologically obsolete, such as the video cassette recorder being replaced by, say, compact disc video facilities, then one company may be able to fill the sales vacuum left by the departing companies. The remaining company may enjoy a temporary increase in both sales and profits, while at the same time minimising expenditure on marketing that product. This is called a 'harvesting strategy'.

Any firm must be flexible and responsive to new stimuli. In essence, it is the future that determines what the firm should be doing now. The dynamic nature of the marketing function becomes increasingly apparent as the marketing department, in particular, attempts to adapt and respond to changes in the environment and to forecast the nature and longevity of these changes. That a product is becoming obsolete is a problem that first confronts the marketing department as sales volume and sales revenue fall. There must be an effective strategy to capture and retain the firm's share of the market. In the first instance, this may consist of attempts to increase the primary demand and profit through aggressive marketing and promotion, price discounting and the development of new users and uses.

The marketing department is, or should be, in the vanguard of the firm's activities. It follows, therefore, that a market-oriented company will have detected that a product is in a particular phase of its product life cycle and will have taken such steps as are necessary to minimise the effects of product obsolescence.

In the maturation phase of the life cycle, the firm will have identified either new products, or possibly a diversification strategy, or new markets and/or new uses for its existing product. It will have planned product extension strategies by preparing to produce the next versions of its existing product. These extension strategies may be simply cosmetic, such as a new and exciting package, or may consist of promotional campaigns to boost sales as the product enters its decline phase. Such measures may be taken to reduce stock and recoup some of the investment, or simply to obtain as much financial contribution as possible in the remaining time available. In other words, the firm will have re-examined and adjusted the ingredients of the marketing mix — which it should have been doing throughout the product's life cycle to invigorate sales and match the competition.

I like the concept of harvesting. It's a fairly new term, but it's a useful one because it describes exactly what happens. Everyone has left the market and the one or two remaining companies can now concentrate on mopping up the remaining sales. Eventually, of course, they'll all leave the market because there'll be no more sales left.

A key term — 'market orientation'. Make sure that you know the difference between this and 'product orientation'.

Note how I take the opportunity to introduce new concepts and terms. At the same time I keep trying to DEEE — define, explain and expand what I have said and, if possible, exemplify.

Introducing the marketing mix reminds us what we're supposed to be writing about. It's easy to get carried away, so occasionally refer back to the question. Ask yourself: am I still answering whatever it is that the examiner wants me to answer? Am I still on track?

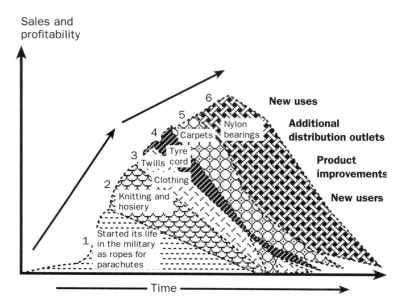

Figure 20 Product extension strategies for nylon

Product extension strategies might be achieved in a number of ways:

- Stimulate increased primary demand, i.e. first-time users.
- Develop additional users, e.g. by appealing to different market segments, different target groups or export markets.
- Increase the number of uses for the product, e.g. the progression of nylon.
- Change the packaging or the size to give the product a new image — a new 'personality'.
- Improve the product quality.
- Increase the product's frequency of use.

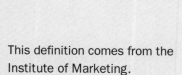

This definition comes from the Institute of Marketing.

Talking about market insensitivity could lead us into the reasons why a company might have been insensitive — someone in the firm has been asleep or events have overtaken them — but that's not what the question is asking. So leave it there.

The primary function of any market-oriented firm is to identify, anticipate and satisfy the market requirements. Failure to recognise that a product is becoming technologically obsolete may reflect market insensitivity. As one product is launched, the search for new products and new versions must begin. There is also a possibility that a firm will undertake the necessary research and launch the product, but that, shortly afterwards, competition appears with similar products, without having incurred the costs of the development.

New products can be acquired by purchasing from another company, by buying another company or by buying a patent. This can be a relatively fast way of diversifying the purchasing company's product portfolio. It can also be very expensive, particularly if established brand names are involved. A large enterprise may, of course, be able to do so more easily than a small firm. The firm may decide to bide its time, however, and perhaps allow the existing product to be phased out; indeed, it may have arranged for planned obsolescence to be built into its corporate plans. At the same time, it might be possible to arrange in-service training courses for its employees and ensure that its staff are as skilled as possible, and prepared and ready to take on a new product. While preparing for the introduction of a new product, however, the firm must look after its existing customers. It must arrange for a continuous supply of spares and the provision of services to those purchasers of the product that has now become obsolete. It must maintain their confidence and goodwill.

The company must also retain the confidence of its workforce and effectively communicate its plans and aspirations without, of course, giving too much away to its competitors. Failure to communicate with its employees and to reassure them may lead to industrial relations problems and the employees' withdrawal of goodwill. It is important, therefore, that the firm engenders confidence in future job prospects and informs the staff of possible production changes and revised training needs. There may be some resistance, but such resistance will be more easily overcome if the staff, or their representatives, are consulted or allowed to participate in and contribute to the decision making.

If you follow the systems approach, which I strongly recommend, then you have to think also about the other subsystems of a company, such as personnel, finance and production. Remember that the question asks how to reduce the effects of product obsolescence, so consideration of the employees is quite relevant.

Related questions

1 It is argued that in a dynamic market place most firms must be market oriented. Explain why this might be so, and discuss the implications for a company manufacturing audio and video equipment.

2 What are the advantages and disadvantages of following an individual brand strategy rather than a family or generic brand strategy?

3 A model is only as good as the data on which it is based. Consider the limitations of a model that suggests that a product is in the decline phase of its life cycle.

4 Not only products but also industries pass through different stages of growth and decline. In terms of strategic analysis and planning, how would you determine whether the product or the industry itself was in decline? In either case, what strategic measures might the company consider?

Pin-point targeting and market segmentation are major considerations in the initial launch and management of a product. Consider the importance of market research and the alternative methods of collecting primary data. Identify and comment on the current classifications of market segmentation.

Tackling the question

Marketing — as you well know — is not just about selling; it is much more sophisticated than that. Marketing is, in effect, a behavioural science; it studies consumer psychology. Market segmentation is sophisticated too. No longer do we use such obsolete terms as 'working class' and 'middle class'. Such segmentation is far too crude, and consumers are much more diverse and, yes, sophisticated. With much greater choice and much greater spending power many consumers are less easily satisfied; hence the importance of detailed market research. Most products — certainly many consumer durables and most FMCGs — are aimed at a particular and specific market segment. Such market segmentation results in benefits for both the company and the customers, but it is only a first step. What does a firm do when it has identified appropriate segments? It must evaluate them and decide which ones are likely to be most profitable, i.e. analyse the cost and revenue implications. Of course, market segmentation calls into question the utility of mass marketing. With pin-point targeting and target marketing becoming more and more the norm, is mass marketing really of practical use — especially in the more sophisticated economies of the world?

Answer

Market research can help to increase predictability and therefore minimise risk, eliminate dubious options, reduce the number of choices available and reveal wastage in certain areas. It helps to focus a firm's resources on relevant aspects of the firm's marketing strategy. Market research has been defined as the systematic, objective and exhaustive search for and study of the facts relevant to any problem in the field of marketing. It provides information in the following areas:

- product studies: developing and testing new products, and measuring consumer preferences for both the product and the packaging. It can provide information regarding the product's design and improvement and how sensitive the demand is to variations in the pricing;

- market analysis: in an attempt to measure current and potential sales, to identify the appropriate market segment and to determine a competitor's share of the market;
- promotion studies: to measure the effectiveness of the choice of media, the advertising campaign and the audience characteristics;
- customer research: into brand preferences, image perceptions and buying behaviour;
- distribution channels: to determine the optimum point of sale, and the method of distributing the product from the manufacturer to the final consumer;
- sales analysis: to appraise sales policies, measure dealer and POS performance, and evaluate sales territories and the performance of sales staff;
- corporate planning: likely trends and changes in customer purchasing patterns, staff needs and export opportunities.

Market data are of two types: primary and secondary.

- Primary data are original data gathered specifically for the current investigation.
- Secondary data are those already gathered and published by someone else.

It doesn't matter what the size of the firm is; it could be Fred's fish and chip van, but Fred needs to know something about his market and who tends to buy what and where and when, if he is to satisfy that market.

Before primary data collection is undertaken, the company should consider the availability of secondary data published by agencies such as HMSO, and the *A–Z of UK Marketing Information Sources* published by Euromonitor. Secondary data can also be gathered from desk research, trade and professional magazines and the government's Market Intelligence Library. For information about overseas markets, foreign embassies can be very helpful. The internal data already held by the company itself should not be overlooked. Another fast-growing source of secondary data is that provided by on-line database services and the Internet. Collection of such data has several important advantages in that it tends to be much easier, less time consuming and much cheaper. However, secondary data do have their limitations, not least that they tend to become obsolete quickly and they may not be as comprehensive as the firm would wish for the current investigation.

If a company intends to undertake primary research, it may do so by commissioning one of the many specialist agencies. Primary research can be undertaken in two basic ways:

This is a fairly standard format, and you certainly need to know the advantages and disadvantages of each approach as well as the pros and cons of each of the survey methods.

- by observation: watching the actions of customers, such as their movements in a retail store and their actions at the check-outs;
- survey methods: this is the most widely used approach and consists of obtaining information by interviewing a number of people (a sample of the particular population under investigation). Questionnaires must be constructed with care to avoid bias and unsolicited or inadequate answers.

Survey methods, in turn, can be divided into four types:

- personal interview. This is probably the best means of obtaining information because it allows the interviewer to establish a relationship with the interviewee and to explain those questions that might be confusing. Such interviews can provide first-class qualitative data. They allow an experienced researcher to determine attitudes and values. However, personal interviews are slow and the most expensive method of data collection.
- postal surveys. While this method tends to be slow in obtaining a response, it is the cheapest form of investigation. The response rate is usually low, often less than 4%, and this may invalidate the subsequent analysis. It is sometimes easier to reach certain groups of people with this method if an up-to-date mailing list is used.
- telephone surveys. This method is inexpensive and it can be quick in obtaining results. It also allows for follow-up calls to be made at little extra cost. For these reasons, it is the fastest-growing method of obtaining primary data. It is estimated that 50–60% of all market research data are collected by this method. Although it discounts people without a telephone and those who are ex-directory, it tends to be a useful approach for gathering data for industrial market research.
- panel data. Members of a representative group of consumers are selected for the panel and each member is asked to maintain a diary of his or her relevant actions or buying behaviour over a time period, e.g. which TV programmes were watched or which cereal was eaten for breakfast. At the end of the specified time, the diary is replaced by a new one and the entries of the original diary analysed. Panels are often used in consumer research for comments about products such as FMCGs.

Each method of primary data collection has it uses and none is superior for all situations. The method used depends on the

Giving a list and then expanding on it is perfectly acceptable. But do remember that the better answers include judgements and evaluation; they offer substantiated and reasoned opinions — so don't be too terse or brief.

nature of the survey, how quickly the data are required, what they are going to be used for, how much funding is available and, most important of all, what the objective of the research is. The surveys themselves will be broken down into sampling frames and the appropriate sampling technique will need to be considered. There are many different types of sample, the most important of which is random sampling.

I'm going to resist the temptation to go into detail about sampling theory and types of sample — stratified, cluster, quota, etc. After all, the question does not ask you to describe how you would actually undertake a market research study.

The aim of market segmentation is to focus the marketing effort more precisely by dividing the total market into several, relatively homogeneous groups. There are four commonly used bases for segmenting consumer markets:

Now we can start focusing on the market segments themselves. You can see that there are many segments in each of the three main groups, so we can begin to pin-point target the consumers we are after. As the target gets smaller and smaller, we shall end up with a very small, niche market.

- geographic segmentation. This is based on population location, movement of populations and type of house — known as 'A Classification of Residential Neighbourhoods' — ACORN);
- demographic segmentation. This is the commonest segmentation. It divides the population into groups according to sex, age, income, occupation, education, household size and family life cycle. The six socioeconomic groups are A, B, C1, C2, D, E. Socioeconomic grading is not a classification by wealth or income only. Its primary purpose is to group together people who have been shaped by a similar education, similar social influences and similar cultural backgrounds.
- psychographic segmentation. This is based on the lifestyle of the potential customers. A recent further categorisation classifies consumers into one of four groups, based on their attitudes and how they spend their money.
- benefit segmentation. This is based on the benefits that consumers expect to derive from a product or from a particular brand.

These segmentations are exclusive. Marketers may aim at one or another segment depending on whom they regard as the primary purchaser of the product, i.e. whoever influences the purchase. The marketing manager may well refine and narrow the segmentation considerably. Each time a market segmentation qualification is added, the target segment becomes smaller and more exclusive. The pin-point target becomes smaller and smaller. Whatever marketing strategy a company adopts, a fundamental requirement is that it must know at which target group it is aiming the product or service. Only then can it manage and manipulate the marketing mix accordingly.

Targeting the relevant consumer is what it's all about.

Related questions

1 What kind of information does the government provide which might be useful to a firm in deciding on a particular course of action? What other sources of secondary data might the company also consider?

2 'Segmentation strategies are likely to succeed when there are substantial differences in needs between the segments.' Explain this statement and suggest how a company can use this concept to its advantage.

3 What criteria might a marketing manager use to determine the point at which targeting products at additional segments is no longer profitable?

4 Undifferentiated marketing is the process of targeting the whole market with one marketing mix. Suggest for which products or services such a marketing approach may be appropriate. Consider also the disadvantages associated with undifferentiated targeting.

Question 47

In a multiproduct company, what are the major areas of consideration in product management and control? Discuss the use and limitations of the product life cycle concept.

Tackling the question

This question specifically requires an analysis of the product life cycle. Remember that every model and every technique has its limitations, and the product life cycle is no exception. Some would argue that it is a very limited model which hardly reflects all the dynamics of product development and product management. Others would argue with equal passion that it has its place in the arsenal of concepts at the disposal of the marketing manager. Perhaps a more pragmatic consideration is the fact that the concept is in the textbooks — and in the syllabus! But remember to state its limitations. Note that the question specifies that the company is a 'multiproduct' company, so it will need to optimise the five Ms — machinery, money, manpower, materials and management. It may not be doing so if it is 'wasting' them on a weak product. Could they be better employed elsewhere?

Answer

Guidance notes

The customer's expectations of a product's performance will be conditioned by a host of factors associated with that product, including its presentation, branding, brand image and personality, the company image, the degree of personal service offered, the prospects of after-sales service, attitudes created by promotion, and economic factors such as price and perceived value. In other words, the product may be seen by the customer in quite a different light from that of the manufacturer or supplier — hence, the importance of market orientation to a commercial organisation.

The majority of companies market more than one product because there is more than one market segment. Such companies are multiproduct companies and many have lengthy product ranges; in which case, products tend to be grouped

Many common examples could be used, such as Procter and Gamble, which produces at least six fabric-washing products (Ariel, Daz, Bold,

Dreft, etc.); three dish-washing liquids, three after-shaves, and many other products ranging from Vick for coughs and colds to Pampers for babies. Or how about Cadbury's, or the Mars group or, even bigger still, Nestlé, with its massive product portfolio? How on earth do they manage such vast portfolios of household names?

together in approximately homogeneous divisions. The product divisions may be organised by:

- raw material used;
- manufacturing process of production;
- distribution channels;
- physical distribution requirements such as perishability or refrigeration requirements;
- salesforce.

Most firms also diversify in some way, if only to spread the risk of product failure and reduce the dependence on one, or a few, major buyers. There are dangers with this strategy, however, including spreading expertise, assets and efforts too thinly. Nonetheless, there are also advantages in multiproduct operations, including a reduction in the costs of development and better utilisation of fixed assets and the labour force.

When a multiproduct firm introduces a new product, it must ensure that the new product does not adversely affect the sales of existing products. A new product that does this is said to be cannibalising the product line. Few products, however, will continue to sell for ever in their existing form. They will require some modification to be made to cater for changing consumer preferences or to cope with the challenge of competitors' goods and technological change. A product may be overtaken not only because of technical improvement but also because of price, design factors and functional performance.

A major concern for management must be the content of the product lines. This concern should generate the need for a formal product policy. Every company has unique strengths and weaknesses, and the optimum product policy must attempt to utilise the strong points and eliminate the weak ones. SWOT (strengths, weaknesses, opportunities and threats) analysis is a significant tool when assessing the contribution made by existing products or determining the technical feasibility and commercial viability of new products. A company's strengths and weaknesses might include such considerations as:

- financial position;
- sales volume;
- channels of distribution;
- research patents;
- raw materials and component parts.

As all products have a limited life cycle, there must be a management resolve to ensure a succession of new or revitalised products. Some awareness of the probable life cycle of a new product may help in assessing that product's commercial viability and the associated marketing tactics that may be required, including the management of the marketing mix. The most important phases are:

- *the development phase*. At this stage there is much technical innovation and research, but there may be initial production difficulties. Channels of distribution are explored and the initial marketing mix and promotional strategies are formulated. Losses are common during this phase, but the foundations are being laid for future profits.
- *the growth phase*. Now it becomes easier to obtain retail outlets. Channels of distribution begin to open up as the market starts to accept the product. Competitors begin to enter the market and they incur lower R&D costs than the innovator. The innovator, using intensive promotional campaigns, attempts to secure and establish brand loyalty, particularly if the product lends itself to repeat purchases.
- *the maturation phase*. This is the longest or shortest phase of the product life cycle. As more and more competitors enter the market, it begins to reach saturation point; there are few, if any, distribution channels to fill. Sales level off and profits begin to fall. The innovator attempts to modify the product, and second-generation products are designed and tested. Promotion of the firm and company image, rather than promotion of the specific product, tends to occur. Emphasis is put on the reliability and integrity of the company.
- *the decline phase*. Sales begin to fall and, in an attempt to maintain sales levels, intensive promotion and merchandising at point-of-sale outlets may occur. This aggressive promotion may reduce profit levels even further. The competition intensifies and firms may now opt for planned product obsolescence rather than allow the product to sap the company's strengths and financial credibility. In addition, firms must ensure that they are not left with unsold stock, so price cutting may occur in an attempt to recover some of the initial costs and, at least, break even.

Product policy must therefore include a programmed timetable for the phasing out of products and the introduction of new products. When a product reaches its maturity stage, the company should be thinking of product extension strategies. The basic ideas associated with product extension strategies are to retain a market share, to provide support for a complementary product, to develop a more varied usage of the product and to modify the product deliberately to meet the needs of identified, potential new users.

Some textbooks may show six or even eight different phases. For our purposes, four phases are quite sufficient. You must learn what happens during each of those phases. A main purpose of the product life cycle is to adjust the elements of the marketing mix as the product enters a new phase — always assuming, of course, that the phase can actually be identified.

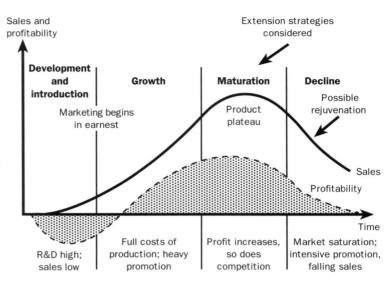

Figure 21 The product life cycle

Here I give the 'downside' — the disadvantages and limitations of the product life cycle. Remember that every model and every technique has its limitations. If you introduce any technique, you simply must know of its limitations and tell the examiner.

Any model of any kind is simply a static representation of a dynamic situation. It cannot possibly incorporate and depict all the eventualities that a firm may encounter in the environment or market place. Models help in planning, understanding and predicting outcomes, but they do have their limitations. So, too, does the model of the product life cycle:

- The life cycle is dependent on the way that the product is managed. Poor marketing may lead to premature decline and death.
- It may not be easy to identify each phase of the life cycle. Depending on the nature of the product and the markets, the sales data obtained may be too little and too late.
- Too much reliance and focus on the life cycle may cause other opportunities to be lost.
- It may be more appropriate for one type of product than another; it is not universally applicable.
- It does not reflect the nature and state of vibrancy of the industry as a whole.

Nonetheless, the product life cycle may help to identify trends and, without doubt, is an aid to formulating marketing strategy.

Related questions

1. What marketing strategy should be adopted for the launch of a new lawnmower, and why?

2. What is the changing role of promotion, and particularly advertising, over the duration of the product life cycle and in each of the various phases?

3. How can the concept of the product life cycle be used in establishing a brand's marketing strategy?

4. 'The product life cycle concept is not truly representative of a real and practical situation. The model is merely a static representation that fails to recognise the dynamic nature of both the environment and the market place.' How far do you agree with this statement?

It may be many years before a product has developed a brand image. Consider why product branding is deemed to be so important and discuss the use of test marketing in the launch of a new product.

Tackling the question

A great deal has been written about the advantages of branding, and from many angles — marketing, accounting strength, production forecasting, etc. A classic case study might include the price that Nestlé finally had to pay to acquire Rowntree-Macintosh with its Smarties, KitKats and a host of other household confectionery names. Branding is a technique basic to marketing practice, and all sorts of concepts could be legitimately considered in this essay — brand extension, brand image, brand loyalty, brand positioning, brand preference. There is also room for ruminating on the fact that test marketing by a corporate brand name might be more successful than that by an unknown company.

Answer

A brand is a name, term, sign, symbol, design or some combination of these used to identify the products of one firm and differentiate them from competitive offerings. The establishment of a brand image communicates certain values to the consumer — quality, reliability, trustworthiness, value for money, etc. It has been suggested that the consuming public may take some brands for granted, and that is a real danger to the owners of the brands, who will have taken years of expensive promotion to establish the uniqueness of their product. Manufacturers have to remind consumers what the brand stands for — every now and again a company promotes its corporate image and not just an individual product.

Some 40% of the buying public are deemed to be 'mainstreamers' — people who do no take risks, who are prepared to pay just that little bit extra for a well-known product

For consumers, branding allows repeat purchases to be made more easily, as they know that they will derive satisfaction from the purchase. For the company, an effective brand allows greater pricing freedom and an opportunity to capitalise on the brand's image. Many customers are willing to pay slightly more for a branded product than for, say, an own-brand label — unless, of course, the own-brand label has developed a similar image of quality.

An American market research study suggests that profit margins for established branded products may be 10–60% higher than for similar unbranded products. However, there has been a marked growth of distributor or retailer brand names that are able to compete most successfully against many of the branded products of well-known manufacturers. The ultimate objective, therefore, of any branding strategy is to provide a guarantee of assurance to the customer.

Possession of an established brand name is, of course, highly valuable, but the value may not be readily transferable to the company's balance sheet. What a brand does is to promise security of earnings over a time period. A brand name or image is worth, in practice, whatever another company is willing to pay for it, and an objective valuation of the brand is difficult to obtain.

that they know they can trust. So they'll buy Heinz products, shop at Marks and Spencer, and buy a British-made car, even if the company is an American one. But branding may take years to achieve and cost millions of pounds; it's a massive investment. A key factor seems to me to be: what does branding mean for the consumer; and what does it mean, in profit terms, for the company?

In a highly competitive market place, success for more and more products clearly depends on creating a favourable general image of the product (or of the company) among prospective customers. The created image, while not the only factor, has a direct bearing on the price; price, in turn, helps to create the brand image. The strength of brand loyalty among customers is measured in three stages:

- brand recognition: the product becomes familiar to the purchasing public, perhaps using free samples and trial packs;
- brand preference: having now had some experience of the product, the consumer prefers it to that of a competitor;
- brand insistence: now the consumer will not accept an alternative.

Many firms invest a good deal not only in developing a brand name for a specific product, but also in developing a corporate image — as a caring company, a trustworthy company, a value-for-money company, and so on. One thing is for certain: they wouldn't do so if it didn't work!

Each of these stages is achieved by the judicious use of effective promotion, including advertising, sales promotion and effective merchandising at the point of sale. Inevitably, these requirements will be expensive. However, the interval between the launch of a new product and the establishment of a household brand name may be a long journey. The vast majority of new product ideas are discarded because they are deemed not to be commercially viable and/or technically feasible. The mortality rate of original product concepts is very high; some estimate as high as 98%. Even when a product appears to be viable and feasible, it may still be necessary to test it out on the

Having discussed 'branding' and its importance, I'm now in a position to make a link with test markets and why they are often — but not always — so important, particularly for firms producing FMCGs.

market and to reconsider the marketing mix as well as the proposed market and segment.

The giant toiletry and food manufacturers, and other manufacturers of FMCGs, have pioneered scientific marketing in the UK, and it is almost axiomatic that new products will be test marketed in a limited area. This limited area is often an ITV region and may be bounded by a natural phenomenon such as the North Yorkshire Moors. The boundaries are often sparsely populated, so there is little drift of the product and its promotion into adjacent areas. It is subsequently easier to collect, record and measure the market research data.

A test market should also represent, approximately, the overall population in terms of socioeconomic groups, sex, age, ACORNs (residential neighbourhoods), psychographic and other market segments and classifications. In addition, a test market should:

- be typical of the proposed distribution outlets;
- contain advertising media that will co-operate;
- have a good record as a test area;
- allow for year-round sales and repeat purchases.

Some companies may use consumer panels before proceeding to a test market, and adapt the marketing mix accordingly. However, the longer the testing period, the greater the probability of a correct assessment being made of what is likely to happen in a national launch, using statistical and inferential analysis of the test data and consumer responses.

For every advantage in business management there is almost always a disadvantage. Again, I make sure I include the disadvantages of a technique. Here are some of the arguments against test marketing.

Test marketing a product does have disadvantages, not least that it allows actual and potential competitors to examine the new product and then to adjust and manufacture an existing or new product to combat the intruder. Test marketing a new product tells a competitor what a company is up to. The competitor may, in consequence, not only revamp its product, but develop promotional and pricing tactics to fend off the newcomer's attempts to gain a profitable market share.

Consumer durables are seldom test marketed because repeat purchases are infrequent and because the innovative company may have huge initial start-up costs associated with production, tooling up and establishing a network of after-sales service agents. To a great extent, such manufacturers operate in an oligopolistic market, in which the emphasis is often on non-price differentials and the development of corporate imagery.

Test marketing is also expensive. The product must be distributed to the wholesalers and retailers in the test market area; promotion and advertising must be designed, and the media selected; merchandising the product at the point of sale must be encouraged; special offers and discounts may have to be introduced. It might be better to forgo the test marketing and commit the test-launch finance towards the national launch costs. On the other hand, a national launch is significantly more expensive. If the company has made mistakes, correcting them at the national stage may be prohibitively expensive and uneconomical.

Related questions

1 Identify the factors that might have to be examined when considering the launch of a product overseas. How does international marketing differ from domestic marketing?

2 Under what circumstances might a manufacturer wish to stimulate demand for a product category rather than demand for the company's specific brand?

3 Why have some companies come to rely more on preliminary market tests and less on full-scale test marketing in evaluating new products? Are there any advantages to such a practice?

4 In a highly competitive market place, what aggressive marketing tactics might you adopt to thwart prospective test marketing planned by a leading competitor?

Consider the nature of marketing and the purpose of models such as the Boston matrix in managing a product portfolio. What are the limitations of such models?

Marketing is not a precise science like physics or chemistry. Essentially, it is a behavioural science which seeks to understand, predict and influence the behaviour of a rather special group of people — consumers. A marketing manager deals less with certainties than with possibilities because consumers are immensely unpredictable in their purchasing behaviour. Hence the use of models such as the Boston matrix (also known as the growth–share matrix) to assist in portfolio management. The Boston matrix has its detractors: too facile, too simplistic, difficult to plot, puts too much stress on market leadership — perhaps. The fact is, however, that it has grown in popularity and become progressively more sophisticated. It is not the only matrix, but it is possibly the most popular and well known. Of course, the model itself is about determining and diagnosing the company's strategic position, and anything that helps a company to do that must have some utility. A model on its own may have little utility; it would be more meaningful, therefore, to relate it to SWOT analysis, the product life cycle and product elimination procedures.

Answer

There is a clear relationship between risk and certainty. It's not a relationship that can be determined with mathematical precision (although, as usual, there are models that try to do this), but we can begin to add numbers to it: for example, when an investment decision has to be made. As we have said many times before, models that attempt to simulate reality — in economics, business studies or engineering — have their uses, but we must appreciate their limitations.

The purpose of marketing is to identify, anticipate and satisfy the consumer's needs and wants. Peter Drucker states that the Siamese twins of management are planning and control; separate them at your peril. Yet, to plan and to control, a manager needs data and information. As the quality and quantity of data increase and improve, so do certainty and predictability. Drucker also states that the two essential requirements of a company are marketing and innovation. The company needs data about the products in the market place to assess the performance, position and potential of its products. Such an audit is part of a marketing manager's brief under product portfolio management. A firm's success in the market place depends ultimately on the products that it offers.

Very few firms produce just one product. There will therefore be a fundamental need to ensure that the firm's basic scarce resources are not squandered. To be successful a company should have a portfolio of products with different growth rates and different market shares. The aim is not only to improve overall profitability, but to ensure adequate cash flow. Clearly, however, every company needs products that generate cash and every product must, eventually, be a cash generator, otherwise it is probably of little value — at least in direct cash terms.

Product portfolio analysis is a key element in strategic marketing planning. The most famous model used in product portfolio analysis is the Boston matrix, which has three features:

- the annual market growth rate, shown on the vertical axis;
- the relative market share of a product, shown on the horizontal axis;
- icons that represent the position of the various products — the size of the icon is proportional to the sales value and sales volume of the product.

The matrix is divided into four quadrants: the stars, the cash cows, the problem children and the dogs. The relative market share indicates the product's share relative to its competitors. A relative market share of 0.2 means the product has only 20% of the leading competitor's sales volume, while 4x means the product has four times the market share of the nearest competitor.

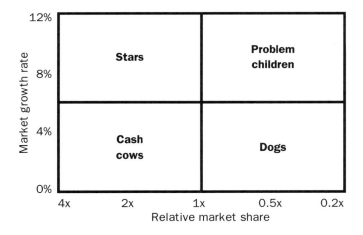

Figure 22 The Boston matrix

Diagrams are always useful and you shouldn't hesitate to use them; the examiner will give you credit. In any case, it's often easier to use a diagram to explain something to the examiner than it is to describe it.

- *Stars*. These are the products with high share and high growth rate; almost certainly the market leaders. They have potential for profitability and more often than not possess a USP (unique selling proposition), but they need large injections of resources to finance rapid growth and promotion. They may, therefore, show a negative cash flow.

- *Cash cows*. These are products with a high market share, but there is not a great deal of market growth potential. Characteristically, such products have developed a personality, particularly in the FMCGs markets, and generate large amounts of cash — often far more than the investment required to maintain that market share. More often than not, the cash generated by cash cows subsidises the investment necessary in the stars.
- *Problem children*. These are the products with a low market share but with high growth potential. They usually require more cash than they can generate. Unless they become leaders, they end up being a liability, for they suck in resources that might be better employed elsewhere. They are called problem children because it is not entirely clear where they are heading. The company might be better off divesting itself of these products.
- *Dogs*. Products in the bottom right-hand corner of the matrix may show a profit, but any profit generated has to be reinvested to maintain the dog's position. These products have no real growth potential and are not going anywhere. Sometimes they are known as 'weak' products because they make little or no contribution, yet tend to sap the corporate strength. More often than not, the company needs to get rid of them. All products eventually become cash cows or dogs.

According to the philosophy behind the matrix, we should kick the dogs, mollycoddle the cows, throw the firm's resources at the stars and give management thought only to the problem children. Consider the fact that dogs can, indeed, prey on the firm's resources; but a dog can also be a faithful companion and give unquestioning loyalty. The dog may not contribute much, but it is part of the family, and it may look good and be impressive.

The need for a balanced product portfolio becomes obvious. The cash cows subsidise the stars — which may, in turn, become cash cows — and the problem children, which may become stars before becoming cash cows (or dogs). The snapshot of a company's product (or services) portfolio shows how those products are distributed on the matrix. Only those products deemed to be cash cows are likely to be net cash generators, i.e. those with a high market share but in a low-market-growth situation. An unbalanced portfolio will have too many dogs and problem children and not enough cash cows and stars. However, evidence suggests that while a large market share may be a significant contributor to profitability, it is not necessary for success. A large market share may be obtained by low pricing and aggressive and expensive promotion, but profitability and cash flow may suffer in consequence.

There is a danger in placing too much reliance on a model. Models help to bring order out of chaos; they help to make the dynamic world and environment in which we live easier to understand; they help us to predict. But no model, however sophisticated or complex, can possibly hope to simulate the dynamic, tumultuous environment of the real world. Models of any kind are merely static representations of dynamic situations.

The Boston matrix, like most models in economics and business and management studies, is not without its critics, and justifiably so. Simple concepts can be oversimplified. The model is very clean and very surgical, and it is a relatively easy task to classify products into one of the groups. But do they really fit so neatly into one of these slots? In any case, while the Boston matrix concentrates on the generation of cash to fund the stars and the problem children, it is, of course, possible to borrow cash, and at times it may make sound business sense to do so. Medium- and long-term profitability may be far more important than short-term cash generation.

There is an assumption in the Boston matrix that products in high-growth areas need more cash and that products with high market shares generate more cash. This is frequently untrue. Other factors may be significant: managerial efficiency, competences and abilities; product innovation; corporate image; the degree of capital or labour intensity; and sociological and legislative pressures. Given this multitude of other variables, many of the basic assumptions of the Boston model may, indeed, be invalid.

> The moral of this story? Use models, of any kind, very carefully and judiciously; they do often help understanding, but they can never be a substitute for detailed analysis and common sense.

Related questions

1 In the Boston matrix, what are the limitations of using market growth rates and market share as a measure of opportunity and performance respectively?

2 Consider how the relationship between sales revenue and contribution might determine the performance of individual products, and suggest why weak products might be retained by a company.

3 Discuss the limitations of models such as the Boston matrix, given that they are no more than static models.

4 If a company had, within its product portfolio, a product that had comparatively little market share, yet the market as a whole was growing quite fast, what measures might it take to remedy this situation?

Question 50

What is the significance of index numbers? With a worked example, demonstrate the difference between Laspeyre's index and that of Paasche. Comment on the limitations of index numbers, especially the RPI.

Tackling the question

Index numbers can be used for almost any area of business management — production, personnel, finance, as well as marketing — in fact, anywhere trends can be determined and comparisons can be made. Here, I am using them to consider prices and consumer expenditure patterns. Index numbers look incredibly complex. They are not. Read the text and follow the number crunching line by line. See if you can work out where I got the final figures from, and then you might try one or two examination questions. Most numerate problems require lots of practice... and the more you do, the better you'll become. It's a bit like learning the techniques of doing, say, a crossword. I have a colleague who has done *The Times* crossword in ten minutes — he's been doing the crossword for years. Me? I couldn't do it if I had all the time in the world. I am not a crossword fanatic. For the exam, however, you have to become something of a number-crunching fanatic! You have to practise... and then practise.

Answer

When we express a relative change in one item as a percentage of a relative change of another item, we are constructing an index number. Index numbers not only express binary comparisons (i.e. comparisons of two things); they are usually used to express a comparison in series. Provided the data are homogeneous, countless numbers of factors can be compared, such as productivity, prices, sales, days lost through sickness or industrial accidents, population changes and usage rates. Probably the best-known index is the retail price index (RPI), which is now tempered by real changes in taxation rates (RPIX).

An index number is similar to an average, in that it condenses a multivariable situation into a single number. The main feature of the index is that, once a base index has been established, it may be used to make comparisons with the starting base. Generally, the starting base is given the value of 100; hence, if the current price index number is 132, the initial index has increased by 32 points since the initial index base was established. A significant and increasingly important use of index numbers is as the basis for wage negotiations, as well as in helping to formulate changes in government economic policy, such as direct and/or indirect taxation.

The retail price index monitors the percentage change in the spending of a typical family on foods and services. The method of construction and calculation of the RPI can be appreciated more readily by considering a very large and representative 'basket' of goods and services in January of each year, and then comparing the cost of this 'basket' in each of the following 12 months. The percentage increase in the total costs, since January, can then be calculated. The 'basket' is changed each January to ensure that it is as up to date as possible, but the percentage changes in the cost of successive 'baskets' are linked to produce a continuous series of percentage changes since the RPI was created.

Some items in the 'basket' account for a much greater percentage of the family budget than others. For example, most households spend (at least in the UK) far more on bread and meat than they do, say, on soap. Therefore, a 10% increase in the cost of bread will clearly add more to the cost of the 'basket' than a 10% increase in the cost of soap. To allow for this relative importance of the various items in the 'basket', each percentage change in price is given a weight to represent that relative importance in the household expenditure of the previous 12 months. The percentage changes in prices are then multiplied by these weights before being averaged.

If it is assumed that the current retail price index is reset at 100, at a later date — after four months, say — and if the contents, services and quantities of the 'basket' remain unchanged, a new index figure can be calculated as follows:

$$\text{Index} = \frac{\text{Current total price}}{\text{Original base price}} \times 100; \text{ or}$$

$$\text{Index} = \frac{p_n}{p_o} \times 100$$

where p_n is the new price and p_o is the old price.

This gives a simple aggregate index. However, no account has been made of the relative importance of the 'basket' of products and services. So, as it stands, it is a little crude. To calculate the index by a weighting method, we can use the following steps:

This looks ever so complicated, but it isn't really. Follow the calculations step by step until you understand them, and you know where all the figures come from.

- Decide the items to be used in the index, their respective quantities and the price per unit.
- Calculate the total cost for each item in the index.
- Add up the total cost column to give the current total cost.

Example:
The personalised RPI for a mythical family, in 1990, is given below.

Item	Quantity	Price (£) (1990)	Price (£) (1991)	Expenditure (£) (1990)	Expenditure (£) (1991)
Meats	4 kg	2.90	3.20	11.60	12.80
Vegetables	4 kg	0.10	0.12	0.40	0.48
Fish	1.5 kg	1.90	2.20	2.85	3.30
Petrol	45 litres	0.34	0.38	15.30	17.10
Mortgage	1	100.00	90.00	100.00	90.00
Energy	1	12.00	15.00	12.00	15.00
House	1	3.80	4.60	3.80	4.60
Services	1	9.80	10.40	9.80	10.40
Total				155.75	153.68

The 1990 figure of £155.75 is, therefore, given an index base of 100. Using the simple aggregate formula, the index for 1991 is:

$$\frac{153.68}{155.75} \times 100 = 98.7$$

The base year quantities, i.e. those for 1990, must be used to reflect the relative importance of each of the items. These quantities are denoted by q_o. In other words, a weighted aggregate index will be obtained. There are two basic formulae for calculating a weighted index, one suggested by Laspeyre and the other formula named after Paasche.

This is all fairly straightforward — assuming, of course, that you know what an index is, and the difference between Laspeyre and Paasche.

$$\text{Laspeyre's index} = \frac{p_n q_o}{p_o q_o} \times 100; \text{ Paasche's index} = \frac{p_n q_n}{p_o p_n} \times 100$$

It can be seen that Laspeyre's index takes no account of any change in the quantities bought, but uses the quantities assumed in the base year for the new index.

Paasche's index, however, reflects a change in the prices *and* a change in the quantities bought in the new index year. Laspeyre's index tends, therefore, to overestimate the change in prices, while Paasche's index tends to underestimate the changes. It does not really matter which is used, except that its use must be consistent, i.e. like must be compared with like. A company cannot use Laspeyre's one year and then switch to Paasche's index the following year. Clearly, the results would not follow.

Example:

Item	Prices (£)		Quantities	
	(1990)	(1991)	(1990)	(1991)
Bread	0.32	0.35	10	10
Coal	3.50	4.20	100 kg	75 kg
Postage	0.10	0.12	8 letters	6 letters
Beer	0.45	0.52	12 pints	8 pints

Laspeyre's formula:

$$\frac{(35 \times 10) + (420 \times 100) + (12 \times 8) + (52 \times 12)}{(32 \times 10) + (350 \times 100) + (10 \times 8) + (45 \times 12)} \times 100 = 119.839$$

Substituting the change in quantity for the given year using Paasche's formula gives us:

$$\frac{(35 \times 10) + (420 \times 75) + (12 \times 6) + (52 \times 8)}{(32 \times 10) + (350 \times 75) + (10 \times 6) + (45 \times 8)} \times 100 = 119.815$$

There is obviously little to choose between the two methods, except that Laspeyre's uses base year quantities, and the given year quantities do not, therefore, have to be frequently updated.

The index of retail prices should not, strictly speaking, be treated as a cost of living index, since the cost of living is determined essentially by households' peculiarities and personal expenditure, and the levels of expenditure in one household may be different from another household. As the RPI is widely used in salary and wage negotiations, one of the main concerns of union negotiators is that the weights in the index may not reflect the actual expenditure patterns of their members. For instance, if an item is weighted less than an individual spends proportionately on it, and the price of that item increases more rapidly than the others in the index, the effect will be less on the index than it will be on an employee's wage packet.

In addition, the choice of items in the basket of goods must be changed periodically to reflect changes in patterns of consumer spending, the demographic structure of society and changes in tastes, fashion, eating habits, etc. Comparing indexes over a number of years, therefore, may present some difficulties because the factors on which the index is constructed will have changed.

And, of course, we would not expect to present a technique or model without mention of its limitations, would we?

Related questions

1   Discuss the criteria you would use to assess: (a) the weighting of an aggregate price index; (b) the base period of an index; and (c) how closely an aggregate index approaches the ideal.

2   Are there any advantages in using Laspeyre's index or that of Paasche? Consider and discuss the criteria that would lead to using one or the other.

3   How far do you think operational or mathematical modelling of any kind can help a production manager in his or her decision making? Suggest what the limitations of such models might be.

4   How important is trend analysis in examining the prospects of a company and determining its strategic direction? What techniques might be employed for such an analysis and what limitations would you be aware of?